Art as Witness

Art as Witness

edited by

Parthiv Shah • Sana Das

Tulika Books

Published by
Tulika Books
35 A/1 (ground floor), Shahpur Jat, New Delhi 110 049, India

First published in India in 2010

ISBN: 978-81-89487-70-6

Design: Centre for Media and Alternative Communication (CMAC), www.cmaconline.org

Printed at Archana, New Delhi

Contents

Acknowledgements 9

Interrupting the Spectacle..........*Sana Das* 11

Images for Change................*Parthiv Shah* 17

I Performance

The Fool's Paradise..........*Gowhar Fazili* 23

Military Calligraphy..........*Parthiv Shah* 28

A Valley Camouflages.........*Parthiv Shah* 34

The Many Moods of an Actor: Nazir Josh, Kashmir..........*Parthiv Shah* 38

Home for Bullets..........*Parthiv Shah* 41

I said to them, spontaneously..........*Inder Salim* 44

Sheen-e-Misha..........*Showkat Kathjoo* 45

Solidarity Football..........*Nandita Haksar* 46

A Daughter Reads Her Father's Dream..........*Salima Hashmi* 50

What is Ready-made in Politics?..........*Inder Salim* 55

Peace, Protest and Prayer..........*Harikrishna Katragadda, Suvendu Chatterjee, Sonia Jabbar, Abdul Rahman Roslan* 61

Hazard..........*Shahzad Noorani, K.M. Asad* 70

Metamorphosing..........*Sara Rahbar* 74

II Behind Bars

The Colour of Khaki..........*Lipton Bhau* 80

'May I take a book with me?'..........*Kian Tajbakhsh* 89

When Prisoners Reform 94

The Costs of Proving One's Innocence..........*Nandita Haksar* 95

Tales from Tihar..........*Iftikhar Gilani* 100

Two Sojourns in Prison..........*Saroj Mohanty* 105

A Fraudulent Matter..........*Lachit Bordolai* 110

From the Underbelly of the Beast..........*Kanak Mani Dixit* 116

III In–Security

Gaze..........*Swapan Nayak, Parthiv Shah* 120

The Knock from the Attic..........*Vibhuti Narain Rai* 128

Battling Impunity..........*Vrinda Grover* 133

Who Was HE?..........*Inder Salim* 144

Despair..........*Sohrab Hura, Shahidul Alam, Parthiv Shah* 145

A Simple Question..........*Temsula Ao* 153

Bullet in the Eye..........*E.M. Jose* 160

Panchnamas of Fear..........*Nandini Sundar* 162

Missing..........*Swapan Nayak, Sonia Jabbar* 168

Disappearances in Nepal 172

Mirrors of Militarization..........*Mukul Sharma* 175

IV Wounds

Surviving Massacre..........*Parthiv Shah, Sohrab Hura, Abdul Rahman Roslan* 182

Hidden Haemorrhage..........*Inder Salim* 186

The Marks of Toil..........*Sohrab Hura* 187

The *Chaddar* and the Mask..........*Suhas Borker* 188

Nanaji's Disappearance..........*Showkat Kathjoo* 189

Who Will Muzzle the Cry from Vidarbha?..........*Suhas Borker* 191

Burma Headed the Wrong Way..........*Daniel Pepper* 192

V The Gauze and the Gallows

The Spy, the *Quran* and the Death Sentence..........*Gowhar Fazili* 196

A Crime and a Criminal..........*Sabrina Lall* 201

The Slayers and the Slain..........*Chittaroopa Palit* 203

The Death Machine..........*Sana Das* 209

Artist under Attack..........*Parthiv Shah* 222

Contributors 224

About 'Art for Activism' 227

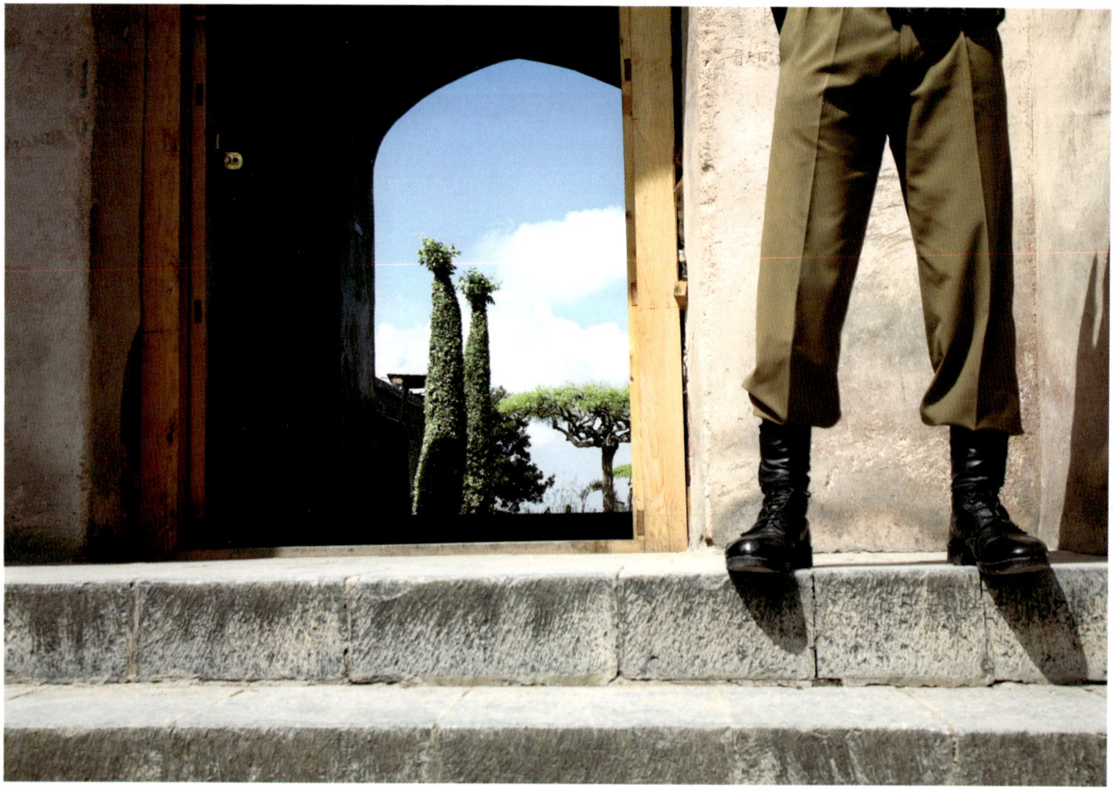

From the *Barbed Wire and Beautiful Skies* series by Parthiv Shah, India, 2008.

Acknowledgements

This collection of photo-essays on jail experience, militarization and the death penalty began as an ambitious and elusive project in the name of 'Art for Activism', at Amnesty International India in 2007, and became the basis for a collaboration with the Centre for Media and Alternative Communication (CMAC). Soon, other artists, writers, advocates, filmmakers, activists, journalists, police officers and professionals came forward to be part of this effort. We thank them for the sincerity of their work, their active company and their patience. Gowhar Fazili from Amnesty International India was a significant creative figure in the project and contributed greatly to the central ideas of the book and its making. He cannot be thanked enough.

Shubranshu Mishra, also from Amnesty International India, 'surreptitiously' became part of this book, thanks to his cross-border connections with writers, poets and artists. Soumya Bhoumik of Amnesty International India and advocate Vrinda Grover generously gave of their time to brainstorm with us on legal cases. Rakesh Kalshian from Panos South Asia contributed with some quirky ideas and suggestions. The design team at CMAC became a steady safeguard against our invariable 'missing-the-bus' style of working. We thank them all. Mukul Sharma, ex-Director of Amnesty International India, who often described us as those with 'fire in their bellies', always picked up the project and put it back on our shoulders whenever we got tired of running after stories and money. For helping synchronize our ideas, plans and deadlines, we thank him. To Tulika Books, we owe our gratitude for being perceptive, appreciative, and for coming forward to publish this book.

We are thankful to all the participating photographers who contributed their works without too many questions regarding when the show would happen, where the photographs would be printed, who would frame them, in which gallery, or when and where the book would get printed – otherwise normal concerns with photographers.

Many of our contributors have shared their personal and painful experiences which have moved us immensely. Without their confidence and boldness, this book would not have been possible. Profuse thanks to them for their trust in this endeavour. Nisha Susan deserves a special mention for her efforts in copyediting and for chasing some of the preoccupied storytellers in this book. Colleagues and students interning at Amnesty International India have indulged the erratic journey of the project conceptually, programmatically and financially.

To all of these people, the working team of *Art as Witness* expresses its heartfelt gratitude and thanks.

Parthiv Shah • Sana Das

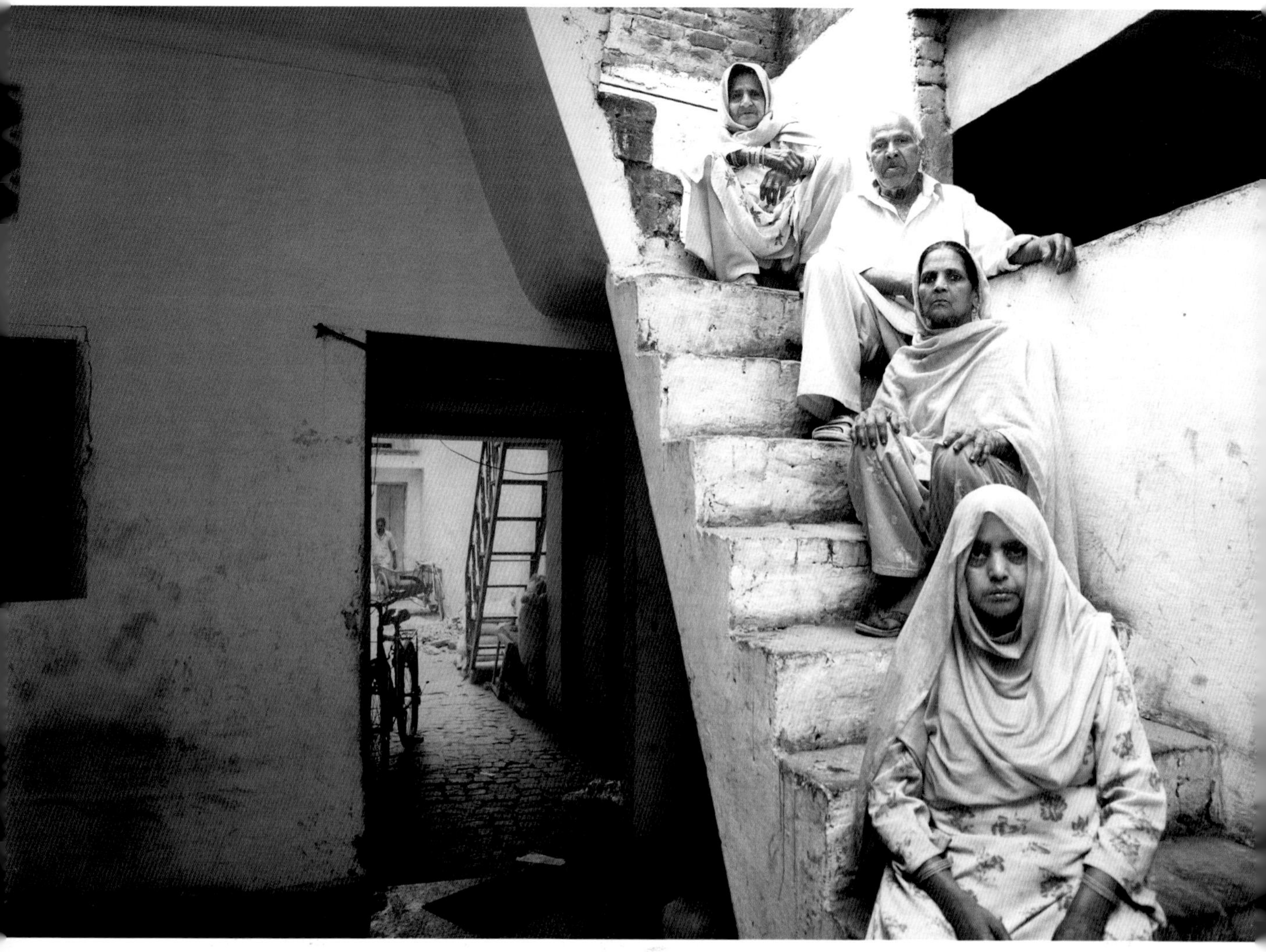

From the *Hashimpura* series by Parthiv Shah, India, 2008. (*Bottom to top, in ascending order*): Zarina of Hashimpura, whose husband Zheer and son Javed were killed by the Police Armed Constabulary at the Muran Nagar canal; Hajra and her husband Abdul Hamid, who lost their son Naem in the same killing; and Hameedan, whose husband was also killed.

Interrupting the Spectacle

Sana Das

When we wedge ourselves between politics and aesthetics, bravely imagining that we have an enabling concept for such an act, what indeed do we want art to achieve? If politics is about constraining the choices of others, what is art? It is particularly ironical to ask this when the 'end of art' has already been announced by various aesthetic regimes, and all we seem to have is a culture of the 'readymade', aided and abetted by technology. More so when artists and philosophers of aesthetics are convinced that in the modern and postmodern world, art is no longer concerned with 'beauty' but with 'fear', 'suspense', the 'grotesque' or 'awesome' – experiences that confound the mind, belie comprehension and are impossible to communicate. That is the juncture at which art is to interject itself vis-à-vis politics. The Kalinganagar killings, the Delhi bomb blasts, the Kandhamal attacks, Gujarat 2002, 9/11, Operation Blue Star, Operation Desert Storm, the Tsunami, the 'War on Mumbai' – these are all moments not of decipherment but of utter bafflement!

There are other questions too, of the 'impurity' of art; of the 'excesses' and 'false movements' of images that undervalue their truth and capacity to enhance experience. The problem with the photographic image is not that it is beautiful but that it is too beautiful, perfected as it is by technology; and its impurity for experience lies precisely in that technological perfection. Thus a very Platonic question emerges: Isn't the written word enough? Why do we need the image? Can an image truly take us to an understanding of an idea, an experience, a concept, in a way that words cannot? And what would it mean to readers if the image was to be seen as that which is 'in the way' of words – as an uncomfortable object intended to trip them – and not a supplement or substitute? In fact that is how the image enters this book: as an obstacle placed 'in the way' of smoothness in order to make the act of reading abrasive, painful, less forgettable. It has to be contended with, and cannot be bypassed to access the 'story'.

The photographs in this book, contributed by photo-artists who have been tracking and recording, for years, the tragedies and wounds wrought by the nation-states of India, Nepal,

Iran, Pakistan, Bangladesh and Burma/Myanmar, directly testify to this shocking combination of the perfect frame and the horror contained within it.

When we invite art into our politics more than as an inducement towards action, art is 'there' as a leaning towards memory, as a beseeching force that revisits the sites and damages of extermination and the grotesque – the numerous obliterations of bodies, histories, images, symbols, culture, memory. How best can art do that – make memory visible – when 'we' are a society without witnesses? By that I mean, we do not hold ourselves accountable to events, to deaths, to destruction – we haven't 'seen' or we are hostile to our own figurations as 'testimonies', and we enter the cycle of forgetting that emerges out of a culture of, what one may call, the 'domestication of death'. Deaths by hanging, bombings, shoot-outs, encounters, starvation and homelessness, in all their presentations of casual, everyday narrations, spectacles and stylizations by the media, appear to the modern mind, by such a logic of domestication, only as startling objects of forgetfulness.

In this situation where the idea of 'we' itself stands in all its fragility, how is art to give appearance or visibility to 'disappearance', to 'memory', to the deadlock of positions and ideas? Mukul Sharma's article in this book, 'Mirrors of Militarization', raises all the doubts of such an authentic 'we', and the senseless circle of violence and irresponsibility that these deadlocks generate. How, we may ask, can art itself become 'witness' or summon us as witnesses, even if that were to be so in a moment of hallucination? What is this book, then, if not such a 'hallucinatory moment' wherein such witnessing and summoning happens – where the event occurs as if today, 'now', and the reader appears at the threshold of the happening, the scene of the event, and leaves it footnoted and marked by gaze, by feeling?

This book is also talking within the narrow gap between the 'cult of the spectacle' and the 'cult of authenticity' in which our times are written. It is tempting to think of the 'spectacle' as the nation's 'protective belt', earning plausibility in the eyes of its people. Surely it is a performance of its own authenticity when the state carries out a 'public' hanging or a 'shoot-out' in full view of media back-up and coverage. These demolition drives of the state that acquire spectacle form are like 'purification rituals', a cleansing or purging of its 'body' of 'undesirables' for 'national safety'. As readers of these events, how do we look at the state's protective belts? You may well ask, what does any protective belt achieve? In the theorization of experience – and here I dare to popularize an idea put across by Vivek Dhareshwar – the 'protective belt' is a set of beliefs, true or false, that, as Imre Lakatos, the philosopher of science would put it, acts as 'immunization' against new experience. It prevents the jolt of new conditions. It preserves the status quo and gives body to our experience in a way that every situation presented before us is verified as either true or false on the basis of these beliefs. With our safety belts always on, we are secure in our old beliefs. Furthermore, we fear the 'falsification' of these beliefs. Thus the 'protective belt', be it for us or for the nation, means security. It also means that this security be made available without the risk of testing or falsifying our preconceptions. In not abandoning what has held our belief–experience 'together' so far, does not the 'protective belt' help us to stay within 'settled' notions about 'terrorists', 'militants', 'feminists', 'naxalites', 'activists', 'criminals', 'government', 'police', 'military', and so on and so forth? When we speak with the 'protective belt' on, we speak with the voice of 'authenticity' which is as 'true' as that of any unproven stereotype. What this book tries to do is to displace the 'protective belt' of beliefs with which readers approach the world of events. It invites them to risk a precarious footing into the world of spectacles, of deadlocks, demolitions and disappearances, without 'decidedness'.

Now, you may wonder if this book isn't a spectacle too? Yes, it is. A spectacle of memory, of obscured spaces, objects, performances and events. The photograph and the autobiographical voice have recognition in our times as masterful instruments of 'proof' in the business of 'authenticity' and 'truth-telling'; but this is not how they stage themselves in this book. They take their place more as a 'trace', as that which captures the differences and discord between forces, which carries the embers of the past in the present – and yet, being a trace, can never be presented fully. Thus, for instance, when we approach the history of capital punishment in the section 'The Gauze and the Gallows', we try to reach this discord at the very heart of truth-telling through the historical use of literary narratives on capital punishment, on the one hand, and narratives of murder-victim families, on the other. By doing so, we are, no doubt, staging its spectacle for the reader, but not as a relic. It is there for readers to witness as *haute couture* developed to the level of fine art, a critical narrative element in the 'task of civilization', and a confounding presence felt by both abolitionists and many who have lost their loved ones to acts of violence and killing. With this logic, Chittaroopa Palit's 'Slayers and the Slain', and the interview with Sabrina Lall, and my own essay 'The Death Machine', are placed as two sides of a tossed coin. In en-framing experiences of imprisonment or a bunker in Kashmir in the form of a film or a poem, we are travelling through the idea with the aid of a 'trace'. Thus the landscape of an event, a phenomenon, a way of life, or a law or a struggle with the past emerges through the forces of facilitation that only such a 'trace' can provide. Gowhar Fazili's short essay, 'A Fool's Paradise', on the metamorphosed faces of Kashmir, gives evidence of this. 'Who Was He?', Inder Salim's poem on a chance meeting with an *azaadi* fighter in Kashmir, perhaps tracks the 'trace' in its most appropriate setting of 'difference' in the Valley, a difference that dare not be remembered and yet cannot be forgotten, and, most significantly, makes us witness to this 'marking' that in a single stroke blurs difference and sameness. But not unlike watermarks, the book runs the risk of elusiveness, of stories and images lying beyond themselves. The fictional, autobiographical, pictorial, poetic and interactive that make up the 'body' of this book carry for us just such a 'trace' of the 'unspeakable', which is fear, terror, hopelessness, horror, despair, amazement and so much more. We will find this expressive range, bordering on the 'absurd', finely captured in a dramatization by the popular theatre and television actor from Kashmir, Nazir Josh. Being a 'presence' that at the same time speaks of 'absence', these texts are not merely what they reveal, but also about what is 'not-there', beckoning us to the 'outside', the 'beyond' of the frame and the word, to the forgotten or the inexpressible – the ineffable. Parthiv Shah's image of three old women and a man on a broken staircase in Hashimpura tugs at and puzzles the conscience for precisely such a conjuring.

The stories and images in this book are nothing less than knockings from the attic of a rotting state – what else can you call a story tumbling out of Hashimpura, a twenty-year-old struggle to give bullet-ridden ghosts a decent legal hearing? Here, V.N. Rai and Vrinda Grover give first-hand accounts of their experience. There are rumblings from prisons in India, Nepal, Iran, Pakistan, Burma, to answer the question, 'Who is in our jails today?' Kanak Mani Dixit's 'From the Underbelly of the Beast' and Kian Tajbaksh's 'May I Have a Book to Read?' demonstrate the prison experience in Nepal and Iran, respectively, against the political turmoil in these states. Lipta Bhau's 'The Colour of Khaki', Saroj Mohanty's 'Two Sojourns in Prison', Lachit Bardoloi's 'A Fraudulent Matter', Iftikhar Gilani's 'Tales from Tihar' and Nandita Haksar's 'Solidarity Football' bring attention to 'who' fills and waits in India's prisons and 'why'. Gowhar Fazili, in an exclusive interview with Kashmir Singh in 'The Spy, the Quran and the Death Penalty', takes us to the countless days he spent in a Pakistani prison as an Indian spy and his encounter with the death sentence. Apart from personal experiences and interviews, the book also carries short information pieces on prison experience and prison reform initiatives in the region. There are desperate petitions from the tribal areas of Chhattisgarh studied by Nandini Sundar; haunting images of prayer, mourning, disappearance and homelessness from the country, its hinterland and neighbourhood, that take us to the underbelly of democracy and security. Like the 'madwoman' in *Jane Eyre* who emerges, after years of being locked up in the attic, to burn the house down and to say without words that she exists, the stories and pictures in this book tumble out from years of storage in forgotten towns, in familiar–peculiar roadside structures, from time-smudged minds. As voices from the attic and not from a decorated sitting room, they are a little disarrayed, a little frightening, unpredictable, discordant ...

These stories are by people seen as having no stories of their own; they represent anti-stories wherein they are themselves negated, caricatured, obscured, made to please or stereotyped. They have either, to use the expression offered by Virginia Woolf, been 'killed into art', that is, beautified into 'art objects' to hang in museums and art galleries, or, contrarily, been made to appear as 'scheming' and 'monstrous' to authenticate the nation's official history and official witch-hunts against activists, doctors, journalists, advocates, minorities, sub-nationalists, naxalites, terrorists, spies and others in various suitable ways. This book is about the stubborn autonomy of the people behind these anti-stories. These are stories that will hopefully no longer stay with the presenters of the book or the authors, but get away from them. Slip away into the consciousness of careless and alert readers, and trouble them like an injury – angry and poking. Like one of our protagonists Balbir Kaur, all the way from Amritsar, 1984, does in Nandita Haksar's account of events, 'The Costs of Proving One's Innocence'. As does our barely literate but worldly-wise Imdongla, the Manipuri woman, who leaves the army officer shaken in Temsula Ao's narrative, 'A Simple Woman'. Stories that will say, 'We have summoned you to our experience! Now you should neither sit nor stand! For a moment, stop!' In fact, herein follows our counter-spectacle, a rupture of the 'spectacle' that marks the book.

The idea is best captured by Stephane Mallarme's prose-poem, 'Le Spectacle Interrompu' ('The Spectacle Interrupted'), depicting the exhibition of a dancing bear by a clown. Jacques

Ranciere, in his book *The Future of the Image*, draws attention to the special moment when the bear stops the clown, in fact the whole performance, by placing his paws on the clown's shoulder, as if to ask the secret of his power over him! This 'accident' within the performance is a powerful gesture of the captive turning on the *madari*, involving not only these two actors at different ends of power-play, but also the audience. So too for our readers: the poignance of being summoned as 'witness' to a moral moment is laid bare before them. How will they respond? As clown or bear? Or both? Are the readers aware if they are 'fixing' other people in their so-called places in the name of the pantomime of 'national security'? Or are they 'fixed' to the voyeurism of 'discipline and punish' as the rightful benefit of citizenship? Do they, like the bear, have the courage – momentary, accidental – to create a 'pause'? If indeed all of us are witnesses, whether called into the courtroom or not, whether we keep our eyes wide open or downcast, glaring or shame-faced, how are we going to respond to the 'pause' that this book represents? And how, in this brief moment, are we going to think a bit more about the secret of our power, and our powerlessness? ... The book is not more ambitious than that. It asks for a pause, and it is within this imagined interruptive space that it offers both fictional and autobiographical accounts, poetry and essay, word as image and image as text. Real-life scenarios have altered since some of these texts and images were prepared, for instance, the grant of bail to Dr Binayak Sen in 2009. Notwithstanding these changes, the evocations in the 'time of the narrative' remain sufficiently porous to grant an entry into the 'trace' of the moment discussed. The two pieces in this book that refer to Binayak Sen's imprisonment – Lipta Bhau's 'The Colour of Khaki' and Nandita Haksar's 'Doctor in Jail' – may be read in that light.

Born out of Amnesty International India's 'Art for Activism' campaign, the book is also about activism for art. The photographs on the vandalism of M.F. Husain's photographs not only stand witness, but also invite the reader to step into the witness-box. Will the readers let these stories prevail? We know that it is the 'politics of plausibility' that will eventually determine which stories will be believed. Or will the voice of Gramscian 'commonsense' prevail, the commonsense that is the sense of the powerful? Will readers be able to separate these stories from stereotypes? Will they mark their reading in such a way as to tell us if we have indeed represented what we set out to? Till such time we shall hold our breath.

Images for Change

Parthiv Shah

The challenge of reaching out to wider audiences and disseminating what may be called 'uncomfortable' information is usually a difficult one. The inability to get across is not always a case of the reader/viewer not knowing the reality (there are times when it is); it is also about dealing with self-delusion, an implosion of images, the all-consuming media – an endless list and not mutually exclusive. The world of rights – the struggles, the 'ugliness' of it, on the one hand, and the strength of being part of it, of learning from it, on the other – is also very much trapped in this context. How can one make these issues part of the social conscience, how can one make them more visible?

My own photographs have dealt with these issues: of freedom of expression, of image perception and representation. My visual journeys as a photographer and curator have led me to work with communities which are trying to find a voice and an identity – the transgender, the mill workers of Gujarat, the communities of men who have sex with men, victims of the Hashimpura massacre in Uttar Pradesh, families of missing persons in Kashmir, displaced people living on the banks of the Narmada – concerns that have preoccupied and have been taken up by rights-based groups.

How does the visual make the connect in a globalized world where everything tends to get labelled or compartmentalized; where one is complacent within a network one is comfortable with, with little awareness of what is going on around? Among the growing middle classes of today's fast-developing economies one can see that people have little time to look around and see beyond their own concerns. How, then, does one approach an audience – viewers, readers – that may not be interested in work that one feels strongly about? Perhaps by using languages and conventions they are familiar with. To that extent, images come in handy to tell our stories; as much as they are our stories, the visual drives home the point that they are theirs too! Visuals have always played an important role in documenting issues, peoples and events – through conflicts, calamities and celebrations. It would not be an exaggeration to say that many of these remain etched in people's minds, constructing structures of memory or nostalgia.

Organizations like Amnesty International which work across the globe raising the issue of rights have felt the need to broaden their platform and reach wider audiences. It is important to fight the battle of rights legally and to raise its concerns in political forums, but it is also important to create public opinion. Books like the one we have put together here can play a vital role in doing this. Through this book Amnesty hopes to draw people's attention to different kinds of rights violations in and around South Asia. There are many ways to communicate on the subject of human rights – through books that are written, films that are made, news stories that are published, the staging of plays, and of course through images that are reproduced. Each of these can achieve and attract a limited constituency.

Through this book we hope to target an audience that in turn can reach wider and diverse audiences, making this a challenge in itself for the working team. To reach a media-savvy audience one has to strike the right balance; even as all the vital issues are addressed, the way they are 'packaged' is crucial. The images in this book have been selected from works of photographers based in India, Iran, Pakistan, Bangladesh, Malaysia and Myanmar. It is not surprising that despite the varied cultures and contexts, many of the rights issues they raise are similar. It has been important for me in selecting and curating this body of images, to ensure that both the local aesthetics and the global implications of the issues are adequately conveyed.

The photographers – both artists and photojournalists – who have contributed to this book are deeply committed to human rights concerns.

Shahidul Alam from Bangladesh has been working on various rights issues for many years. His images in the book deal with domestic violence. They take the viewer on a journey to an unseen world where no one goes, where no one hears or speaks a common language.

Swapan Nayak documents the internally displaced people of the North-Eastern states of India, victims of ethnic rivalry and violence who have become refugees in their own country.

Sohrab Hura's evocative black-and-white images, *Land of a Thousand Struggles*, depict the harsh realities of the rich–poor divide in India. While there is rapid growth of high-rises in the major cities, many live below the poverty-line, often working for less than the minimum wage and in abysmal conditions.

Sonia Jabbar has been working in Kashmir to bring the issue of disappearances to public attention. In this book her images are of families that have lost their loved ones and of the sense of void left behind. The women in her photographs – wives, daughters, mothers and sisters – are protagonists who have a long struggle ahead.

Harikrishna Katragadda, a photojournalist, was in the USA during the Iraq war. The Republican Party held a convention on the theme 'Fulfilling America's Promise by Building a Safer World and a More Hopeful America' in New York City in August 2004, seeking the re-election of George Bush. The images he created then, against the background of the New York skyline, capture the protest in a unique visual language.

Abdul Rahman Roslan has been working with and photographing Burmese refugees in Malaysia. With a large number of them having had no choice but to leave their families behind, these refugees remain lost and stranded.

Daniel Pepper works in Myanmar/Burma in Southeast Asia, a country of about 50 million people which has been under military rule in one form or another since 1962. 'The military's strategy for the last ten years has been to bring the entire civilian population under direct control for forced labour and monitoring', says Kevin Heppner of the Karen Human Rights Group, based in Thailand; '... but the villagers don't want to live under military control. So they evade the troops, leaving the villages before they arrive. They live with very little or no relief or aid.' The result has been thousands of refugees, and a growing humanitarian crisis.

Salima Hashmi's work focuses on the sufferings of women, especially under the Zia-ul-Haq regime in Pakistan, considered one of Pakistan's most repressive eras, the after-effects of which can still be seen. Hashmi treats photographs within her art practice as an advocacy tool, while her paintings are usually abstract figures of women which reveal the political and social uncertainties under which the people of Pakistan live.

Shahzad Noorani's photographs deal with child labour – a reflection of the absolute poverty of the developing countries. Ecological disasters and the decline of traditional economic activities have subjected South Asia to an uprooting process of unparalleled dimensions. Criminal networks profit from this and their main victims are children.

K.M. Asad has worked with child labourers at the dockyards by the Buriganga river in Dhaka. A large work force has developed in this area. The children of this community aspire to develop their lives here, while the workers' dream is that their children will grow up to help them in their trade.

Suvendu Chatterjee has been photographing the people's movement in Manipur, a small state in the northeastern corner of India which has witnessed deep social and political turmoil. His photographs evoke a visceral response.

Sara Rahbar was born in Tehran, Iran, but the revolution in Iran and the start of the Iran–Iraq war caused her to flee her birthplace. 'Our foundations lay,' she states, 'but our houses have burned to the ground. Building castles in the sky for a species that cannot fly, brick by limb we tear it down. Thinking that we are moving forwards, yet moving backwards all along. Gajar woman and golden toys, we wait for dawn.' Her images evoke memory, longing and inertia in inhabiting the tensions of dual disjuncture.

I sincerely hope this book will open a window to viewers/readers who don't usually get to see such images, and who are perhaps simply not familiar with all that is happening around them!

Performance

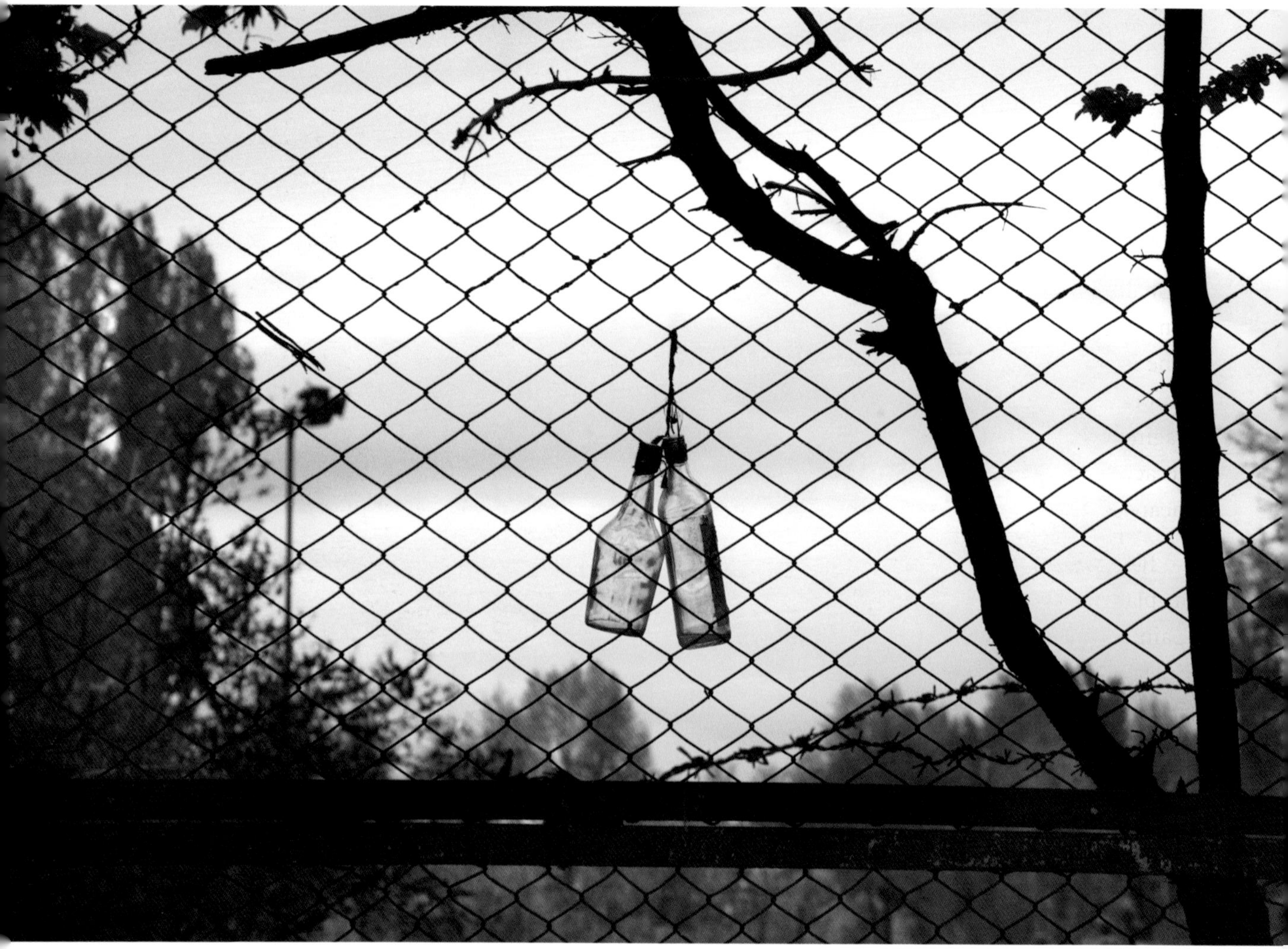

From the *Barbed Wire and Beautiful Skies* series by Parthiv Shah, India, 2008.

The Fool's Paradise

Gowhar Fazili

The tragedy of life is not its hopelessness but that it is tantalizingly pregnant with possibilities: so many possibilities that most will have to fade into oblivion even before being fully known, let alone realized. (Ghalib would either have agreed with me on this or sued me for plagiarism.) What one is able to grab is so little that it amounts to practically nothing. Writing is one way of raging against this fruitless battle of refusing to accept inevitability. It is on the fringes of near-nothingness that our hopes rest.

It hurts to look at Kashmir from an airplane in spring. But to experience this pain you probably need to be a Kashmiri (please overlook the parochialism being unleashed). It is the beauty that slices your heart. If you are not a Kashmiri, or not someone sensitive to the situation there, the view is merely beautiful. From the sky, Kashmir appears in the form of emerging greens and lushness behind multilayered plumes of clouds.

Hopes and clouds are enmeshed in Kashmir. I wonder if this has a longer history. My memory goes as far back as the late 1980s and refuses to pierce through the haze any further. If I force myself to look further back, beyond 1987, all I seem to recall is the mixed pain of days at school and the childhood bliss of long, lazy winter holidays. As children we would resort to special prayers and incantations to stretch the winter holidays longer by making it snow for the good part of the spring. This happened year after year, so my faith in this regard is unshakeable.

Beyond these memories, I must take recourse to images evoked by Bollywood films of the 1960s to 1980s, and their unceasing romance with Kashmir. Bollywood is the haze through which all views of Kashmir must pass. That is the Kashmir of dazzling greens, dreamy blue lakes, snowy mountains, lazy pony rides, and love songs around flowerbeds and in *shikaras*. In all these movies the Valley is empty of its people and their concerns. The local people appear, if at all, only as a benign backdrop to romances from elsewhere. They seem to occasionally materialize as a *Kashmir ki Kali* (1964), a mainland girl lost and raised in Kashmir, or as the boatman in *Jab Jab Phool Khiley* (1965), a naive fellow with whom a *malken* (lady) from the mainland falls in love while taking a pony ride. The Kashmiri language in these films is a funny blabber, exactly as it would sound to an outsider unfamiliar with the local language. Kashmir seems so peaceful in these movies, why wouldn't one willingly trade the real-world memory for the cinematic? The Kashmir of (India's) desires is a land shorn of its people and, along with them, its problems. For what is the 'Kashmir problem' but its people? (Perhaps this is a problem with the genre. Perhaps people from Goa, Shimla, Ooty and other cinematic destinations feel the same.)

Like in a tragicomedy, when Kashmiris do finally arrive on the cinema screen in the 1990s, they turn up as horrifying 'terrorists' or their unfortunate family members, as villains or victims, as gullible misled youths, or simply as a backdrop to the war between heroes and villains – the Indians and the Pakistanis. It has been a long process of becoming, from near non-existence to an existence of some sort. But one wonders if obscurity would have been better. (Once again, apologies to Ghalib for I am skirting too close to '*Na hota mein to kya hota*'.)

What would it be like if the movies of the 1960s were shot in present-day Kashmir? The camera would find it hard to keep out the bunkers and security personnel that dot the place. It would also capture the irony and ease with which the symbols of violence have become a permanent feature of the Kashmiri landscape and – if there is such a thing – the mindscape. In the early 1990s these symbols used to look like temporary aberrations. Now they have become naturalized to the extent that their absence would create a sense of loss: a gaping hole, a hollow nothingness. For instance, during my last visit home, I found the massive bunker at the mouth of Court Road missing. Consequently, the traffic was moving with such ease that it felt like the world was about to come to an end.

Most of the bunkers have been 'jazzed up' with fluorescent camouflage paint-jobs that render them striking rather than obscure them. Maybe we need a new word, 'camouflaunt', to describe the phenomenon. After all, bunkers are not supposed to look like ticket booths at a circus. When one imagines a true and honest bunker, a classical bunker and an authentic one, the image is of the menacing bunkers of the early 1990s, made out of pure jute sacks filled with sand. Since then the bunkers have undergone so many changes that one could do with a brief history. The corrugated tin roof was a necessity from the very beginning, given the treacherous weather and hostile terrain, not to mention the untrustworthy people. But it took them a couple of winters to realize that the jute bags weren't good enough. They needed to be protected by a plastic cover to last through the snowy winters. I guess they had no idea then what a long haul it was going to be, or maybe it was just a resource crunch. It took many, many long winters to perfect the bunkers to the local requirements and soon heating systems had to be installed. No wonder the bunker had to draw from the local tradition of a makeshift *bukhari*. Slowly but steadily, the bunkers evolved into brick-and-concrete structures with barbed wire coiled around them and a full-fledged net to bounce off grenades and other aerial attacks – mostly local invectives from the irritated traffic. (Kashmiri curses are known to be among the most potent in the world.) Road blockades and diversions have changed from simple rocks pulled off the pavements to a wide range of fancy metal frames.

One could look at the present stage of evolution of the bunker in two ways. Either it is the triumph of the native to which even brute symbols of violence have had to submit. Or, one could look at it as a cruel joke that bunkers are here to stay – not just for long – but forever. We must quickly erase this latter thought, and not let go of either hope or humour.

People tell me of times when Bollywood blockbusters used to première in Srinagar. Such must have been the viewership! And maybe this had to do with tourism. Cinema halls are another way of tracing Kashmir's recent history. Like many other buildings of public utility – the indoor stadium, colleges and schools, hotels and heritage sites, anything that had a roof including the partially built World Bank-funded facility meant for mushroom harvesting – cinema halls have been turned into garrisons and torture cells.

In the absence of contemporary cinema, what is the language that would do justice to the mood of contemporary Kashmir? It is not easy to write about Kashmir in a serious mode. Any attempt to do so would fail to represent the complexity and irrationality of the situation that prevails. If one were to make sense of the events that have passed since 1989, no logical explanation could capture it completely, for it is a world gone mad.

I am not trying to say that nobody is responsible for the suffering, or that everybody is responsible and thus escape the burden of belling the cat. But the dynamics of what happens or has been happening is too complex to make rational explanation possible.

There is a language that local people resort to while communicating this impossibility – a language that makes the surreal and tumultuous situation at least bearable. It is the language of the absurd. *Bhand-e-pather*, a traditional form of theatre in Kashmir, has deployed this technique for centuries now to engage in political critique. It has survived some of the most oppressive regimes in human history. Its sustained survival is due probably to the genre it works with – the absurd. *Bhand-e-pather* engages in extreme frivolity, even what may be considered vulgarity by the refined, only to be able to talk about cruelty that is beyond human understanding.

In its traditional form, it was performed at fairs associated with local shrines and temples. It was on the decline even before the 'trouble' started in Kashmir, as newer forms of entertainment, such as television and cinema, became popular. But the conditions that prevailed in Kashmir during the early 90s made assembly, not to speak of public theatre, impossible. The *Bhands* (the performers) went underground. However, an innovation by Nazir Josh, from Budgam, especially thrived during times of extreme political trouble. He was successful in appropriating the form and using it in serialized form for television. Three of his serials, probably the most popular in their times, were *Bale Totma*, *Hazar Dastan* (alternatively called *Ehed Raza*, after its lead character played by Nazir Josh) and *Juma German*. Bale Totma was a vulgar fellow who would perform song-and-dance routines to comment on the prevailing social ironies. *Hazar Dastan* was a caricature of political regimes, with particular reference to the Farooq Abdullah government, his rise to power and his coterie of stupid *wazir*s. Juma German was a World War veteran-turned-policeman who would engage in extreme violence to control petty crime. He was extremely brutal but comic, armed with instruments of local domesticity such as the *kanger* (firepot), *soi* (an itch-inducing weed traditionally used to discipline deviant juveniles), etc., to inflict punishment on his victims. *Juma German* was aired on television in the early 90s, when police and paramilitary brutalities were rampant. Somehow, even while extreme censorship was in place, Nazir Josh's serial was aired uncensored for over 30 episodes, as was his earlier *Hazar Dastan*: a direct comment on rigged elections, corruption, and the inefficiency and immaturity of the political class. The beauty of Josh's work lay in his genius in producing a language which simultaneously talked to people of all classes and alienated none. It is said that even the people who were the butt of his jokes would enjoy the serial in the privacy of their homes.

Josh operated within the constraints of a *sarkari* (state) medium with all its bottlenecks, bureaucracy and interference from *sarkari* agencies that have nothing whatsoever to do with art – and survived.

Nazir Josh and his work provide us an exemplary take on the question of whether it is possible to position oneself both inside and outside the conflict even while, to borrow Zizek's phrase, not being malevolently neutral.

Military Calligraphy Parthiv Shah

From the *Barbed Wire and Beautiful Skies* series

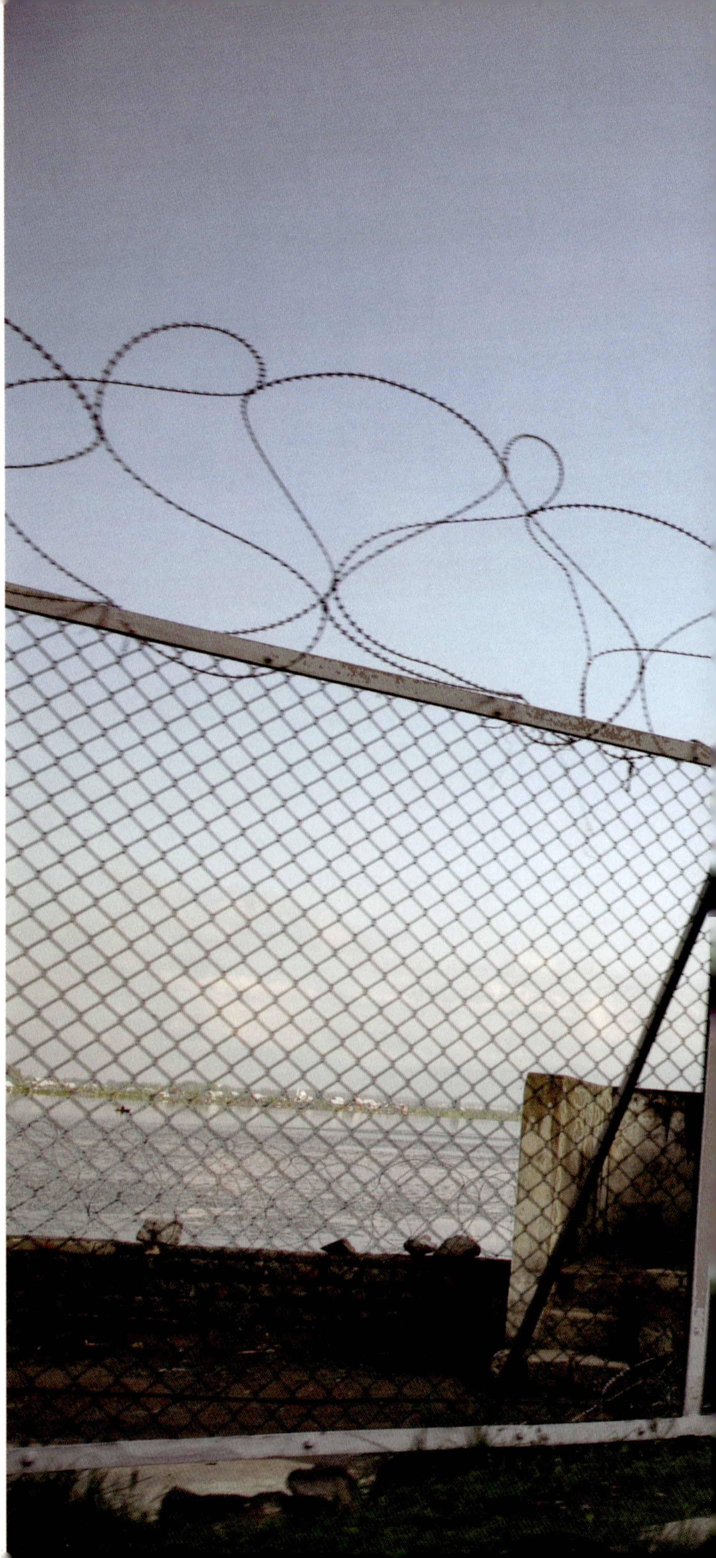

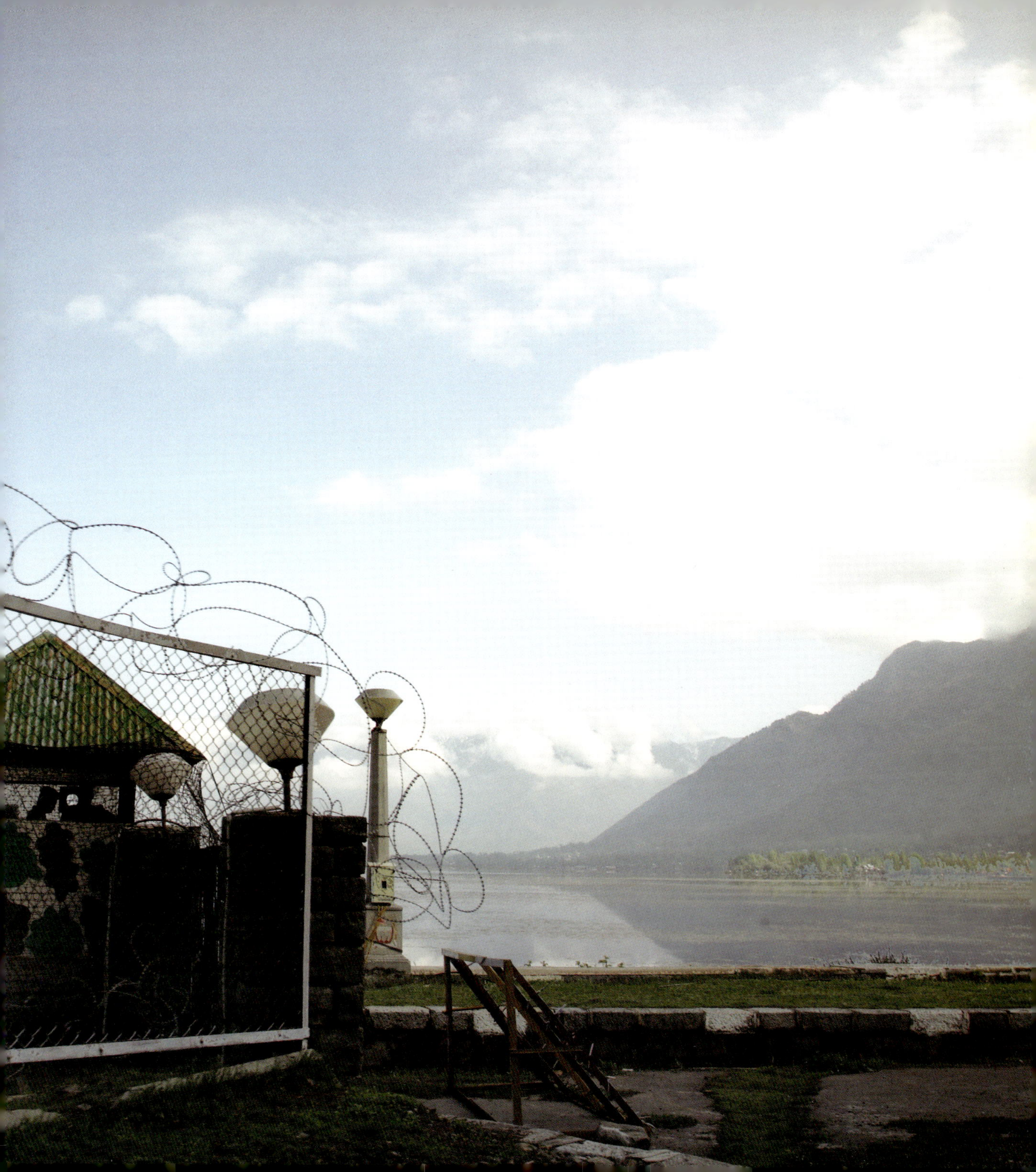

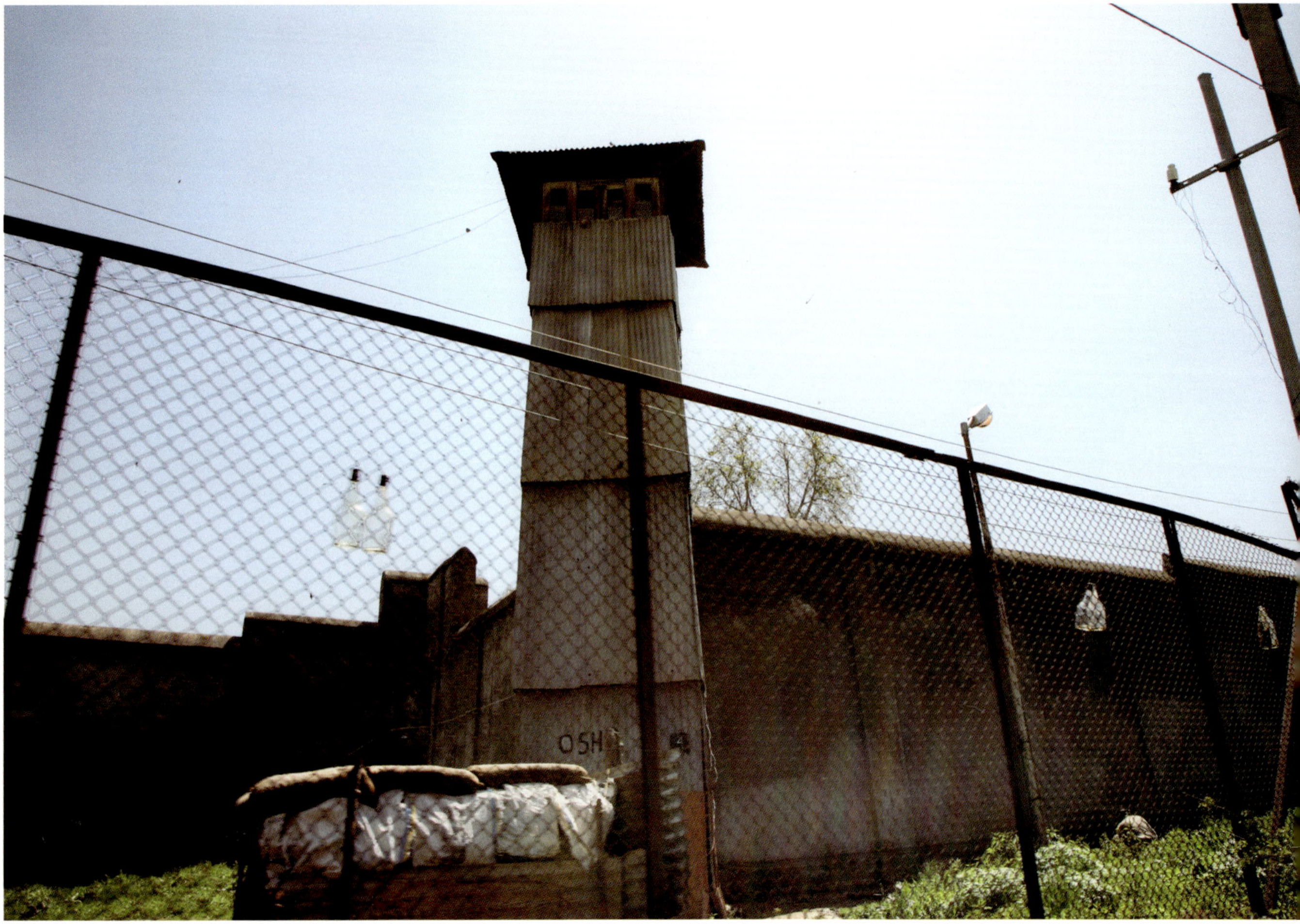

Central Jail, Kashmir. By Parthiv Shah, India, 2008.

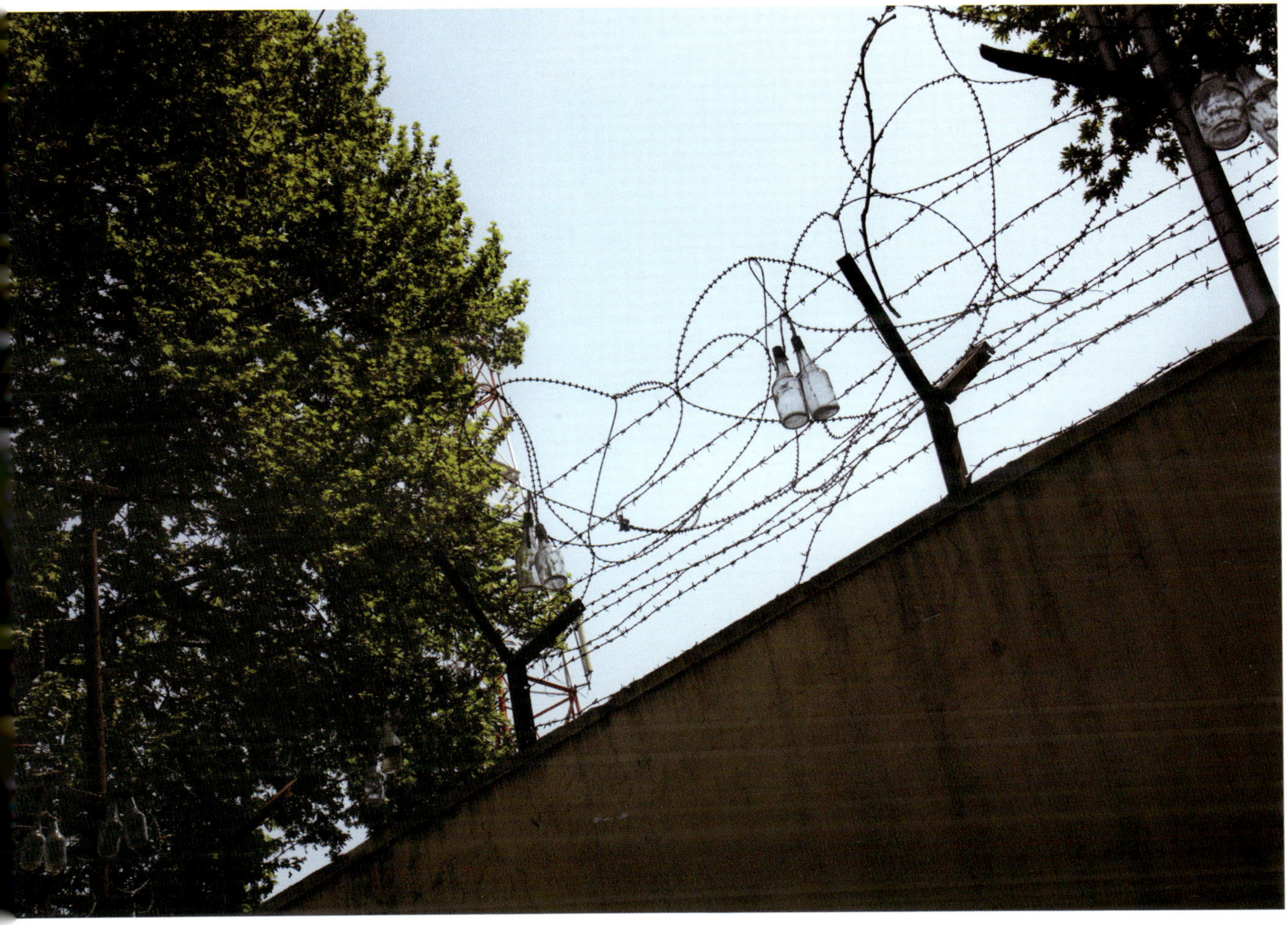

Chinar trees, bottles and razor-blades are Kashmir's new sky-line. By Parthiv Shah, India, 2008.

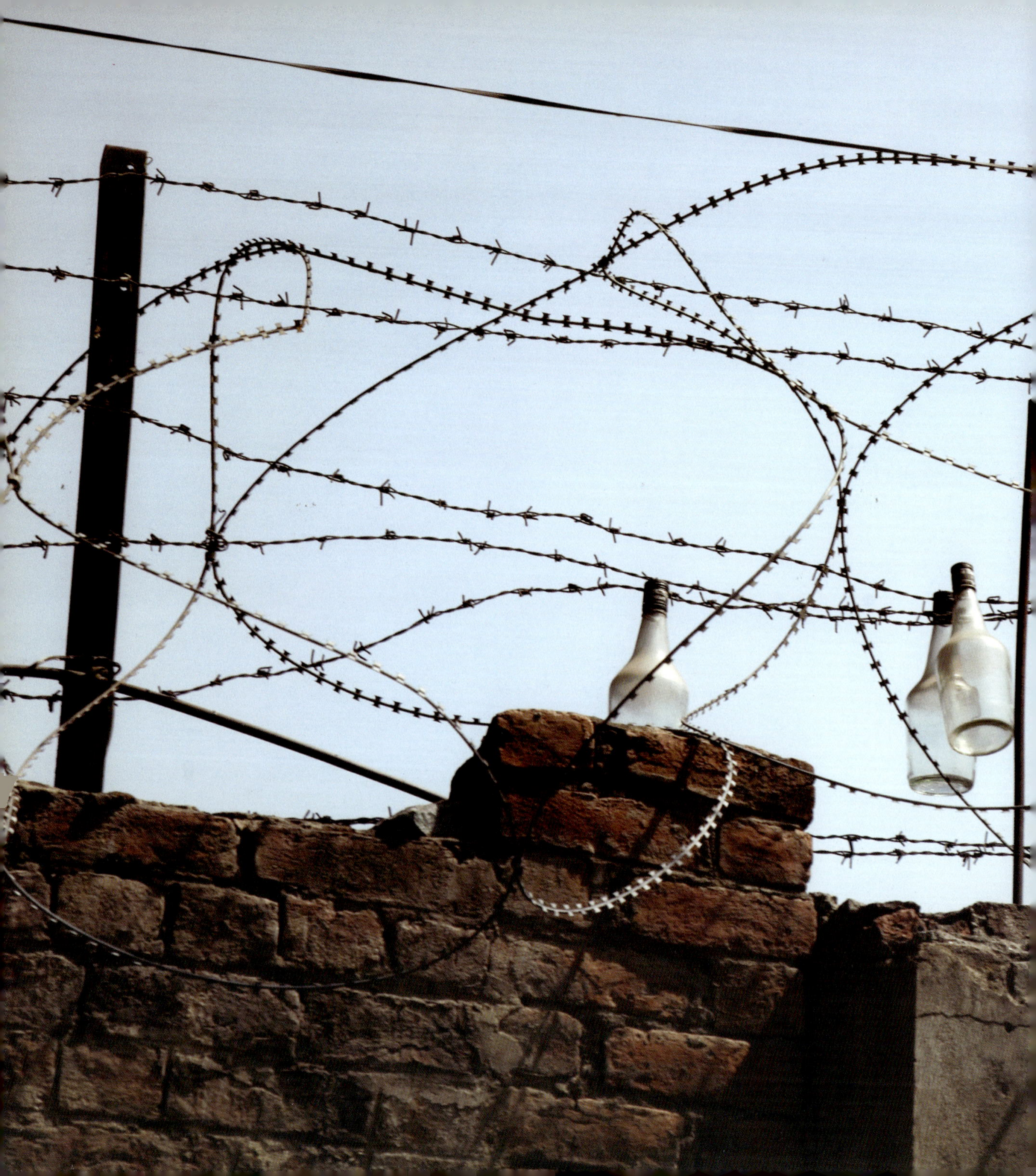

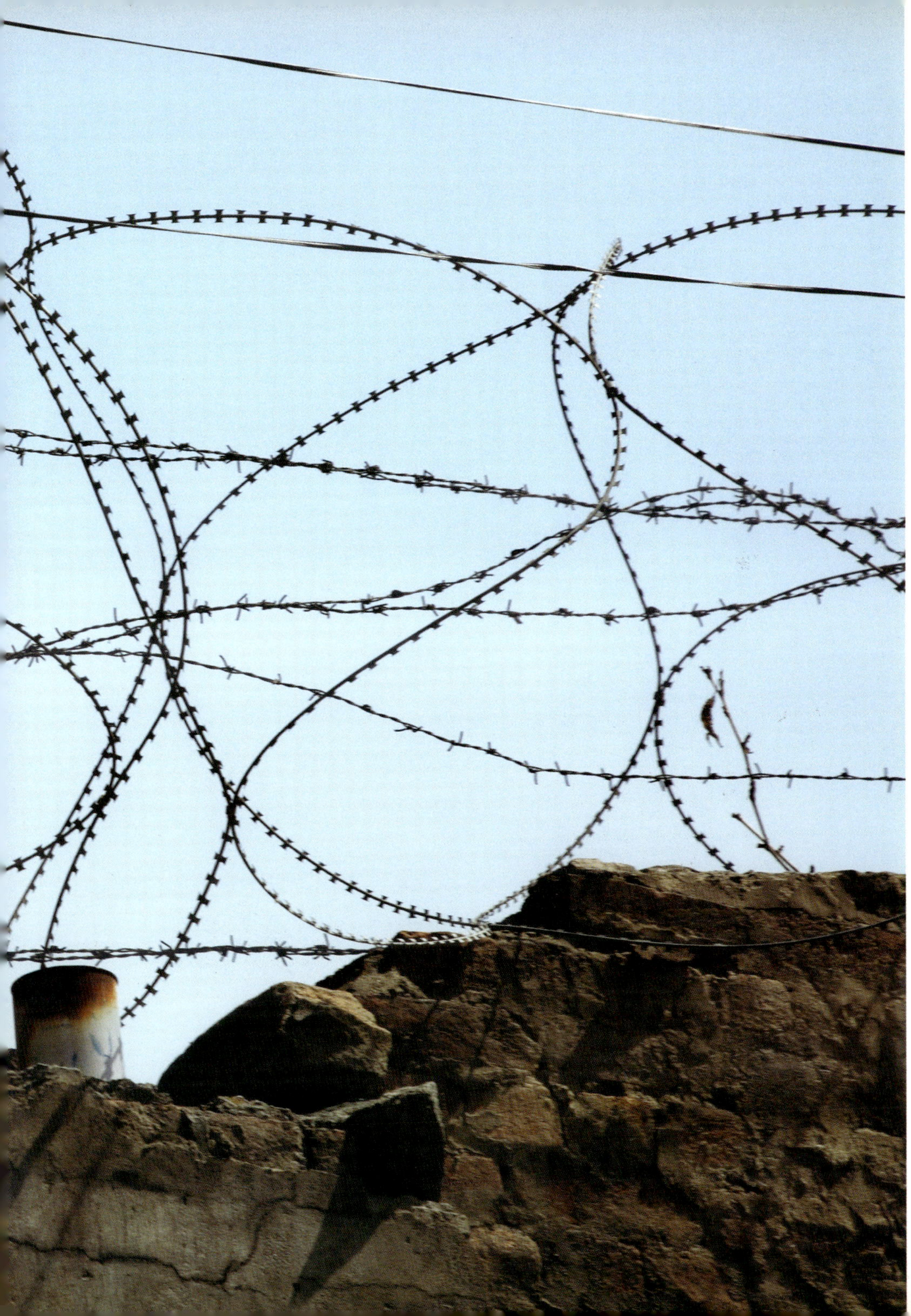

A Valley Camouflages Parthiv Shah

From the *Barbed Wire and Beautiful Skies* series

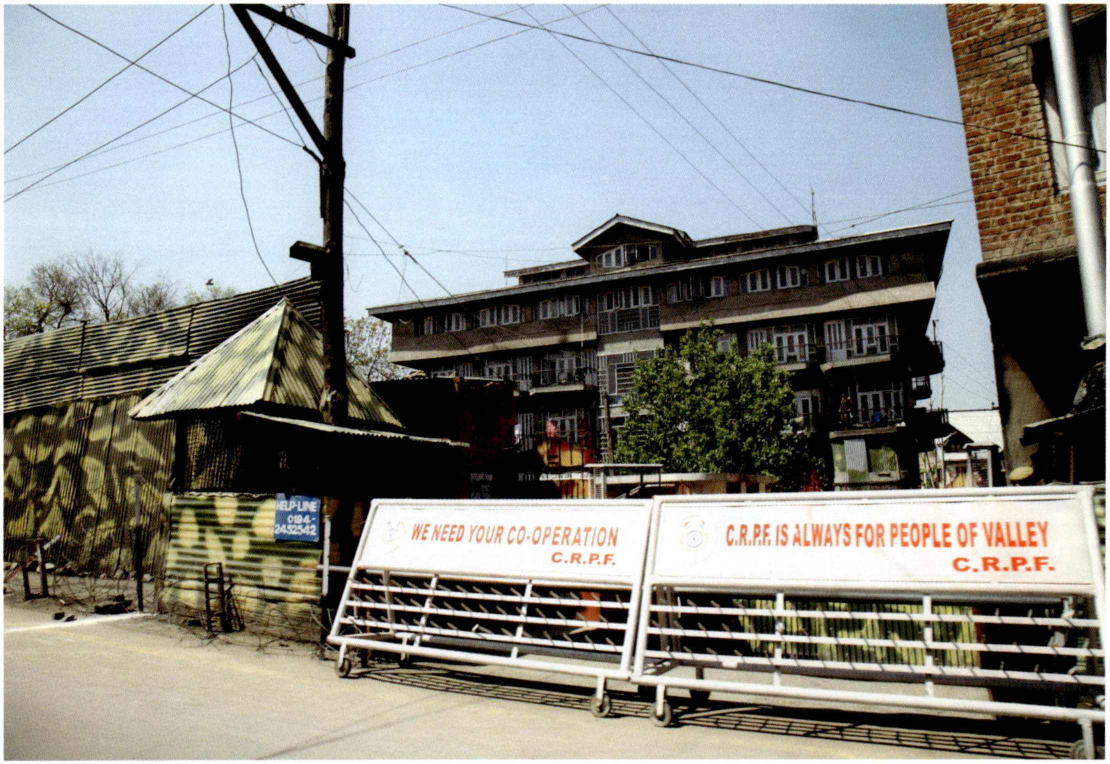

Firdous Cinema, now a resting place for the armed forces. By Parthiv Shah, India, 2008.

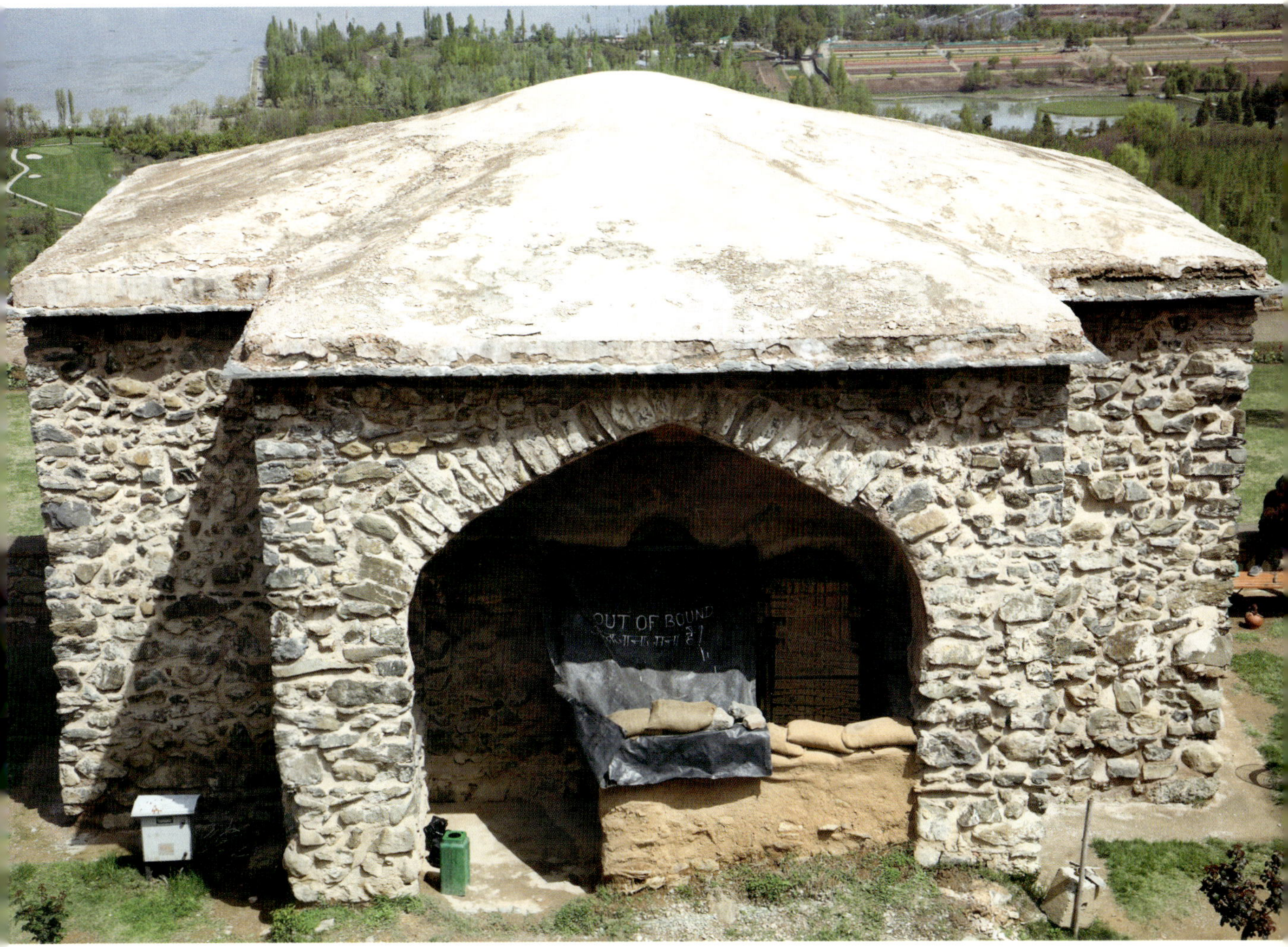

'Out of bounds', a bunker inside Pari Mahal. By Parthiv Shah, India, 2008.

Overleaf: Kashmir Valley from a bunker, this is what the soldier sees. By Parthiv Shah, India, 2008.

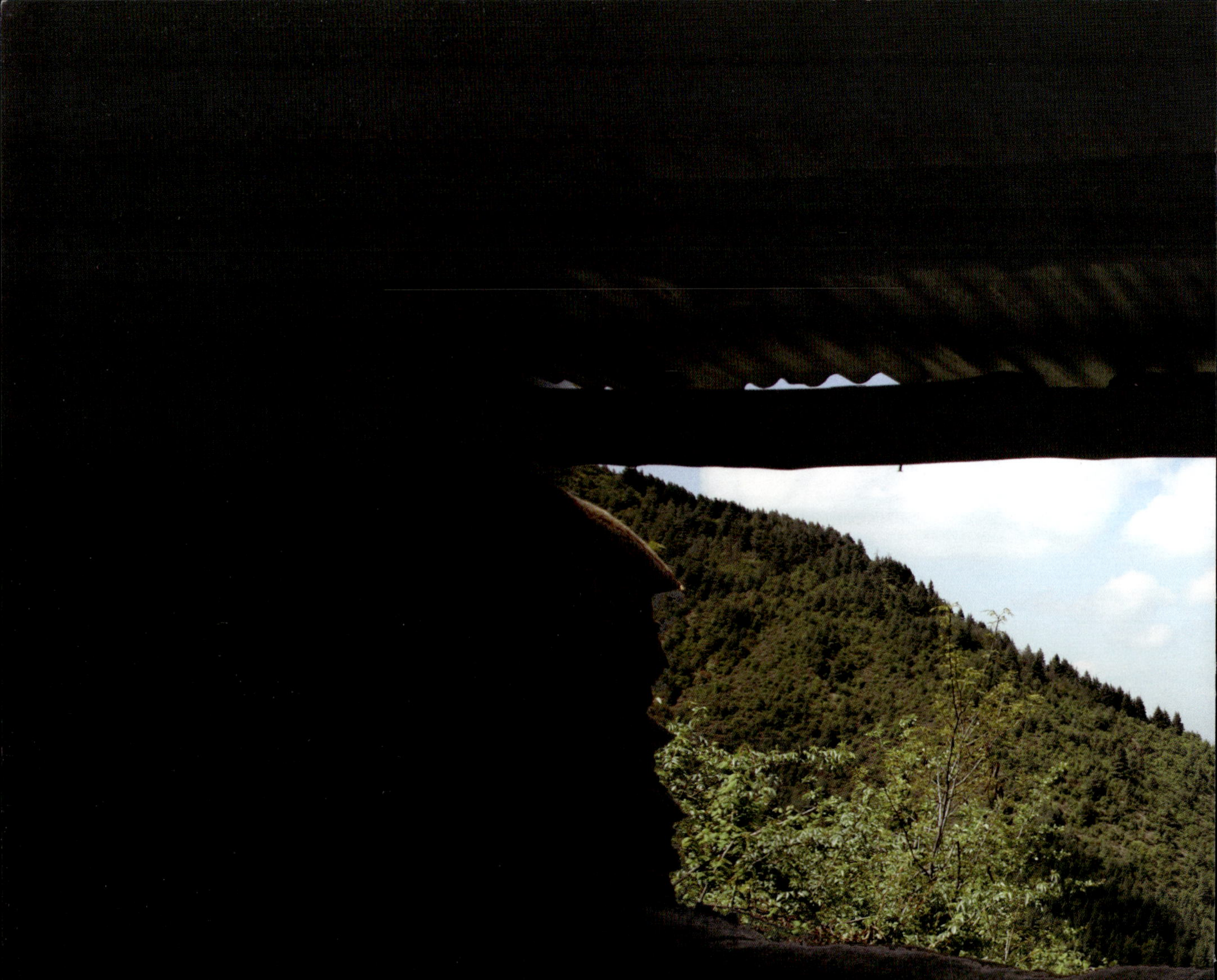

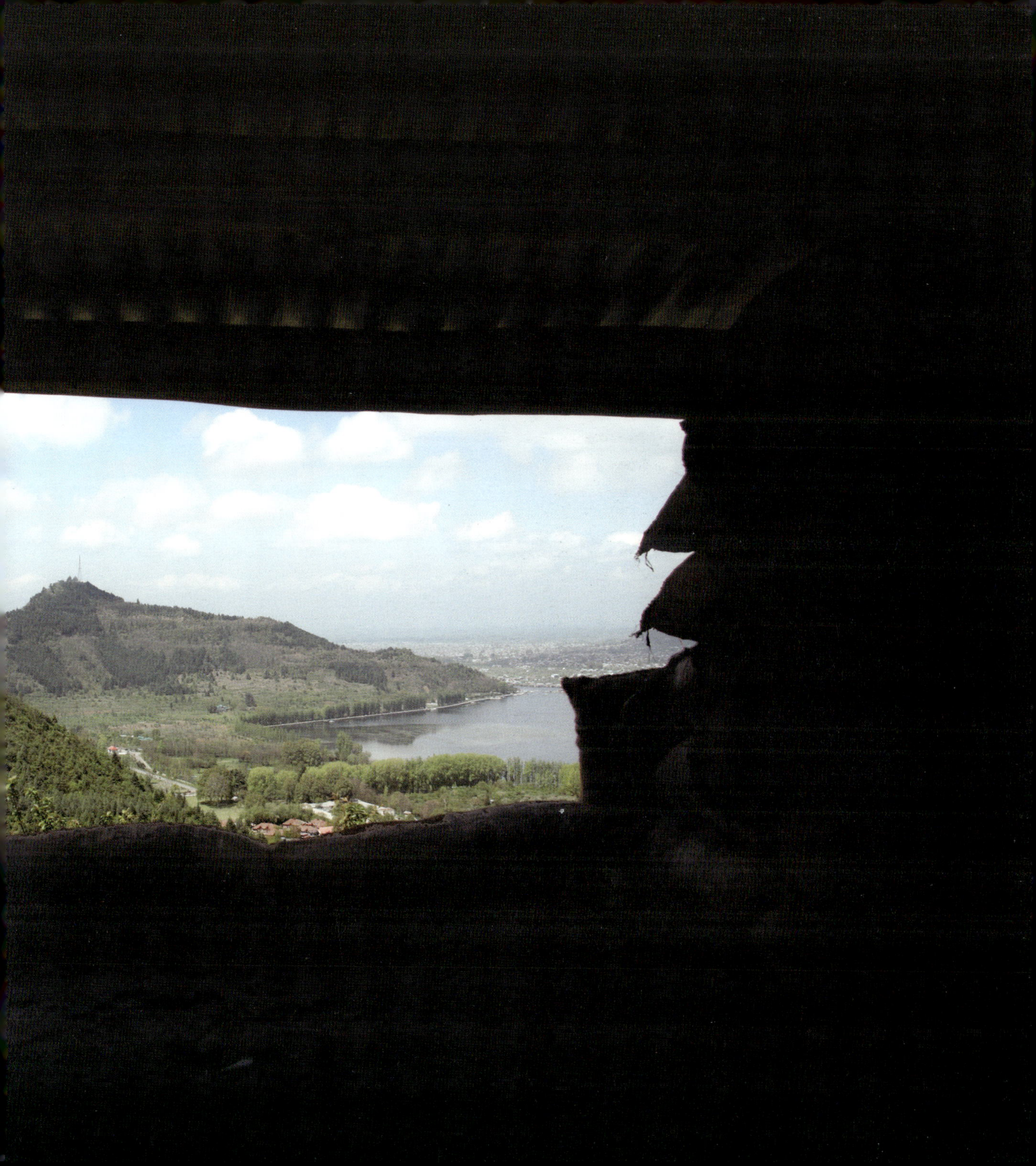

The Many Moods of an Actor: Nazir Josh, Kashmir

Parthiv Shah

From the *Barbed Wire and Beautiful Skies* series, 2008

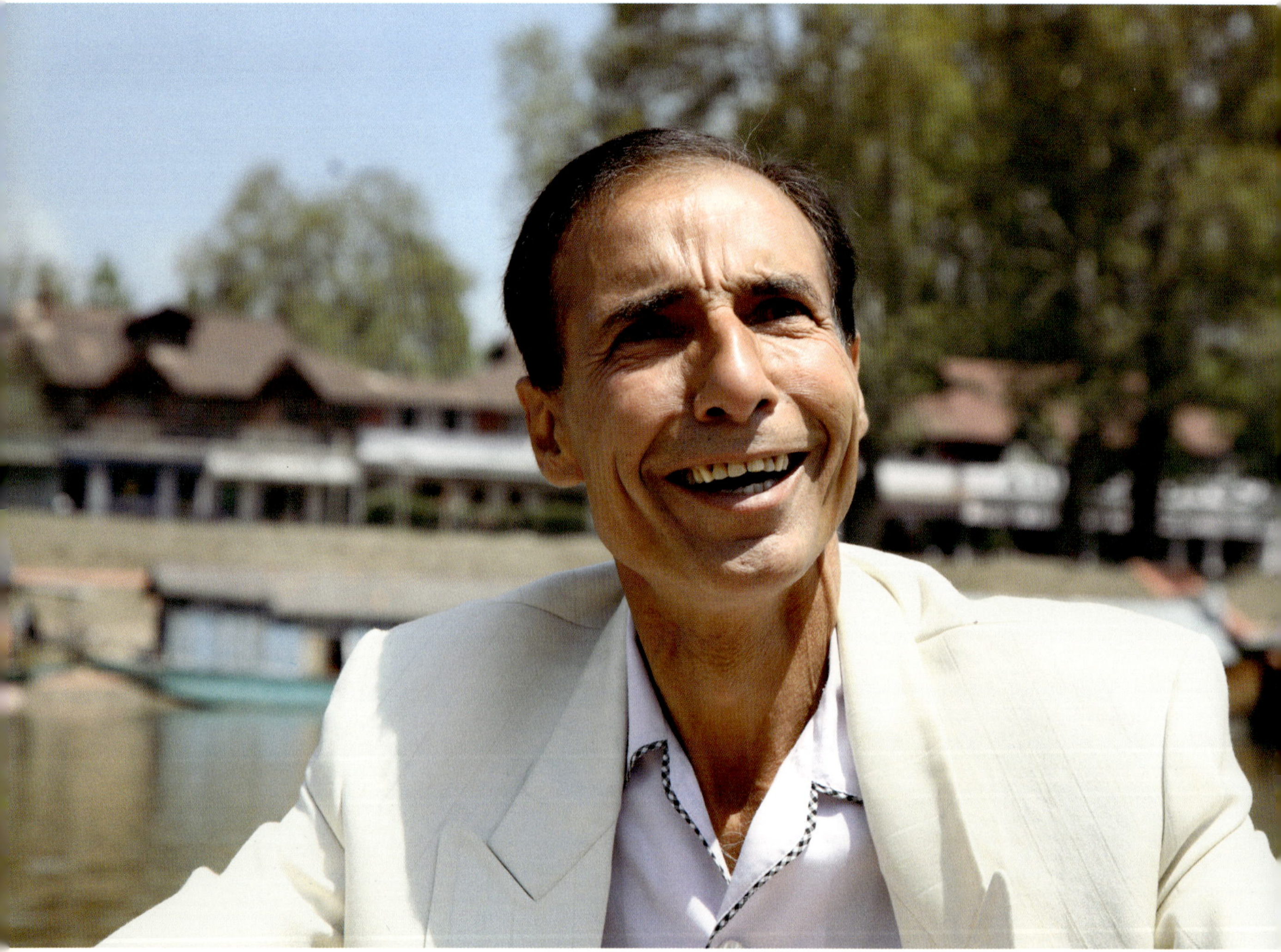

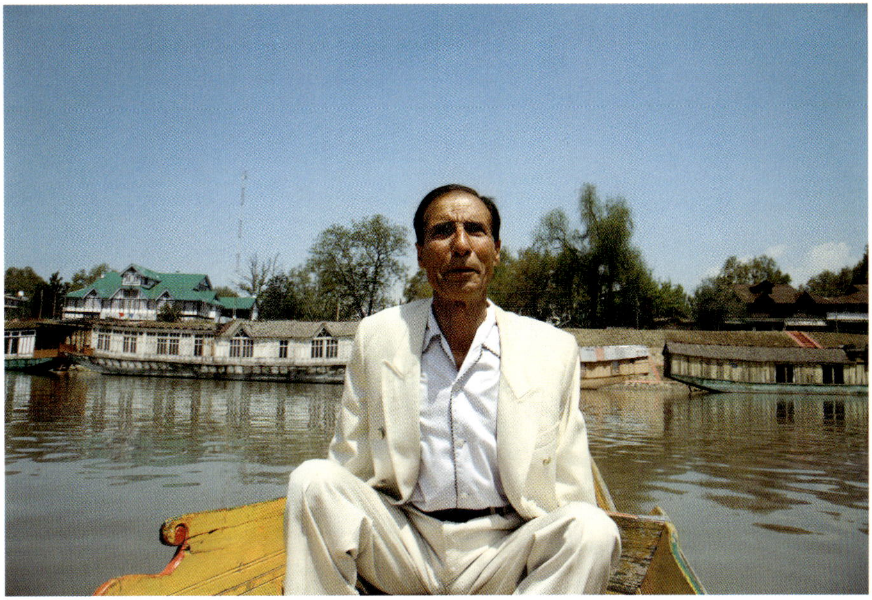

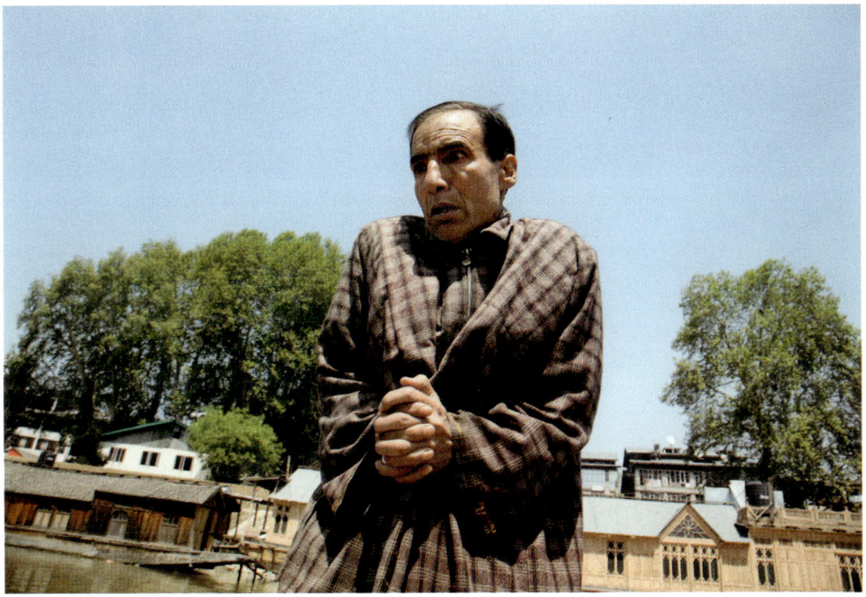

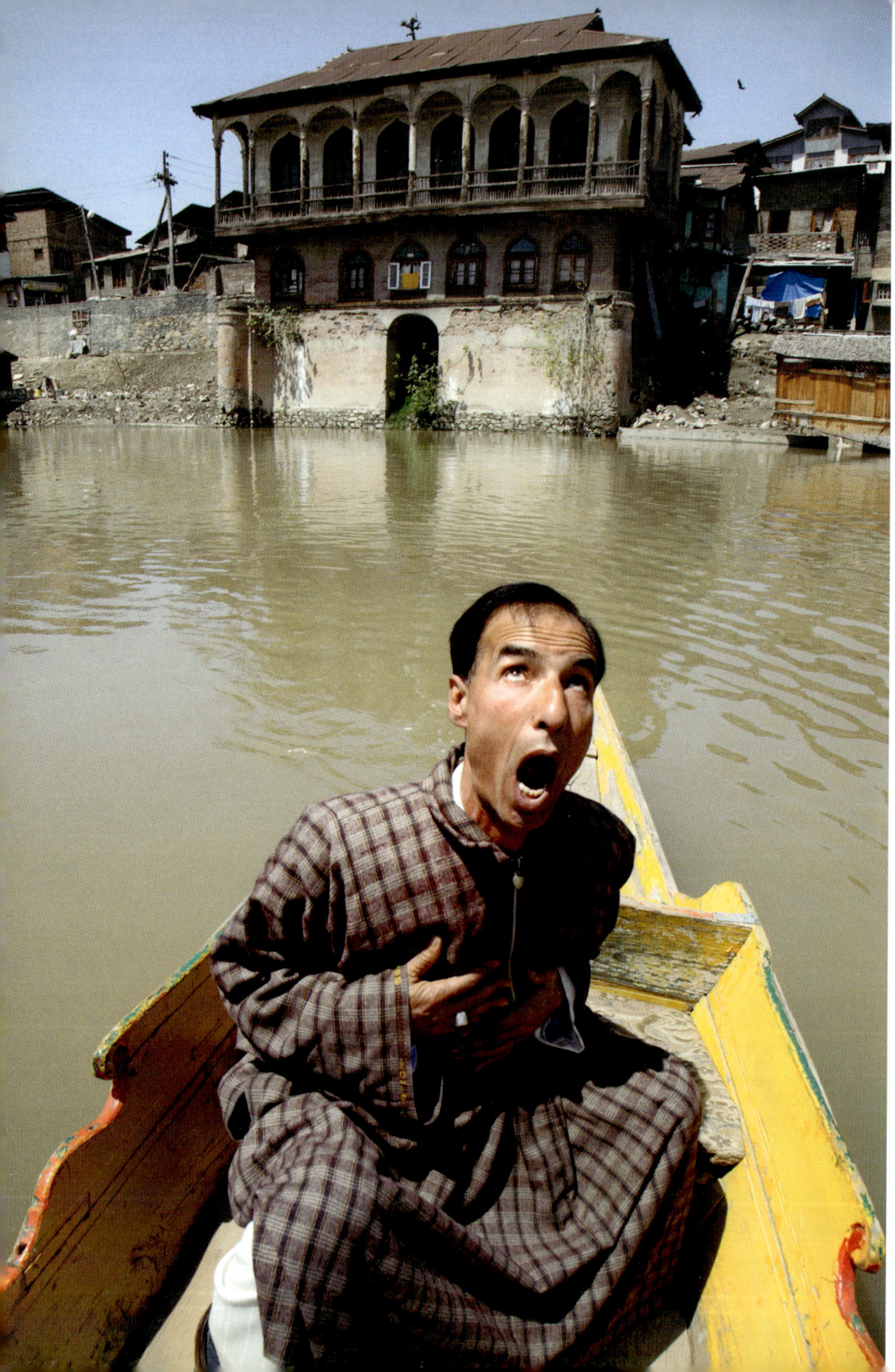

Home for Bullets Parthiv Shah

From the *Barbed Wire and Beautiful Skies* series, 2008

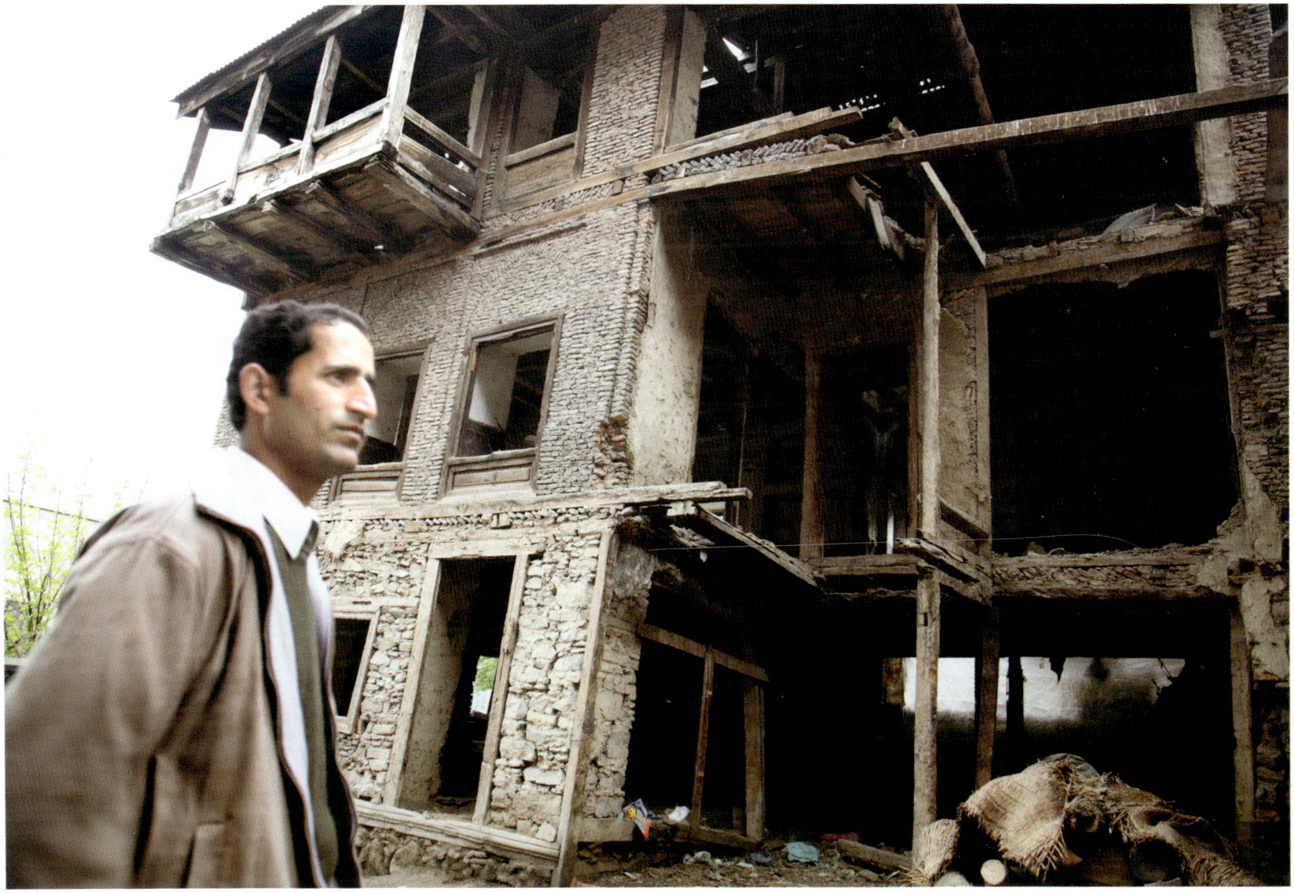

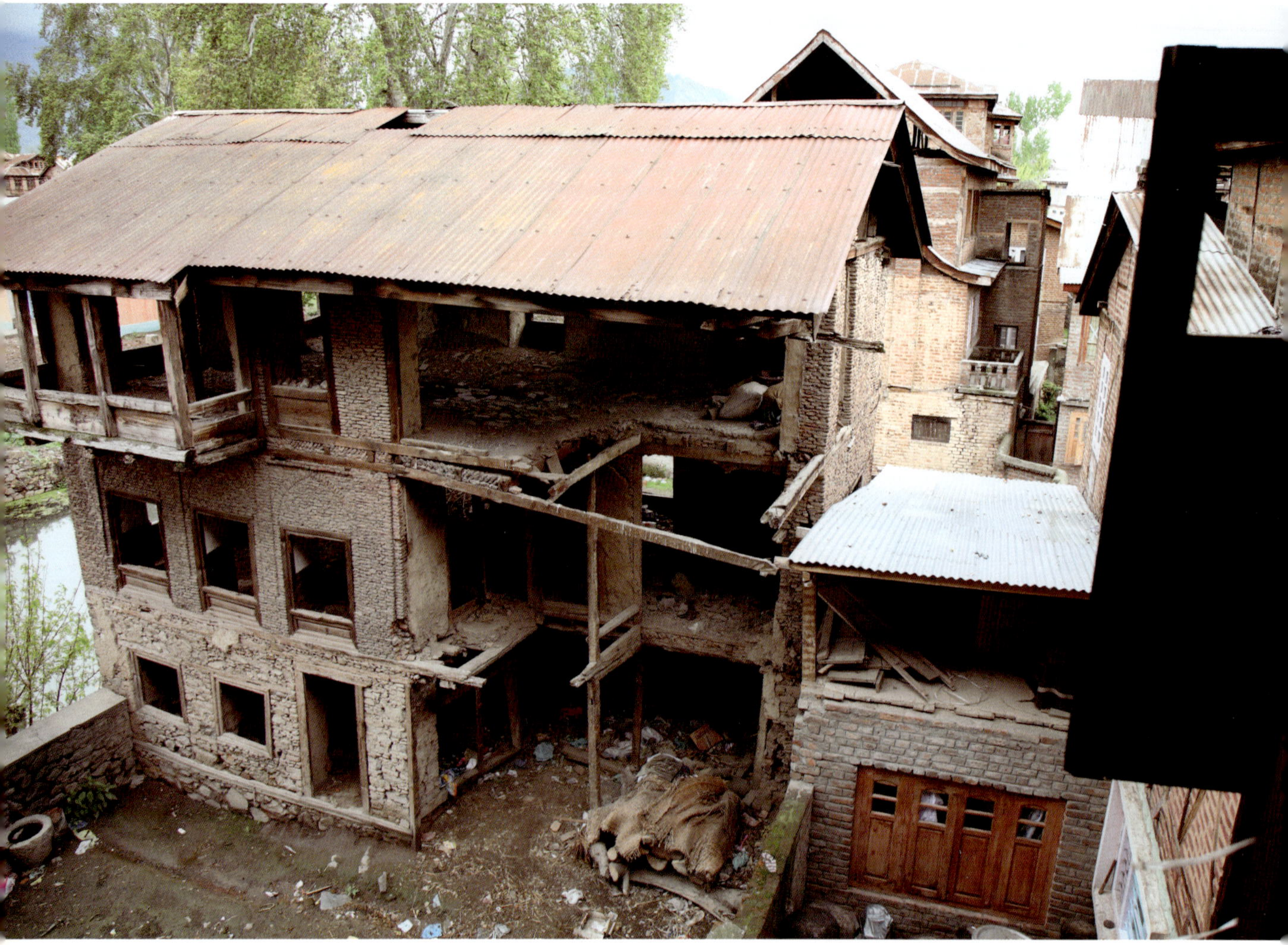

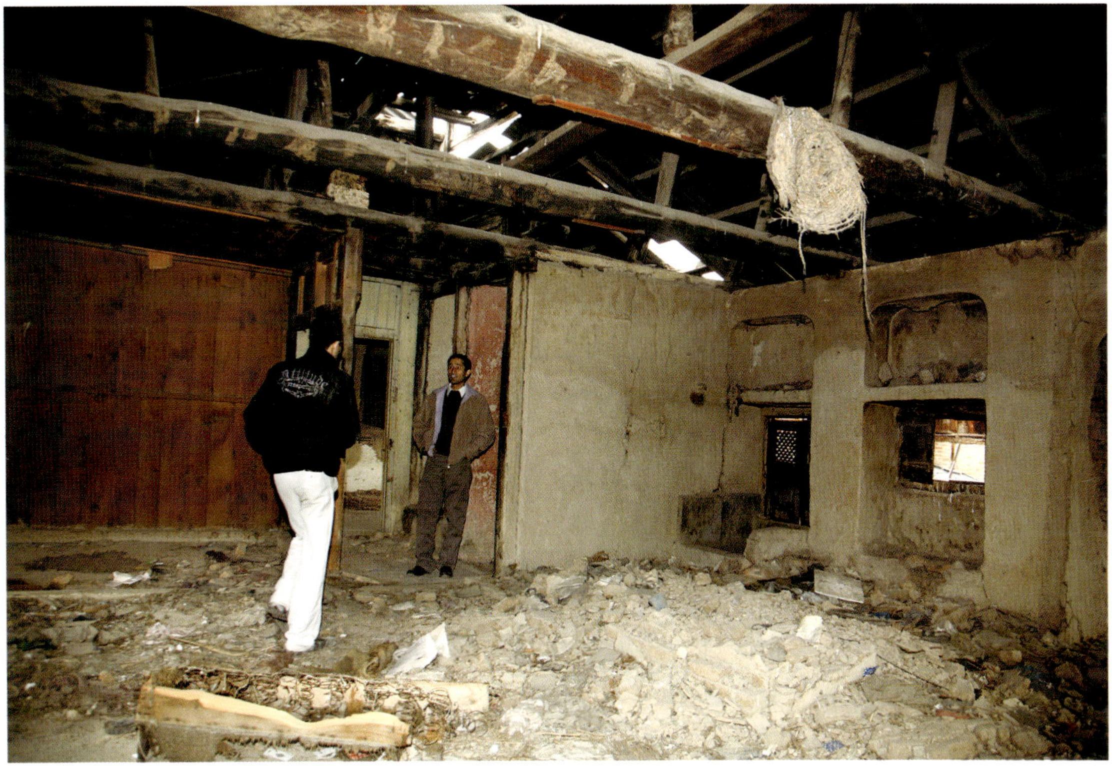

I said to them, spontaneously

Inder Salim

I said to them, spontaneously
Take away your Kashmir,
Just take away, it is all yours.

They laughed, then looked
At each other's faces with disbelief,
But grabbed quickly: the Azadi

Freedom in their hands was water
As pure as one drinks
At the beginning of a river.

Their hands were as big as the valley itself
And they dancingly moved towards
Their homes like the river itself.

This freedom, still water-like,
Not a just born baby as yet,
So they went to martyrs' graves first.

There they quenched the thirst of
The dead, who by technique
Drank a water within this water.

This freedom still water-like,
Had to be taken to a place like
Secretariat, if one goes by the Theory.

But they instead kept on gazing at its
Myriad faces, which perhaps delayed
Its instant shelving into structures.

That was the time it revealed its
Unpredictable face, which unnerved even
Those who held it lovingly in their hands.

Its sudden surge inundated all the
Barbed wiring and dead walls,
Crossing new frontiers.

New thoughts, new soil and old
Seeds were passing through the
Alimentary canal of earth's friendly worms.

All the shit of all the animals
unanimously dissolving their egos:
'Love' was declared: the only God.

Sheen-e-Misha

Showkat Kathjoo

The shrine of Mia Shah Sahib, situated along the backwaters of Dal Lake in the interiors of Rainawari, has fostered the cultural ethos of the neighbourhood for centuries. The *urs* of Mia Shah Sahib, observed at the shrine, had come to be revered as an expression of the culturally shared and celebrated pluralism in the Valley. The shrine was also noted for being a part of both Hindu and Muslim beliefs in the Valley. The occasion falls every year on 21st December, marking the death anniversary of the sage. Being a common celebration of Muslims and Hindus, the day is celebrated with equal zeal and passion by both. It is known to mark the commencement of the winter season in the Valley and it is also believed to symbolize the snowfall in winter; so much so that the Valley would always receive snow on this day, if only for a brief span of time. This shrine is also locally popular by the name of *Sheen-e-Misha* ('Snow of Misha'). The day evokes a passion for snow.

The celebration would be followed by special preparations of fish in both Muslim and Hindu households. This would be shared with the family, distant relatives, as well as among neighbours. The shrine would be decked with lights, candles and garlands. Then, towards the evening, children as well as adults would gather together to light fire-crackers. This was the favourite part for the children in the entire locality of Rainawari. The residents of the opposite bank of the river would also come across and participate in the evening get-together.

There was certainly an atmosphere of implicit reconciliation among the people, with a valuable cultural legacy and a secular space being expressed through these common festivities.

Solidarity Football

Nandita Haksar

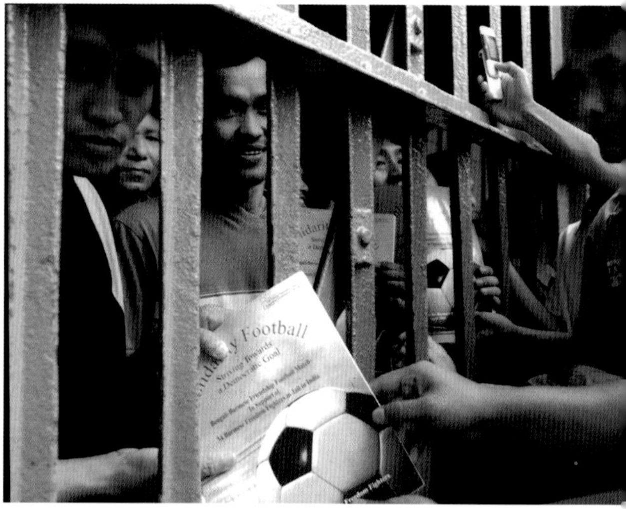

Burmese freedom fighters behind bars being greeted at Presidency Jail, Alipore, West Bengal, by the Solidarity football team and human rights activists. Photo courtesy: Mizzima News Service.

There were more than 500 people in the air-conditioned press room of the Netaji Subhas Chandra Bose indoor stadium in Kolkata. These men (and two or three women) represented various sports clubs all around the city and they had gathered together at the invitation of the maverick Sports Minister of the West Bengal government, Mr. Subhas Chakravorty.

In beautiful flowing Bengali, the Minister told them of the plight of the Burmese people living under the most brutal military dictatorship the world had ever known. He appealed to them to mobilize people for a very special football match: the Bengali–Burmese Friendship Football Match to be played in solidarity with thirty-four Burmese freedom fighters who have been languishing in Indian jails for the last ten years.

His short appeal opened a floodgate of memories for the audience, and the atmosphere was electrified as people got up and pledged to support the Burmese resistance. Speakers expressed their sorrow that the Bengalis who had stood by the Vietnamese, the Palestinians and the South Africans had not done enough for their neighbours. Others reminded the audience of the historical connections between Bengal and Burma.

Within the next few days, thousands of people received invitations to the Solidarity Football Match organized by the Sports and Youth Services Department, Government of West Bengal. And on 26 April 2008, the

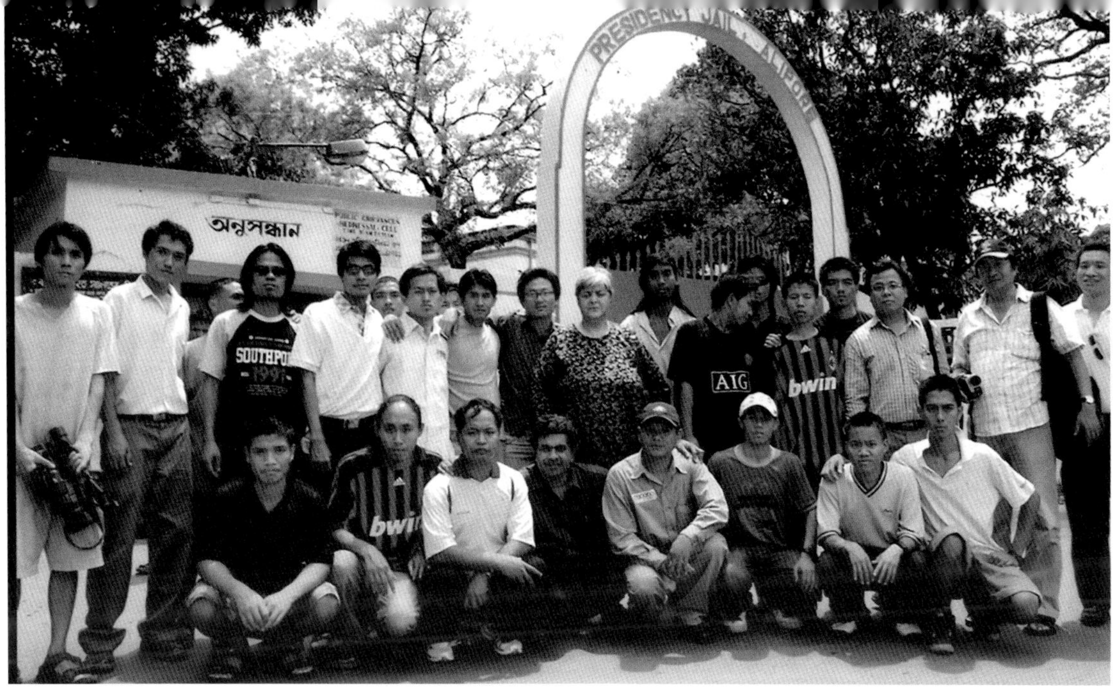

The team of Burmese refugee football players outside Presidency Jail, Alipore, with Supreme Court advocate, Nandita Haksar. Photo courtesy: Mizzima News Service.

famous East Bengal ground witnessed a unique event in the annals of the human rights movement. Many people gathered around the huge hoardings in English and Bengali announcing the event, and inviting people to show their solidarity with the Burmese freedom fighters, then in the Presidency Correctional Home, Alipore.

The Sports Department brought out pamphlets with a picture of Daw Aung San Suu Kyi on the cover, giving details of the Burmese struggle for democracy and information on the thirty-four Burmese freedom fighters incarcerated in India since 1998.

The Indian government had arrested them alleging that they were gun-runners, but soon after their arrest the media had exposed the fact that these men were members of the Arakan Army and the Karen National Union who were engaged in a life-and-death battle with the Burmese junta.

The men had been arrested at Landfall Island where they had been lured by an Indian military intelligence officer who had promised to give them a base and betrayed them to the Burmese junta. Six of the Burmese leaders had been shot dead and the others were detained in horrific conditions

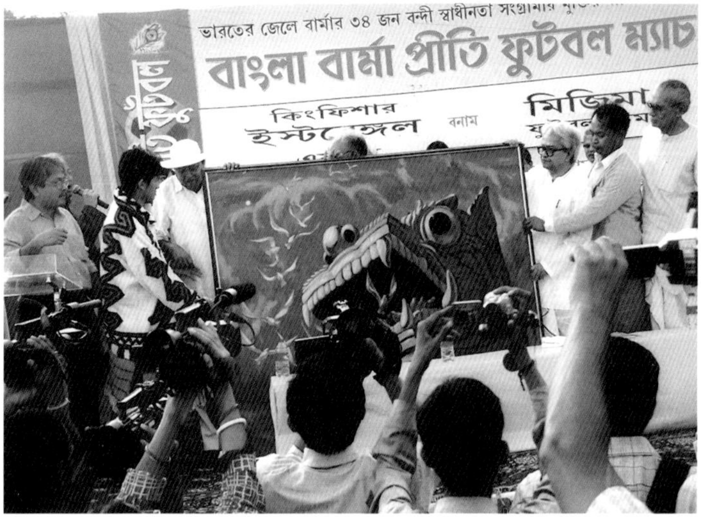

Sports Minister, Mr Subhas Chakravorty, gifting a work of art with the distinctive Burmese dragon to the Burmese football players. Photo courtesy: Mizzima News Service.

in Cambel Bay in the Nicobar Islands, and later transported to a jail in Port Blair, Andaman Islands. There they remained for six years without being chargesheeted and under threat of deportation. On one occasion, their imminent deportation was stopped by the intervention of the National Human Rights Commission and the UNHCR.

These men come from small towns and villages of the Arakan states. They are from poor families and many did not get an education because they were too poor to pay the fees. There is not one among these young men who had not witnessed or endured torture, or seen their villages burnt to cinders. Some of them live with memories of women being raped by the Burmese army while parents watched helplessly, unable to protect their daughters.

These thirty-four Burmese freedom fighters could not understand why they had been put into jail in democratic India. For them it was unimaginable that India should side with the Burmese generals instead of supporting the movement for democracy.

After days, weeks and months of imprisonment, having endured humiliation and abuse, they welcomed the news that some Indians had formed a Solidarity Committee for Burma's Freedom Fighters at the initiative of the legendary Dr (Col) Lakshmi Sahgal, founder of the first women's battalion in Asia under the leadership of Subhas Chandra Bose's Indian National Army. It was the Solidarity Committee that approached the Sports Minister and he had responded with whole-hearted enthusiasm. In fact, the entire Left Front government turned up at the stadium and the match was inaugurated by Biman Basu, Chairman of the Left Front.

The Solidarity Match was played between Kingfisher East Bengal Club and the Mizzima football team, consisting of Burmese refugees living in India. The match was preceded by a band and the atmosphere was more like a carnival. And Biman Basu promised to fight for the release of the Burmese freedom fighters.

After the match, the Burmese football team, accompanied by Indian human rights activists, visited the freedom fighters in jail. It was perhaps the most moving scene the jail authorities had witnessed. The spirit of Burmese resistance could be seen as the prisoners and Burmese exiles together sang songs born of their freedom movement. For a few moments the prisoners could forget their pain, their terrible uncertainty about their future, and many dared to hope again that the new solidarity and friendship would soon lead to their release.

The thirty-four Burmese freedom fighters continue to be on trial in Kolkata.

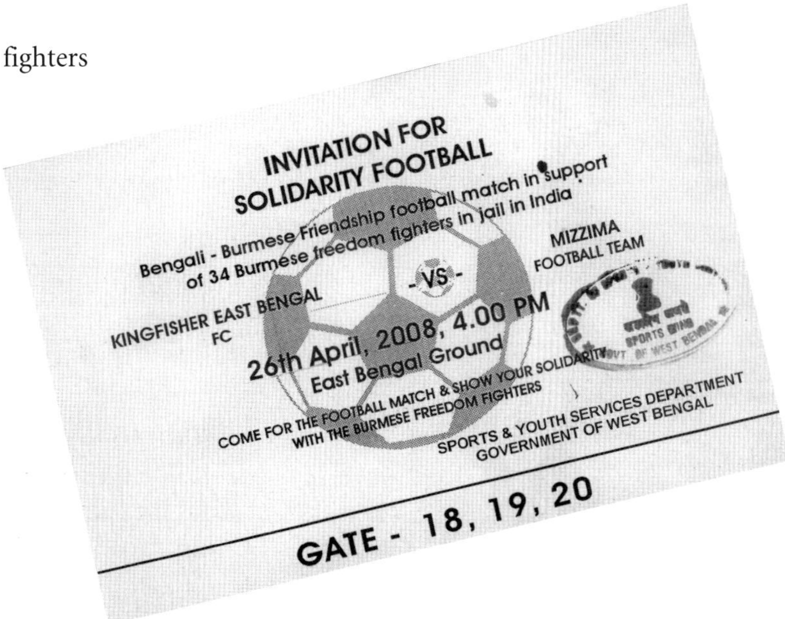

Ticket for the football match.
Photo courtesy: Mizzima News Service.

A Daughter Reads Her Father's Dream

Artist and writer **Salima Hashmi** from Pakistan responds to the globally celebrated poet and her father Faiz Ahmed Faiz's poem, '*Mere Des Kay Naunihaalon ke Naam*', through photographs.

Woh ghunchay jo shabnam ki ik boondh ko
Khilkhilanay ki ummeed lay kar
Hamesha tarastay rahay
Woh laal o' gohar
Jinhay gudureeyon kay andhere say baahir
Chamaktay huay din ki har ik kiran
Jagmagaanay se pehlu bachati rahee
Jin kay nanhe dilon kay katoron mein
Mehr o' mohabbat ka rus
Koi tapkaanay wala na tha
Jin ki mehroom aankhen
Un ki maaon ki soorat
Mere des ki saari maaon ki soorat
Aane walay dinon mein
Hansi kay ujaalay ki rah tak rahi hain

میرے دیس کے نونہالوں کے نام

وہ غنچے جو شبنم کی اِک بوند کو
کھلکھلانے کی اُمید لے کر
ہمیشہ ترستے رہے
وہ لعل و گہر
جنہیں گدڑیوں کے اندھیرے سے باہر
چمکتے ہوئے دن کی ہر اک کرن
جگمگانے سے پہلو بچاتی رہی
جن کے ننھے دلوں کے کٹوروں میں
مہر و محبت کا رس
کوئی ٹپکانے والا نہ تھا
جن کی محروم آنکھیں
ان کی ماؤں کی صورت
مرے دیس کی ساری ماؤں کی صورت
آنے والے دنوں میں
ہنسی کے اُجالے کی رہ تک رہی ہیں

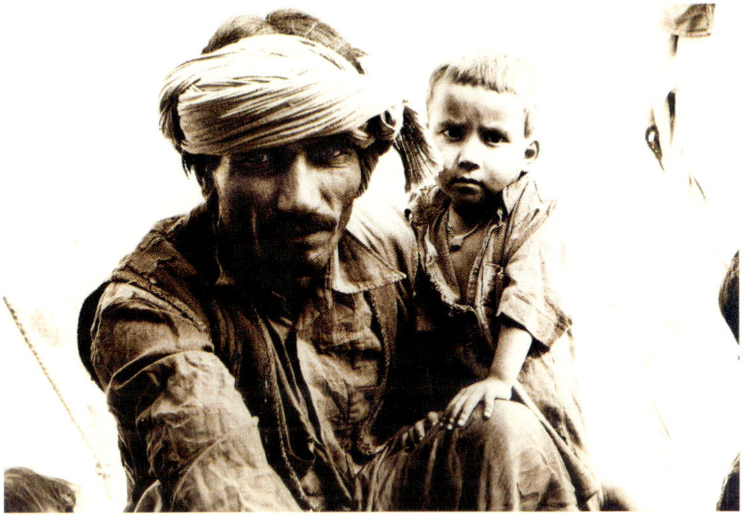

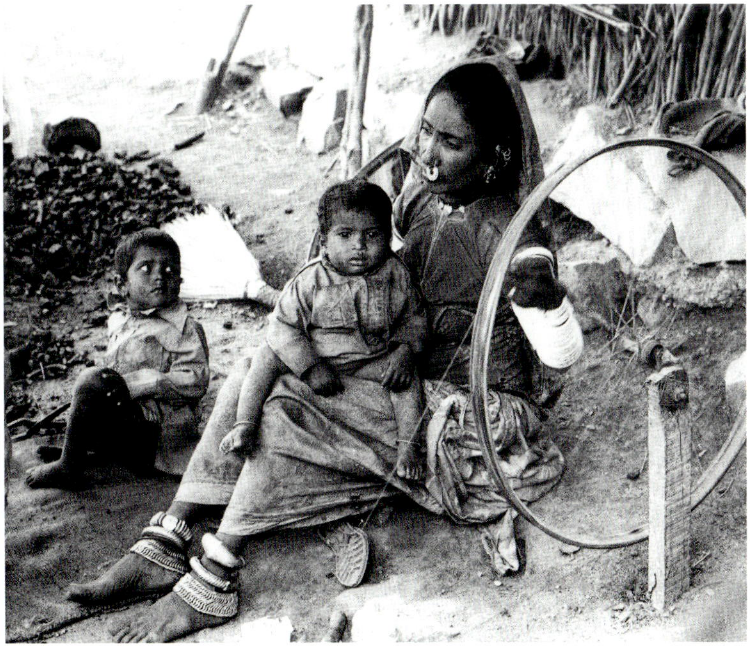

By Salima Hashmi, Pakistan.

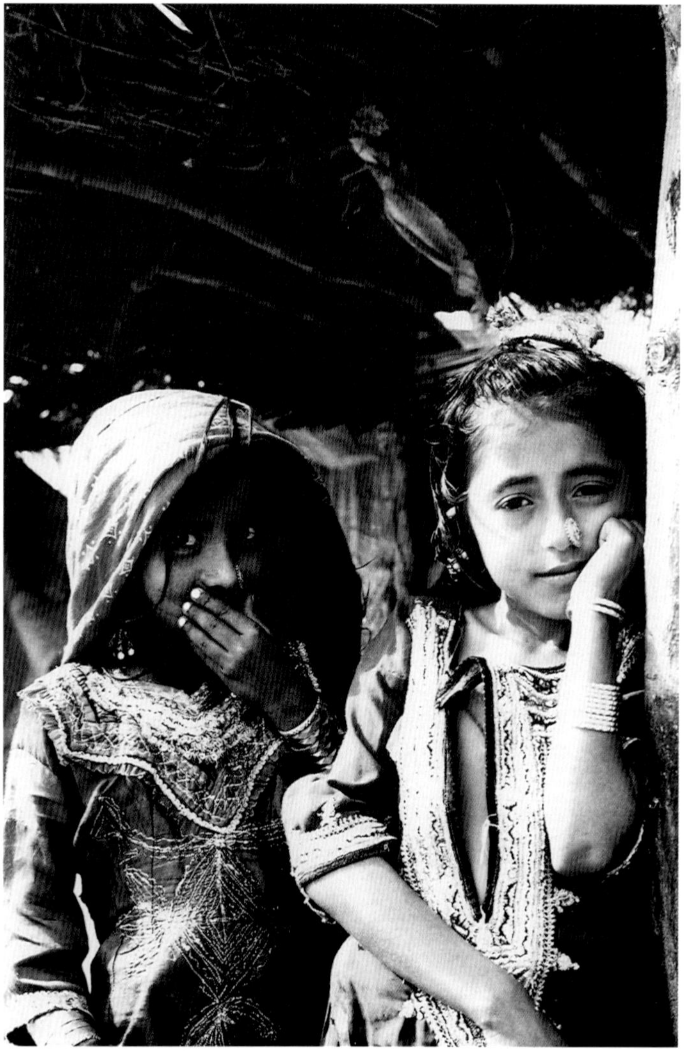

By Salima Hashmi, Pakistan.

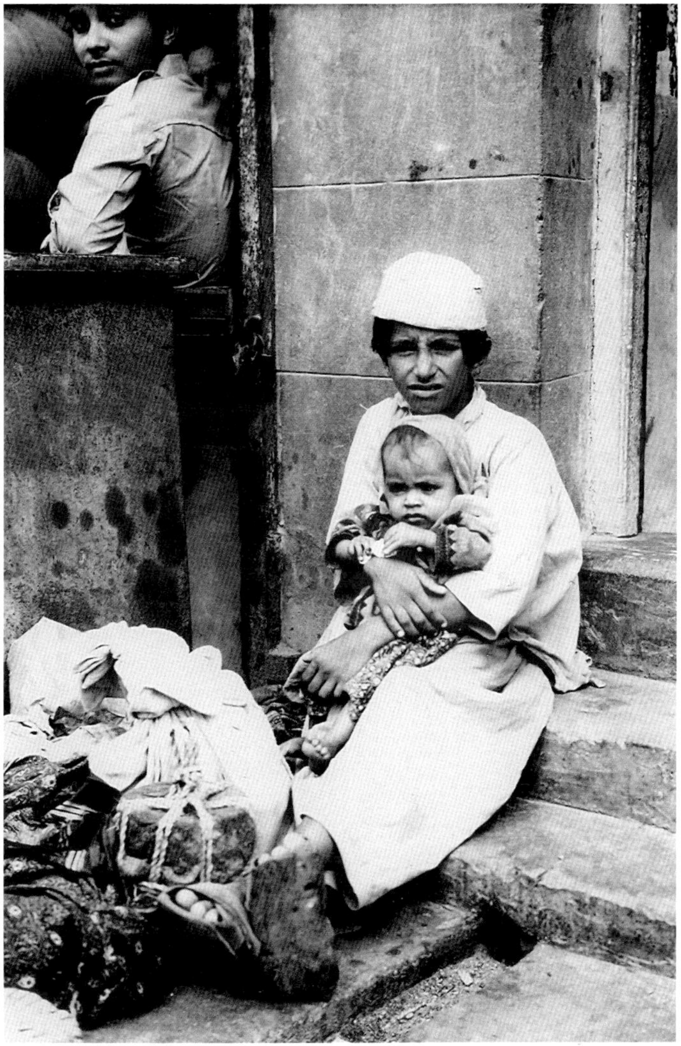

By Salima Hashmi, Pakistan.

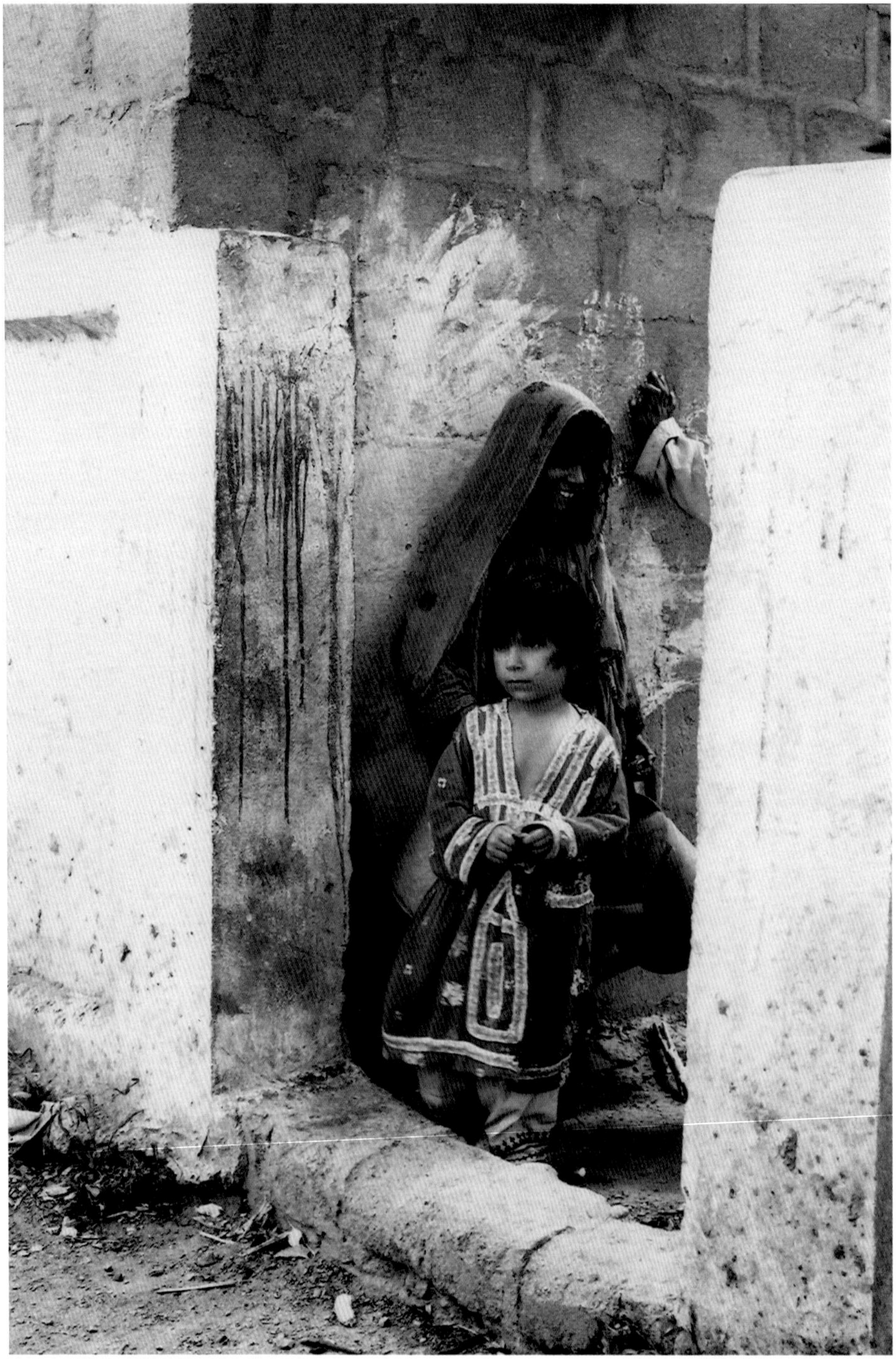

By Salima Hashmi, Pakistan.

What is Ready-made in Politics?

Inder Salim

Félix Guattari's use of the term 'ready-made' is multiple, endless, overdetermined. Indeed there exist numerous other ways in which this term has been used to define politics even. The term itself is a ready-made now. I use this term very carefully, since I am using it in the present context of Kashmir. Although a little vaguely, it does border simultaneously on various other connected issues. So, first an amateurish beginning into the pedagogy of the term 'ready-made'.

The term 'found art' – more commonly 'found object' (French: *objet trouvé*) or ready-made – describes art created from the undisguised but often modified use of objects that are not normally considered art. Often this is so because they already have a mundane, utilitarian function. Marcel Duchamp was the originator of this art form in the early twentieth century.

If 'birth' implies that we have been almost thrown into a ready-made world, which is nevertheless changing, then the body in itself becomes a site of the ready-made. Everything is culturally and economically valued and passed on to the next generation as virtue. However, the next generation automatically verifies it and revalues each and every object and concept. But it often takes an artist like Duchamp to point out that value-making mechanisms can go wrong unwittingly if we don't fix a critical gaze on each and every thing that goes into making us.

Derrida's writing circulates a discourse of what is and is not of art: writing out of frame, something that is hovering at the edge of the painting and beyond. Earlier, the real function of the ready-made was perhaps limited to the sphere of art only, but what we cannot ignore is the fact that the production of an art object often reflects the politics of a particular time. Be it in the economy or in aesthetics, art and cultural expressions swim through waters of every kind. Certainly, ready-made as a concept could not have come into being during the Renaissance, and therefore, when the sweetly dissolvable character of aesthetics reached its saturation point, it automatically began to justify the concept of ready-made. The ready-made was already in existence when the alchemy of art was busy churning newer art forms as per the conventional norms, which are also pregnant with significance (but that too can function as ready-made in a different sense).

So a ready-made is usually found in a public space which is heavy with historicity and, therefore, a ready-made battle zone. A ready-made is both visible and invisible, both in matter and as a concept.

So a ready-made in politics can only happen if politics, both creatively and willingly, allows itself to be used as ready-made. Politics conventionally has generated 'the other' as waste material, which is almost similar to e-waste in the present context. If e-waste is considered a necessary recycling component of technology by the environmentally conscious masses, then the mountains of political waste too can be recycled. This way it can disseminate its commitment to our society with a fecundity that we have not witnessed before. If politics is an automatic, machine-like thing, then it is the function of a ready-made to guide us in such a way that other hierarchies too fall in line.

Just as we apply a little bit of Foucault or Derrida in our systems of thought, we can use this concept of the ready-made by Duchamp as well, which was in fact necessitated by a crisis in western art at that time. For those who don't know, he submitted a simple white urinal (titled *Fountain*) as a work of art to the Society of Independent Artists, of which he was a board member. The selection committee automatically dismissed it as a joke: not only was it signed lethargically as R. Mutt, but the name was unheard of in art circles. The moment the urinal was dismissed as a work of art, it gained reputation as a deliberate act of subversion. It succeeded in generating a tremendous discourse on art and aesthetics at the time, which art critics today find relevant as never before. The found object, which could sometimes be even worse than a urinal, can give us a lesson that everything has a value. Even nuisance has a value, called nuisance value.

Needless to say, the story of present-day civilization is the story of human journey directed by a series of wars of the past. A soldier's simple helmet with a hole functions as a 'ready-made' on the pedestal that mocks the whole machinery of war. The 'war' too is a ready-made for people who have controlled human beings for thousands of years. They have never thrown it out, which could have enabled them to see its other function as well. One needs an impulse to return to the dead, to lift the discarded, to realize the potential of trash, which was hidden earlier. Great philosophers, saints, musicians and poets did this by speaking on themes of peace and love. But, as they say, who cares? Warmongers have still not granted the status of WASTE to WAR, which could have enabled it to enter ART. It will be naïve on my part to expect them to abandon war projects suddenly. These days, one notices how guerrilla war techniques unnerve the ruling elites who like 'real' war games. Or at least I presume so. One can talk about their success in Nepal where the king ('right-winged' Lord Vishnu) was on the run.

What is even worse about war and counter-violence is that those who return alive are usually so traumatized that they are unable to speak about it. At best, a story-like thing comes out, or some anecdote about a miracle escape during bombing. And if they are changed at heart, it is futile to expect anything from them. It takes a little for a Nazi policewalla to become an anti-Nazi policewalla. Hence one gets the feeling that there is no one to tell us about what actually happens in a war. And whatever exists in the form of literature and art is so insufficient that we are tempted to repeat the question again. How can we abandon violence, or throw it out as trash, so that it becomes READY-MADE? The question is a desire.

DESIRE has uniquely helped human beings to shape the politics around them. It is because DESIRE has achieved the status of TRUTH that it guides humanity to some future. Images, signs, symbols function endlessly only where desire is struggling to come out of previous modes of oppression. If the agenda of religion is to curb desire, the capitalist's agenda is to invent territories and control it. A mystical approach to DESIRE is oriental in design and has its own powerful thought mechanisms of the past, which we constantly revisit as ready-made(s) – as and when we are stripped bare by capitalism and religious bigotry. One instantly thinks of Mirabai while reading Luce Irigaray who talks about the feminist mystic as one who is 'autonomous', 'remains within herself ', and 'communicates and returns home'. What is home? The fourteenth-century Kashmiri mystic and saint-poetess, Lal Ded, says, 'I am crossing a big sea in a big boat with the aid of an unspun thread. I feel death approaching me, I yearn to go back home.' There is a death-wish that one needs to internalize if one finds some readiness to enter the signifier of a 'ready-made' in discourse. At that moment, the ready-made will however cease to behave as a ready-made, even as Derrida suggests in 'Writing out of Frame': the body, in fact, has a frame but it always crosses its own territory to merge with the other's. The merging is Desire. Watching this game of territory-merging from a closer distance gives in, ontologically, to acclaim of the mystic qualities that immortalize the core human spirit.

In our socio-political set-up we have endlessly encroached upon the territories of others. That is our history of tears of which no one has written. The saddest part is that we keep on inventing newer and newer 'others' to tighten our grip on 'power'. Here, Indian society is unfortunately riddled with the tragic continuity of the caste system which justifies oppression in the name of religion. The struggle of the Dalits is on, and no sane person on earth can deny their right to dignity and social elevation on the basis of equal distribution of resources. It needs to be noted that Dalit assertion has been non-violent with some success, and the credit for this goes to Dr Ambedkar whose thoughts emerged from non-ritualistic Buddhism. Also, that the recent success of Tibetan protests against Chinese aggression and occupation is the result of creative means that are non-violent. So, is non-violence a 'ready-made' that we can re-enter?

But again, unfortunately, we keep discovering newer forms of the Dalit. If we consider that an artist, a poet, a musician, an actor, is a Dalit because that breed is visible only when they are bought by the corporate(s), then, in that sense, the first Dalit is the TREE – voiceless and therefore without power. So we need to cut thousands and thousands of trees to host the 2010

Commonwealth Games in Delhi. This is happening along with the removal of lakhs of poor labourers and migrants living on the banks of the Yamuna river. The river in Delhi is already dead. Dead.

Performance

Now, what is ready-made in politics? The reader of this little text piece is free to answer this herself or himself. I usually introduce myself as follows: **tHIS** indersalim STUFF from KASHMIR … with Love. I emphasize the word 'stuff '. Inder as Hindu and Salim as Muslim: a mask of 'the stuff '. The only visible face of the stuff, the only sign that is willing to negotiate the conflict, be it in Gujarat or Kashmir, or even an environmental issue.

If there is no choice but to enter the room, I would prefer to enter it through a window. I want a new politics, new urgency to deal with pending issues. I want people to go within and realize the inner potential of their existential core. But is that possible if we don't let our thoughts mingle with the thoughts of the other?

I think of the Bollywood song, '*Ghungroo ki tarah … ghungroo ki jagah to hai pairon mein. … Kabhi masjid mein, kabhi mandir mein, bajta hi raha hoon mein*' ('Like an anklet I make music, whether I am in the company of my friends or foes, my place is near the feet. … Whether it is the mosque or the temple … I make music'). This is how I can talk about this indersalim stuff.

This indersalim stuff can't go out and indulge in violence. Therefore, this indersalim stuff cannot join a struggle that is heavily using the language of violence to counter the violence of the state. This indersalim stuff can't justify violence in any form. If violence is inevitable, then it has to come from within, almost creatively. It cannot hurt the other in any way. When Van Gogh was angry with his friend Paul Gauguin, he amputated his own ear. That too is violence, but it has a 'self ' in it – the personalized, which can also be political.

So what is to be done? Can these freedom struggle movements become creative in their pursuits and abandon violence? There must be a way out to achieve the goals. If there is a will, there must be some possibility they have left unexplored. The trouble is that violence in the present form is strengthening the hands of those who are at the helm of affairs. So the movements meant for realizing goals turn into excuses for the state to suppress them in the name of 'law and order'. There has to be rethinking.

Let us take an example. Sanjay Tickoo, from the Kashmiri Pandit Sangarsh Samiti (KPSS), said some time ago that Kashmir is a 'disputed territory'. 'The law says that if the number of persons who abstain from voting exceeds the number of persons who cast their votes, the polling gets cancelled. This could be used as a referendum against India in international forums, if Kashmiri leaders know it', he said, adding, 'I will make people aware of the law as part of the election boycott campaign.'

Now, I wonder why this idea has not come from the Hurriyat itself. We know that whenever an election is held in Kashmir, all the protesting (militant) parties in Kashmir strictly demand a complete ban from traders and office-goers. The people fear them, and abandon their trade and duties. Now this new kind of thinking can make a real change in the Valley if there is a real awakening among the people of Kashmir.

Can a freedom movement become a 'ready-made'? How and with what changes in its agenda? Can environment and freedom of thought become part of its manifesto? If yes, then this indersalim stuff too can join a freedom struggle in the changed format. That too is Desire.

I quote Michel Foucault: 'As the archaeology of our thought easily shows, man is an invention of recent date. And one perhaps nearing its end' – and with some optimism.

I also quote Nund Rishi / Sheikh Noor-u-din Noorani (Sheikh-ul-Alam), the saint-poet in Kashmir, who said, 'As long as there are forests, there is food.' This slogan, which is widely used by different agencies in Kashmir to highlight environmental awareness, can also be internalized for some real effects.

I guess that can happen only if the so-called terrorist parties club their issues to create a new agenda, a new politics, a new art, a new awareness for a new life.

The slogan can be *Sazrah, Pazrah te Azadi* (Simplicity, Truth and Freedom).

Peace, Protest and Prayer

Harikrishna Katragadda ● Suvendu Chatterjee ● Sonia Jabbar ● Abdul Rahman Roslan

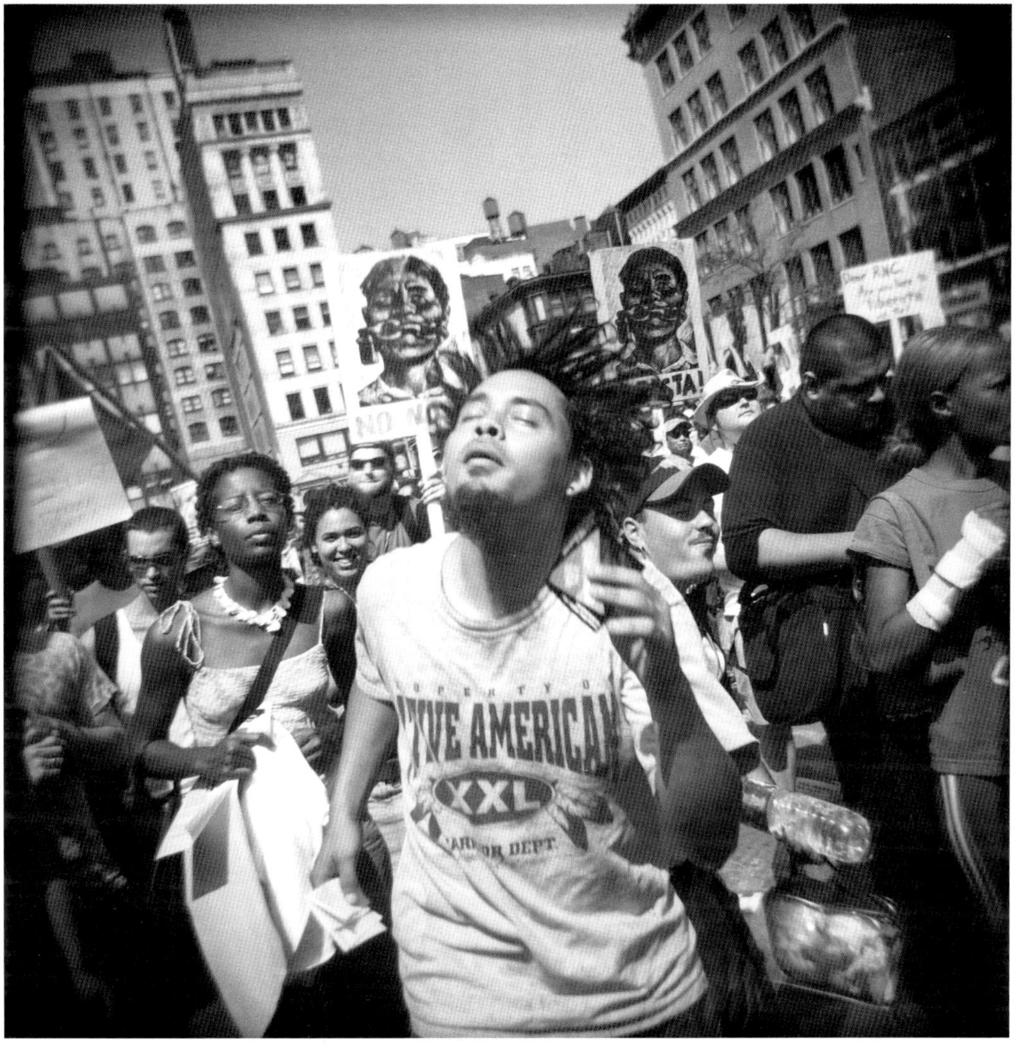

The Republican Party convention on 'Fulfilling America's Promise by Building a Safer World and a More Hopeful America' faced unprecedented protests in New York City. More than 1,800 people were officially arrested, the majority on minor charges. By Harikrishna Katragadda, India, 2004.

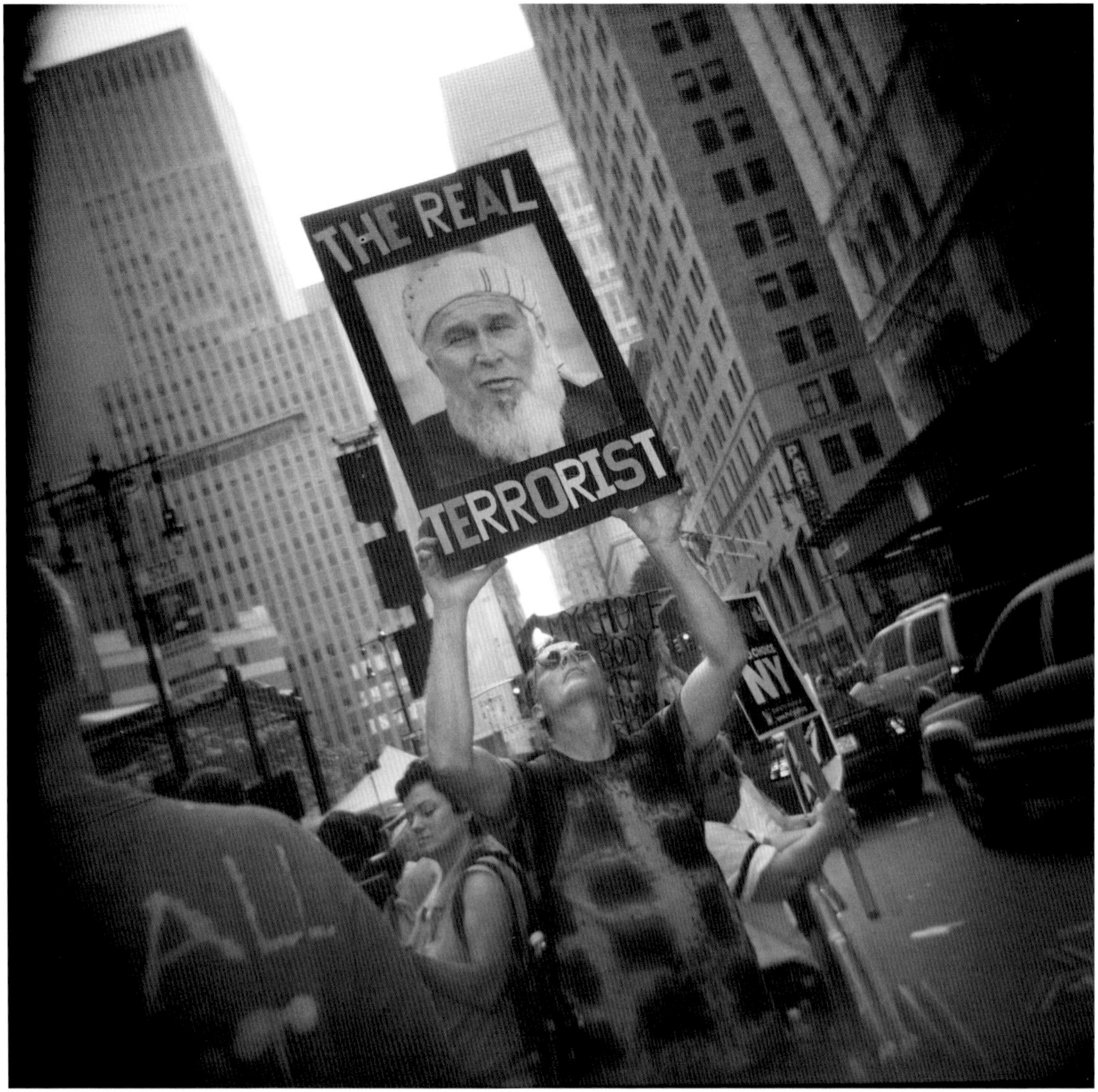

A protestor mocks George Bush's hawkish policies, New York. By Harikrishna Katragadda, India, 2004.

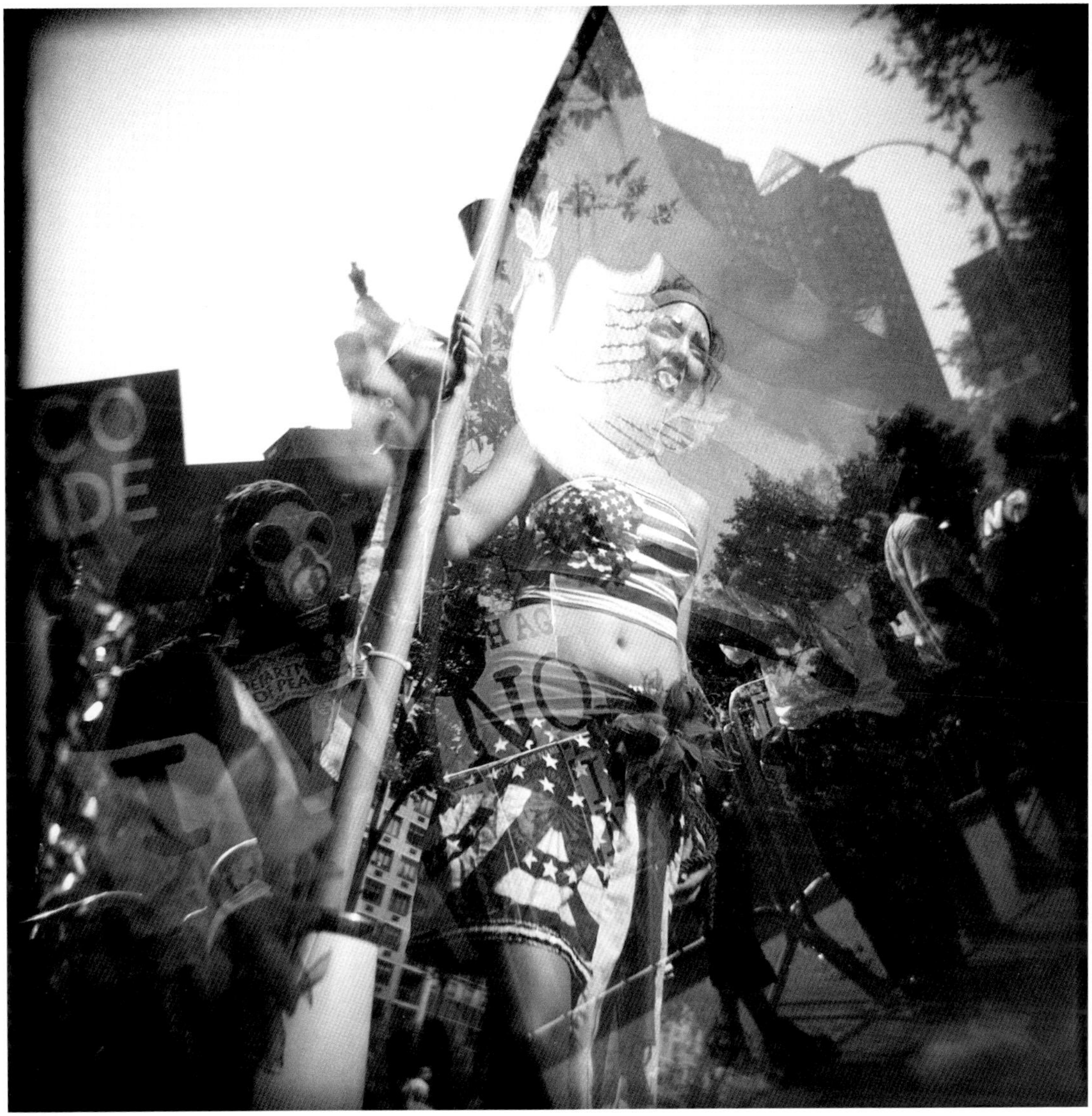

Peace protestors at Union Square in New York – historically the start or end point for many political demonstrations. By Harikrishna Katragadda, India, 2004.

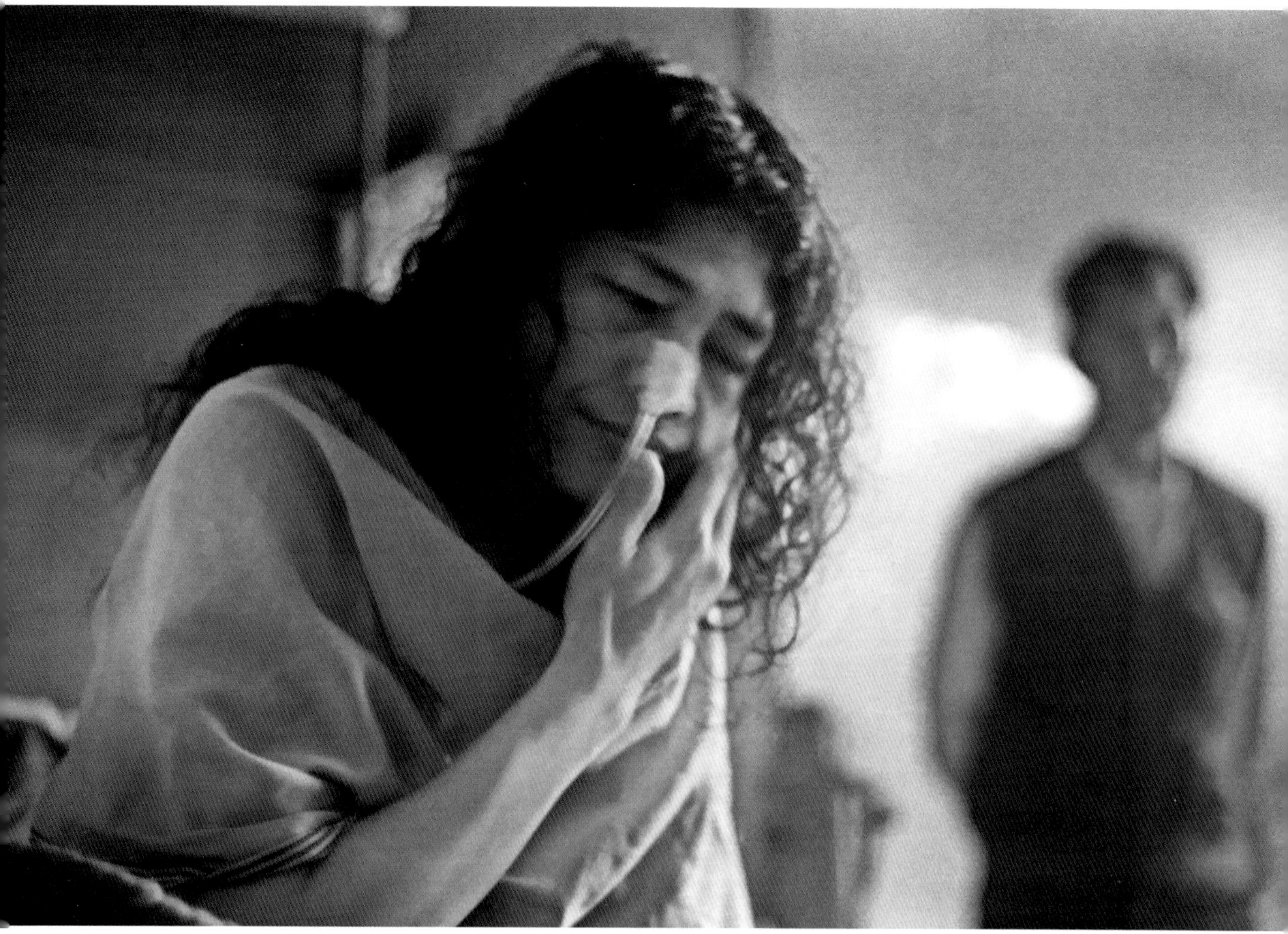

Irom Sharmila at Imphal Medical College, Manipur. She has been fasting for the last seven years, demanding withdrawal of the draconian Armed Forces Special Powers Act (AFSPA). By Suvendu Chatterjee, India, 2005, DRIK.

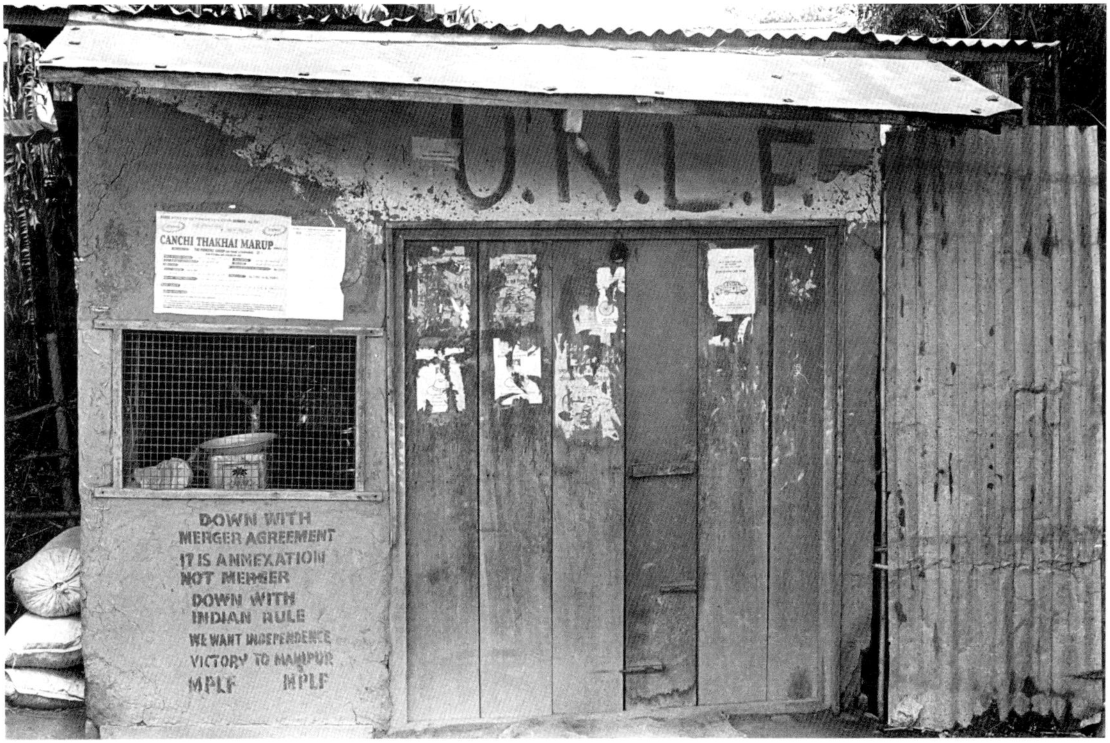

Militant outfits in Manipur campaign for secession from India. By Suvendu Chatterjee, India, 2005, DRIK.

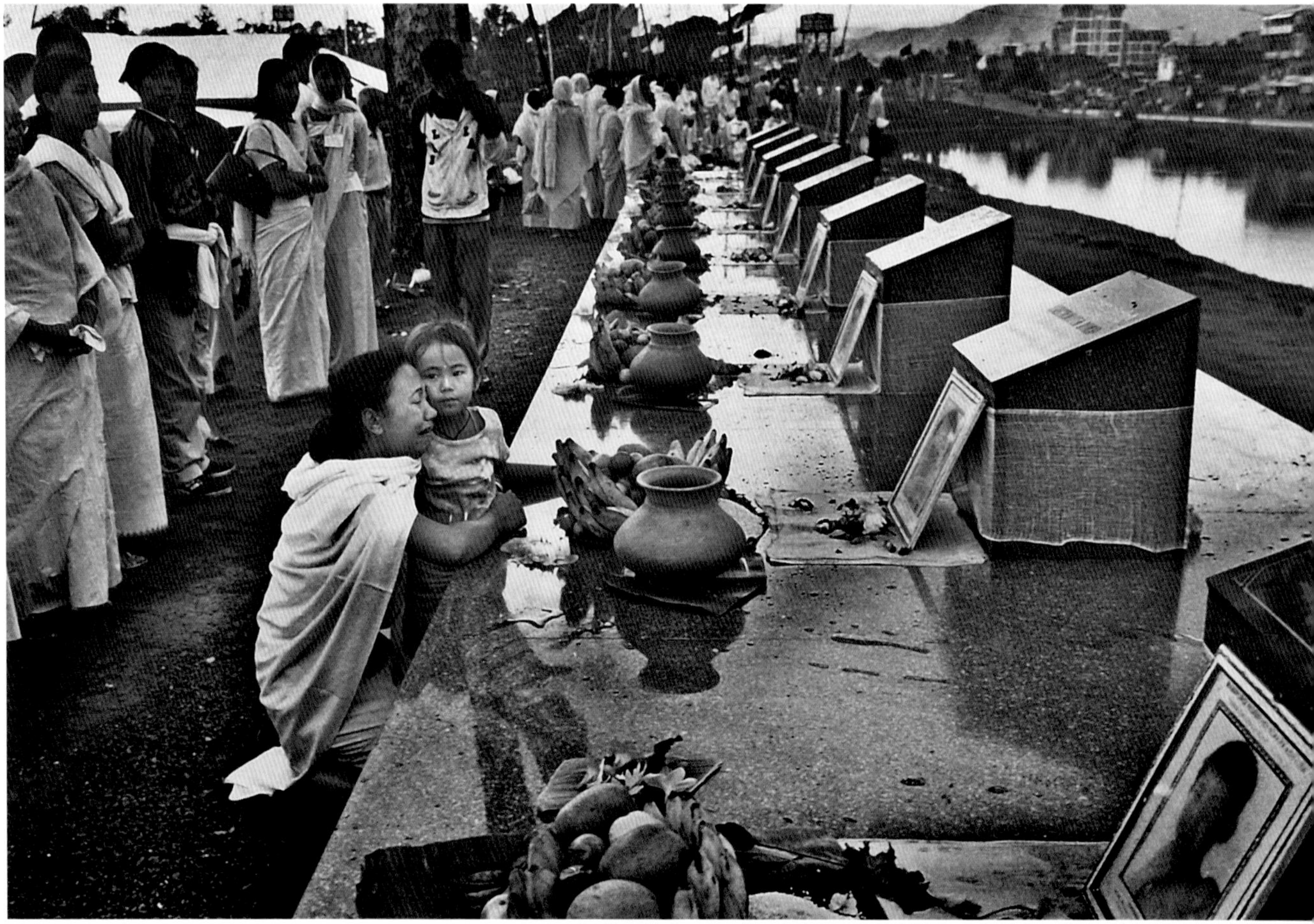

Imphal: grieving mother of posthumous child in front of a picture of her late husband Amom Rajen Meeti who was shot dead by CRPF personnel on 18 June 2001. Eighteen people sacrificed their lives for the territorial integrity of Manipur in the firing by the CRPF. By Suvendu Chatterjee, India, 2005, DRIK.

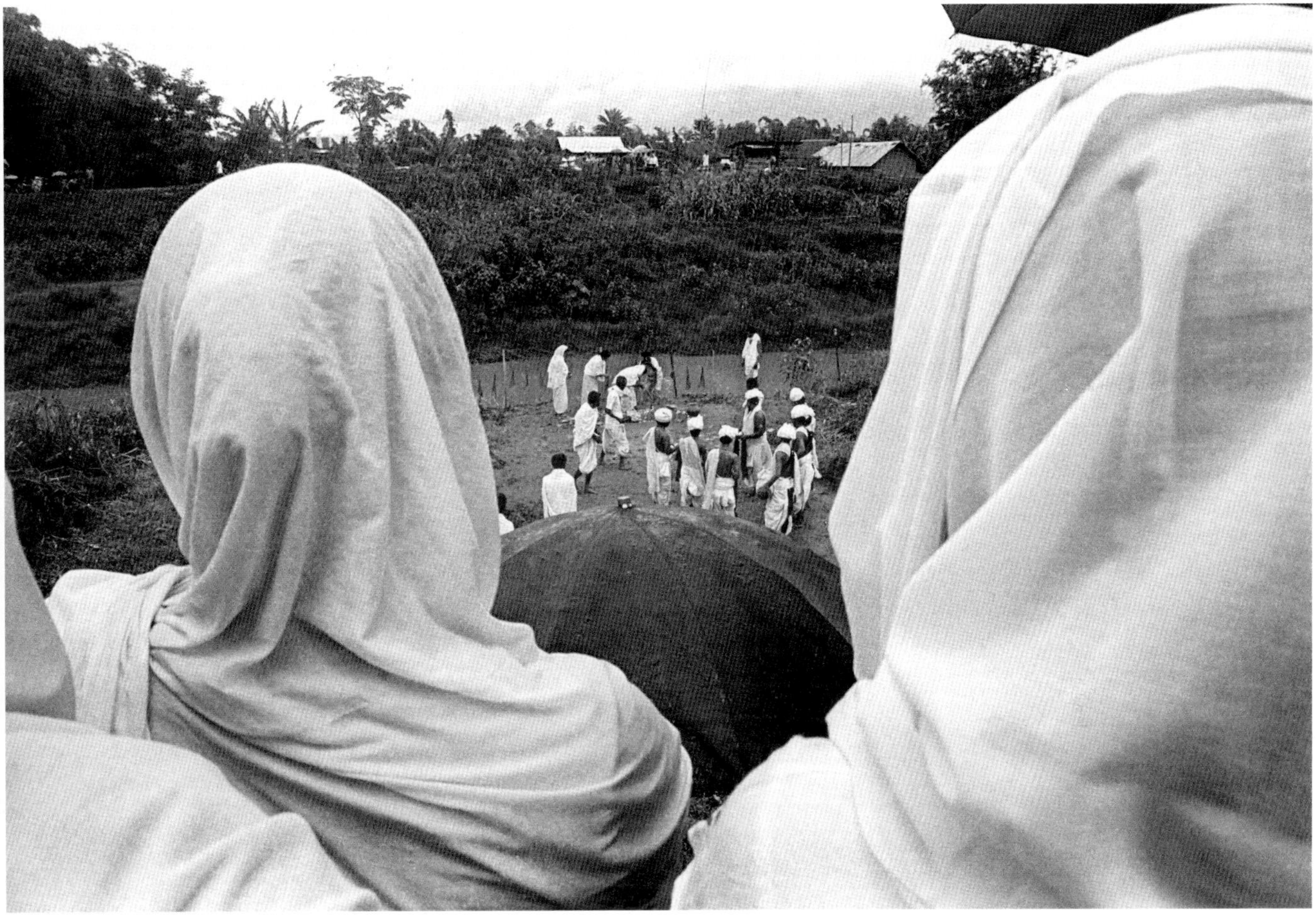

Funeral rites of a common villager, 30 kilometres from Imphal, the capital city of Manipur. The man was shot dead by paramilitary forces in the name of counter-insurgency. Fake encounters are rampant in Manipur. By Suvendu Chatterjee, India, 2005, DRIK.

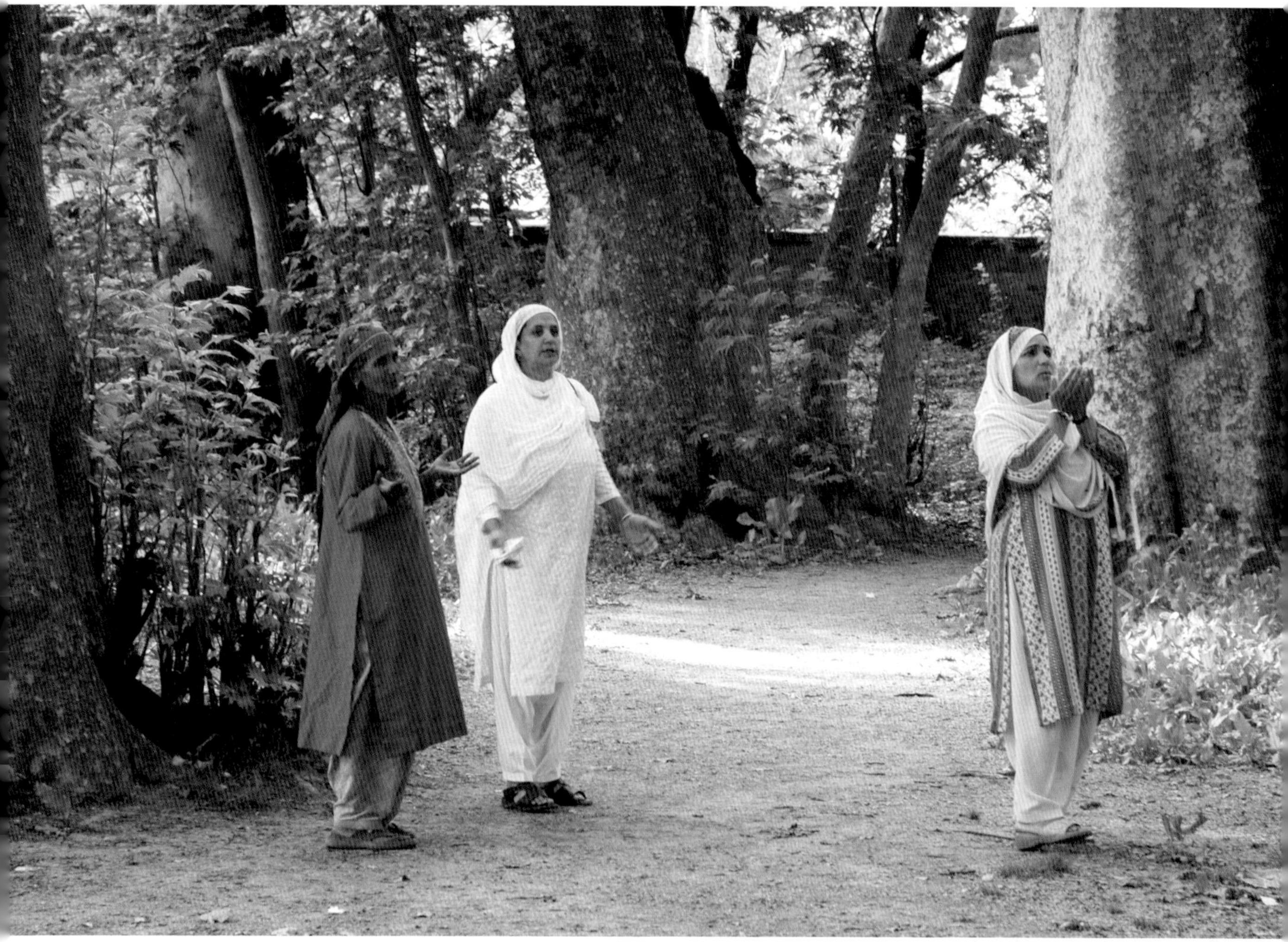

Bakhti, Parveena and Suraiyya, all mothers of disappeared sons, pray at a shrine in Tragpora, Baramulla District, Kashmir. By Sonia Jabbar, India.

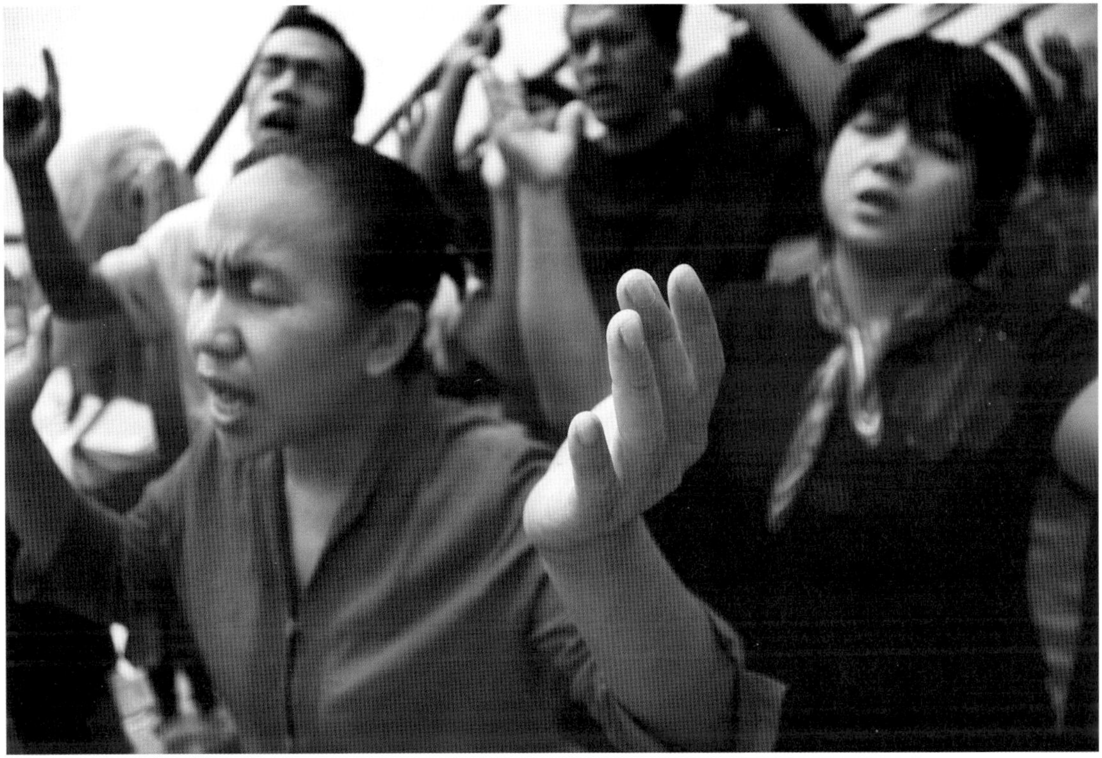

Refugees offer prayer in a makeshift church at one of the many camps set up by the displaced Burmese population in Malaysia. Chin refugees from Burma have sought shelter in Kuala Lumpur, the capital of Malaysia. By Abdul Rahman Roslan, Malaysia, 2007, DRIK.

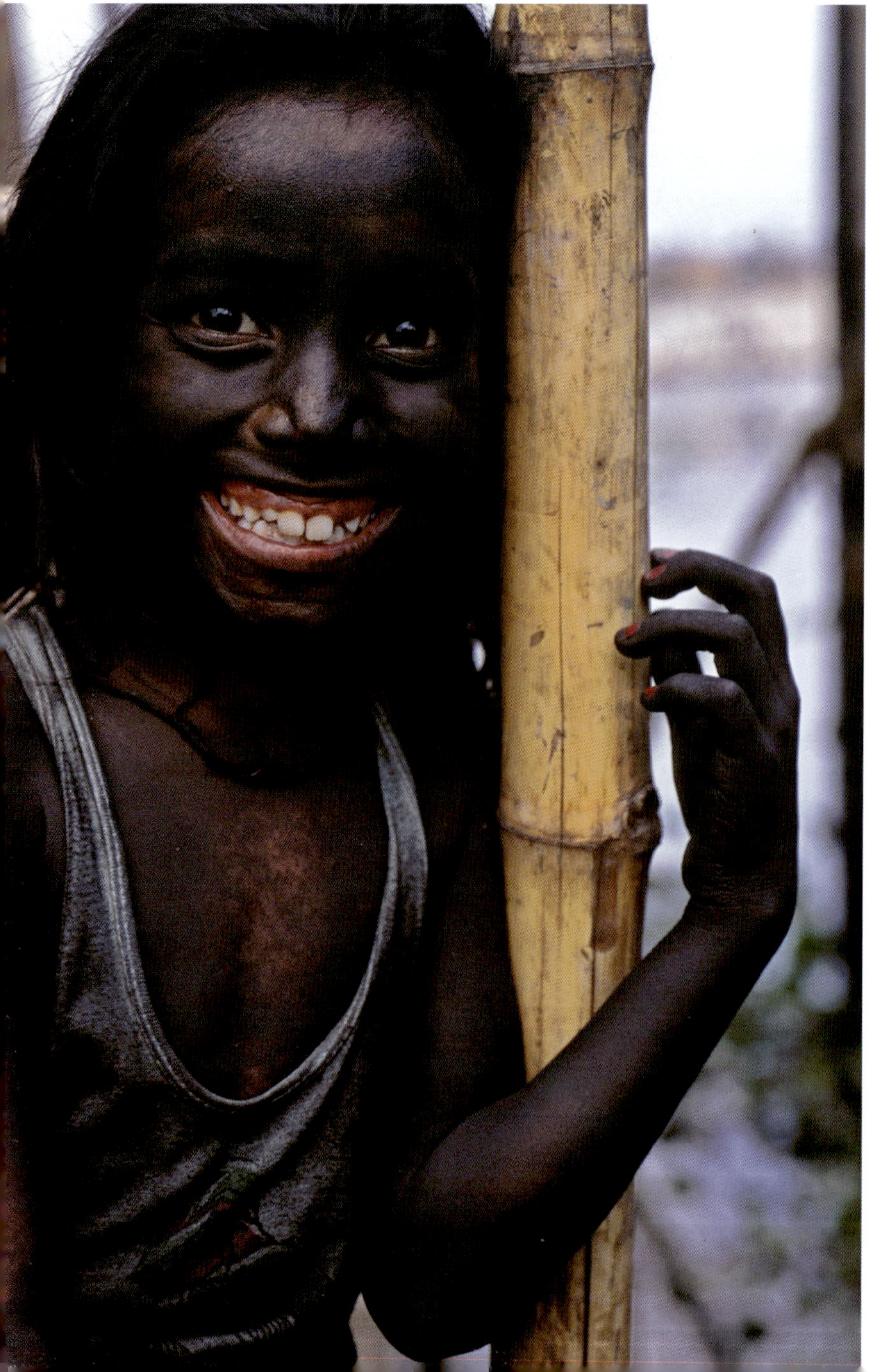

Hazard

Shahzad Noorani
K.M. Asad

Leaning against a bamboo near her home, Sathi (8 years old) smiles. Her face is blackened with carbon dust from recycled batteries. Often she looks so black that children in her neighbourhood call her a ghost. She works in a battery recycling factory at Korar Ghat on the outskirts of Dhaka. She earns less than Taka 200 ($ 3.5 approx.) per month. She lives with her mother and older sister in a little bamboo structure constructed over the river Buriganga, which alone cost them Taka 410. It is a constant struggle for her family to meet other monthly expenses with the remaining Taka 300. Even after working all day in the hellish environment of the battery recycling workshop, they often have to sleep on an empty stomach. Wiping her eyes, her mother says, 'I don't know what to do. I feel so sorry that I cannot send my daughters to school.' Hundreds of children dismantle used batteries to recycle them in similar workshops on the outskirts of Dhaka. They extract the carbon rod from the centre of the batteries, the zinc casing and the coated brass contact cap. All the recycled components are then sent to manufacturers of new batteries and to the wholesale market. In the process of breaking the batteries, the children inhale carbon dust throughout the day. They get between Taka 10–15 per day. They work barefeet and very often step on sharp objects like tin or shards of glass that cause serious infections. As they spend a good part of the day working in a polluted environment, inhaling harmful gases and particles, they often remain sick. By Shahzad Noorani, Bangladesh, DRIK.

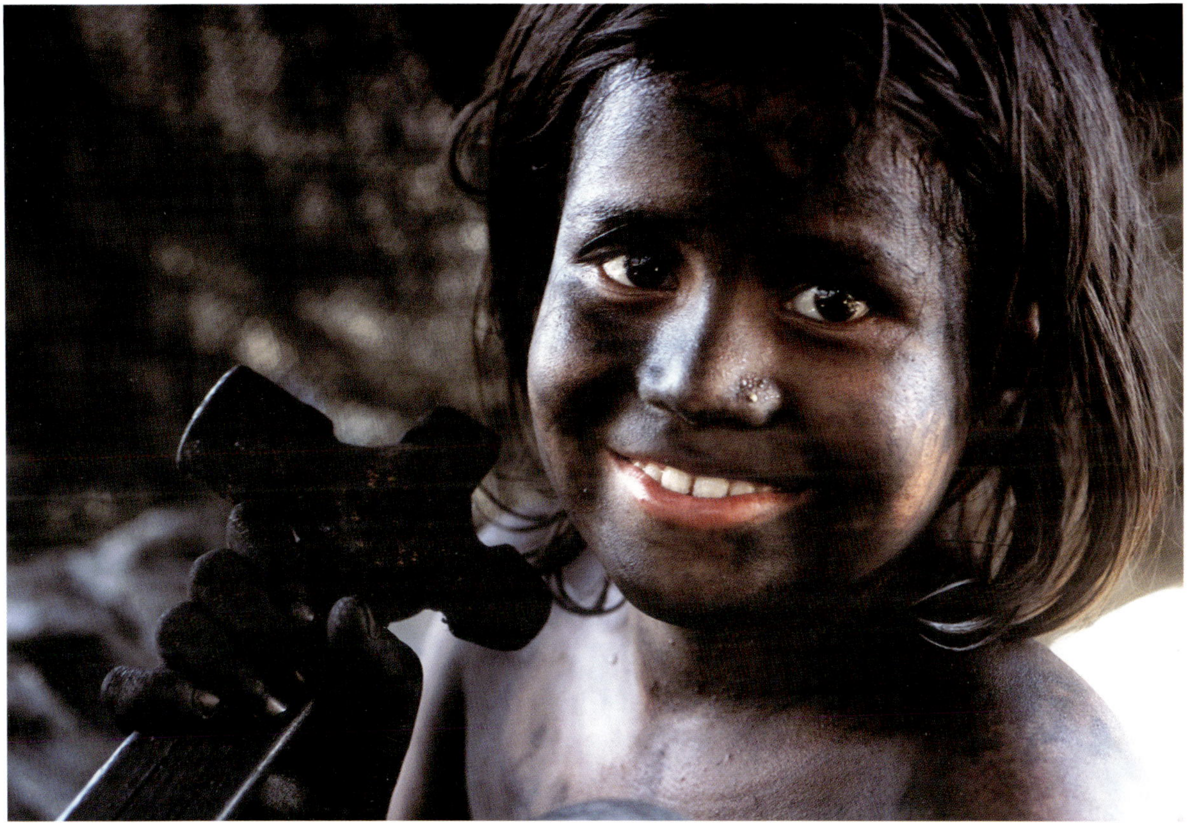

Using a heavy hammer, Rubina (9 years old) breaks used, D-size batteries. Her face is coated with the black carbon dust that puffs out of old batteries as she bangs them. Besides her big white eyes, the only other clean part on her face are her bright red lips as she keeps licking them when they get coated with carbon dust. For over 10 hours of work daily, she gets between Taka 10–15 (US$ 1 = Taka 60), depending on the number of batteries she can break. Rubina's mother complains about her unemployed husband: 'Don't I know that these children are supposed to be in school, but what can I do! We barely survive even after putting the entire family at work. If only their father wasn't so useless, we would have been different.' There are hundreds of other informal factories and workshops inside and on the outskirts of the city of Dhaka, the capital of Bangladesh. The industry employs thousands of women and children who dismantle used batteries to get reusable parts and tiny pieces of metal out of them. Once separated, these materials are sent to battery-manufacturing factories and workshops that either reuse them or melt them to make other useful products. While breaking the used batteries, children inhale fine carbon dust particles throughout the day. Depending on how much work they do, each of them gets between Taka 5–15 per day. It takes a child 4 to 12 days to earn just US$ 1. These children face some of the worst conditions of life anywhere in the world. None of them goes to school. Although they work hard and need nutritious food, they hardly eat. It's amazing they still look happy and manage to crack a smile every now and then! By Shahzad Noorani, Bangladesh, DRIK.

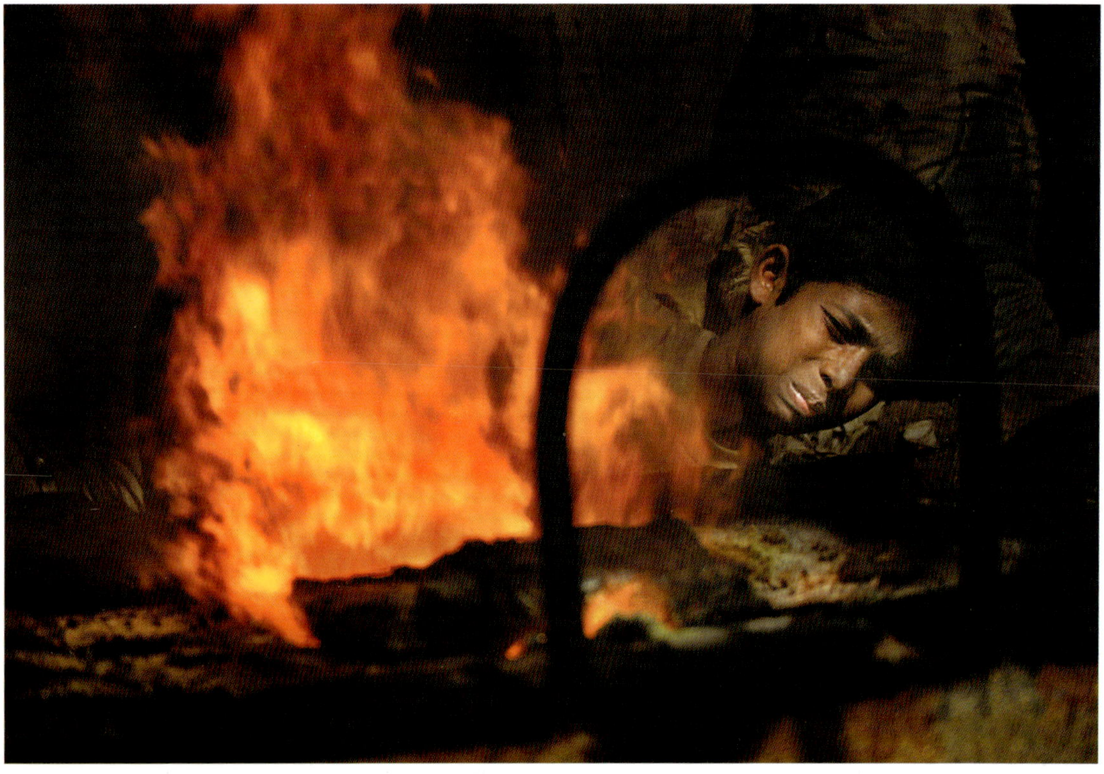

Child labour at the dockyard in Sadarghat, Dhaka. According to the UNICEF Asian Child Labour Report 1999, there are some 40 industries in Bangladesh which use child labour, often under hazardous conditions and with little regard for health and safety. By K.M. Asad, Bangladesh, 2007, DRIK.

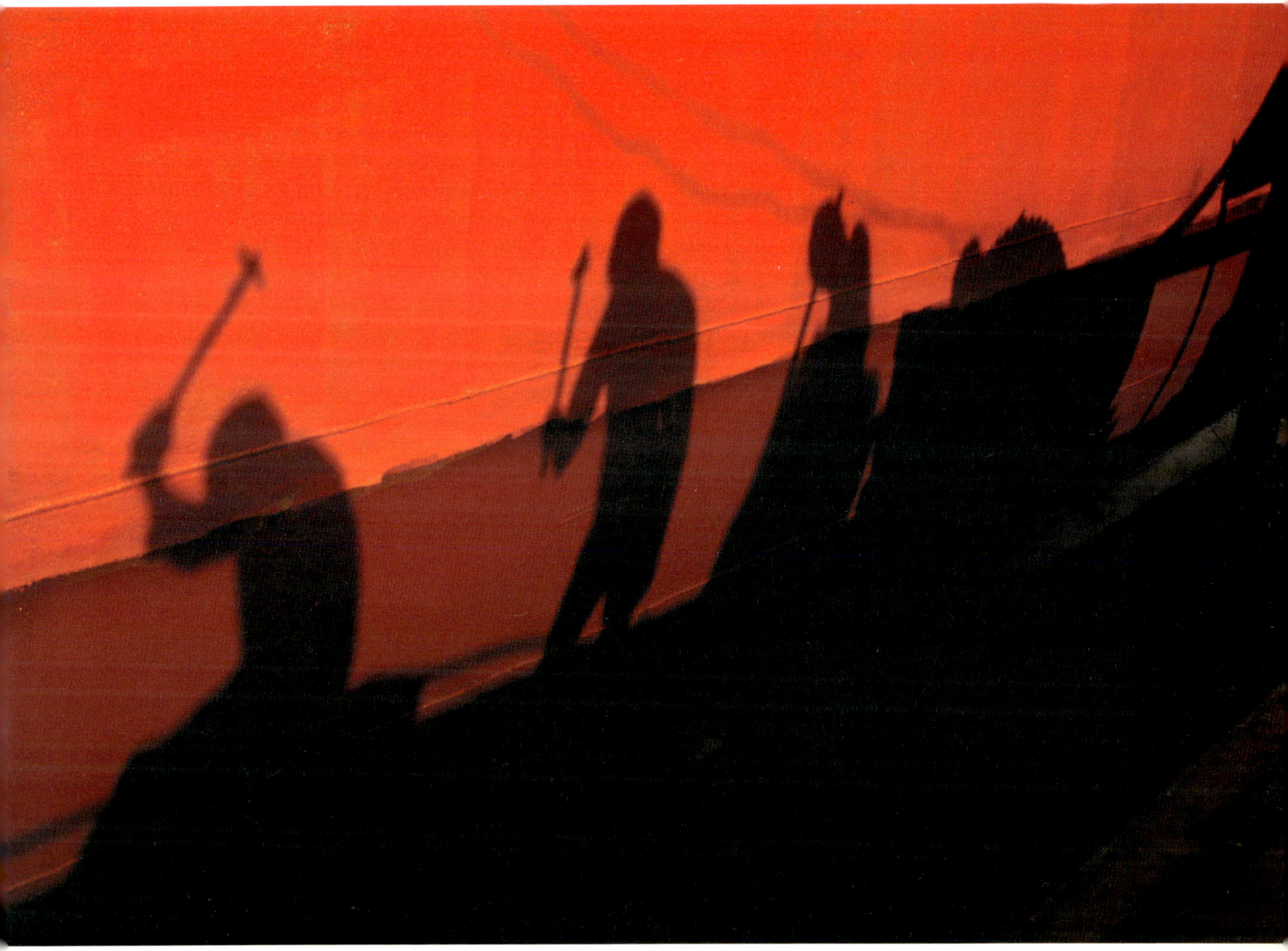

Silhouettes of workers at the dockyard in Sadarghat, Dhaka. By K.M. Asad, Bangladesh, 2007, DRIK.

Metamorphosing

Sara Rahbar

Like a mirror my work reflects my life, my geographic locations, my history, my present, my environments, my memories. My goal is to educate and to show another perspective.

My work addresses identity and the notion of borders – both cultural and geographic – and questions the concept of belonging. I am opposed to symbols such as the national flag, and feel that they keep us divided and separate from each other. They put into place this belief that we are so different from one another. I do not believe in the borders created by devotion to a flag, a country or a religion.

The only thing I wish to do with these symbols, that have created so much strife, is to shed them.

Through my work I invite viewers to look at the bigger picture and be alert to the way we view one another. My work encourages them to move their focus away from cities, states and countries, and to see the world at hand. My aim is to have people re-examine the concept of coexistence, as opposed to tolerance, and begin seeing things in a new light, with a new perspective. It is thus important to begin focusing on our similarities rather than our differences, and to remind ourselves that we have built these imaginary borders ourselves, and only *we* have the power to take them down.

We are constantly metamorphosing, transforming, reshaping. Our foundations remain, but our houses have burned to the ground. Building castles in the sky for a species that cannot fly, brick by limb we tear it down, thinking that we are moving forward, yet moving backwards all along.

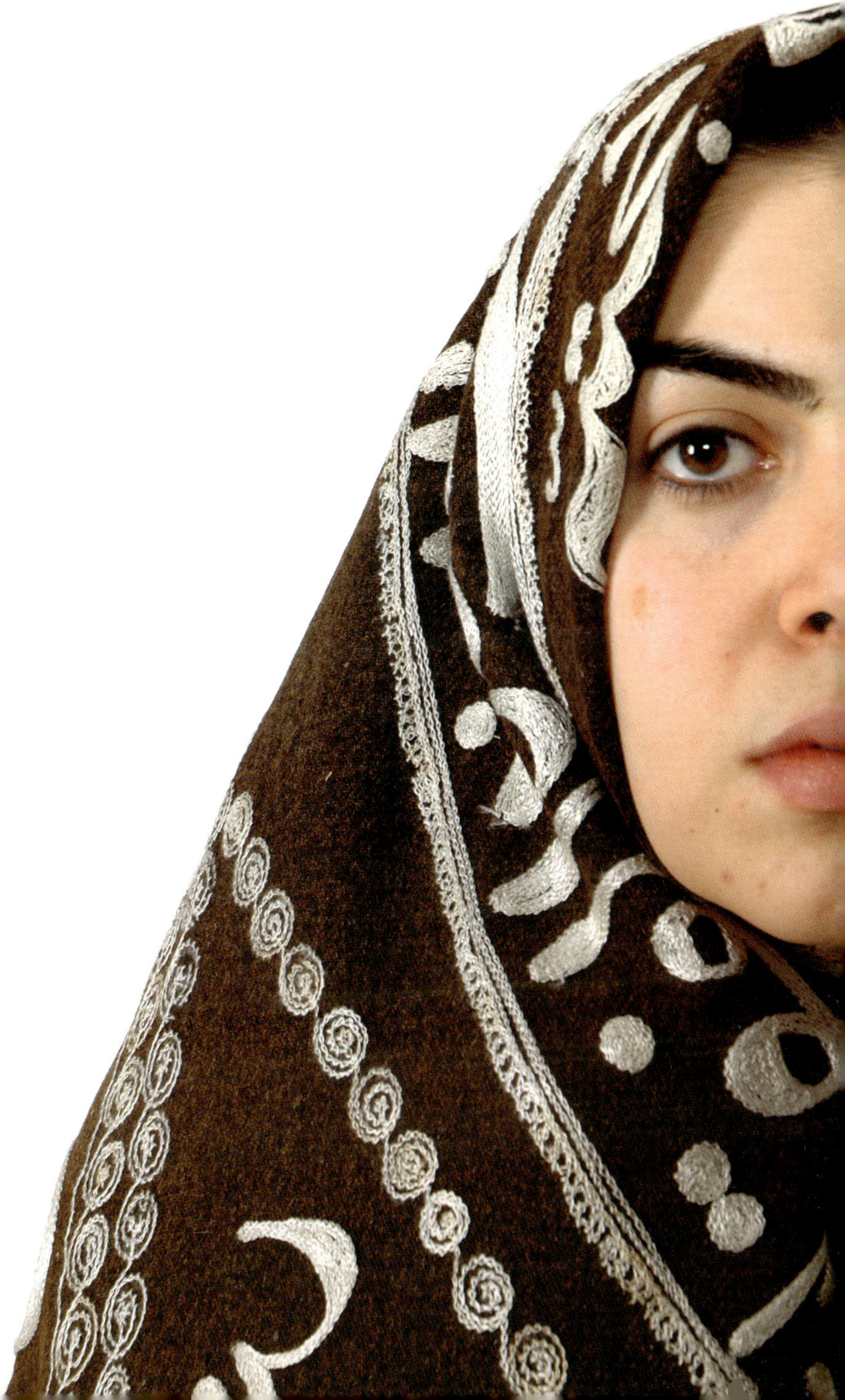

From *Oppression* series 2,
a series of 12 images.
By Sara Rahbar, Iran, 2007.

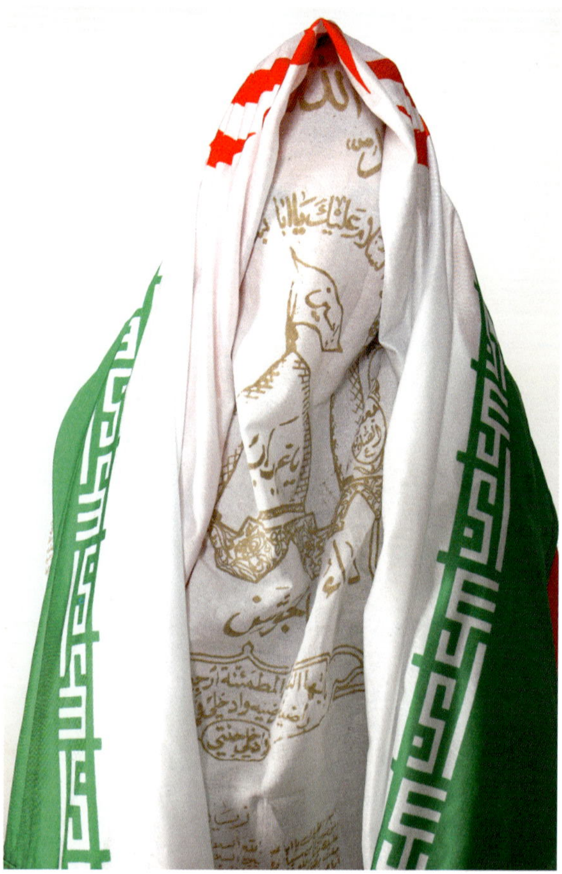

From *Oppression* series 2, a series of 12 images.
By Sara Rahbar, Iran, 2007.

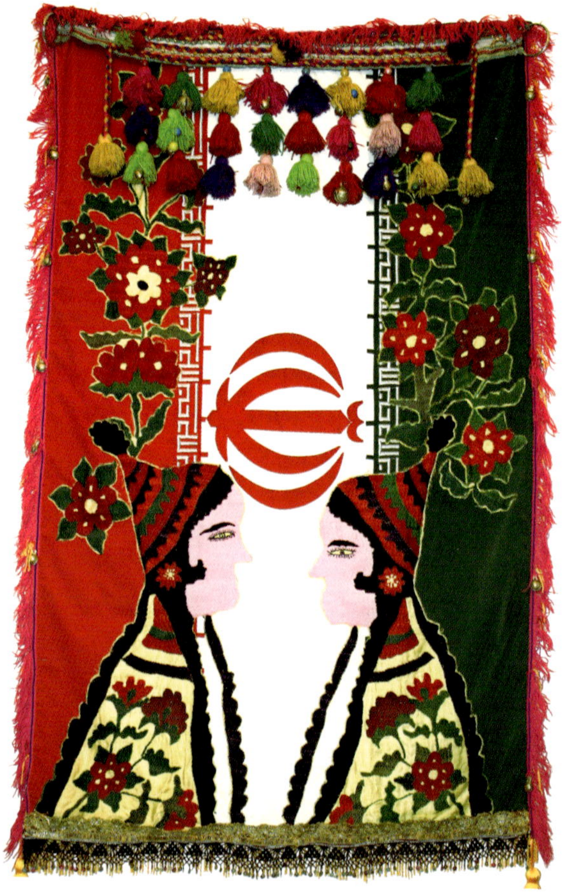

Women textile. By Sara Rahbar, Iran, 2007.

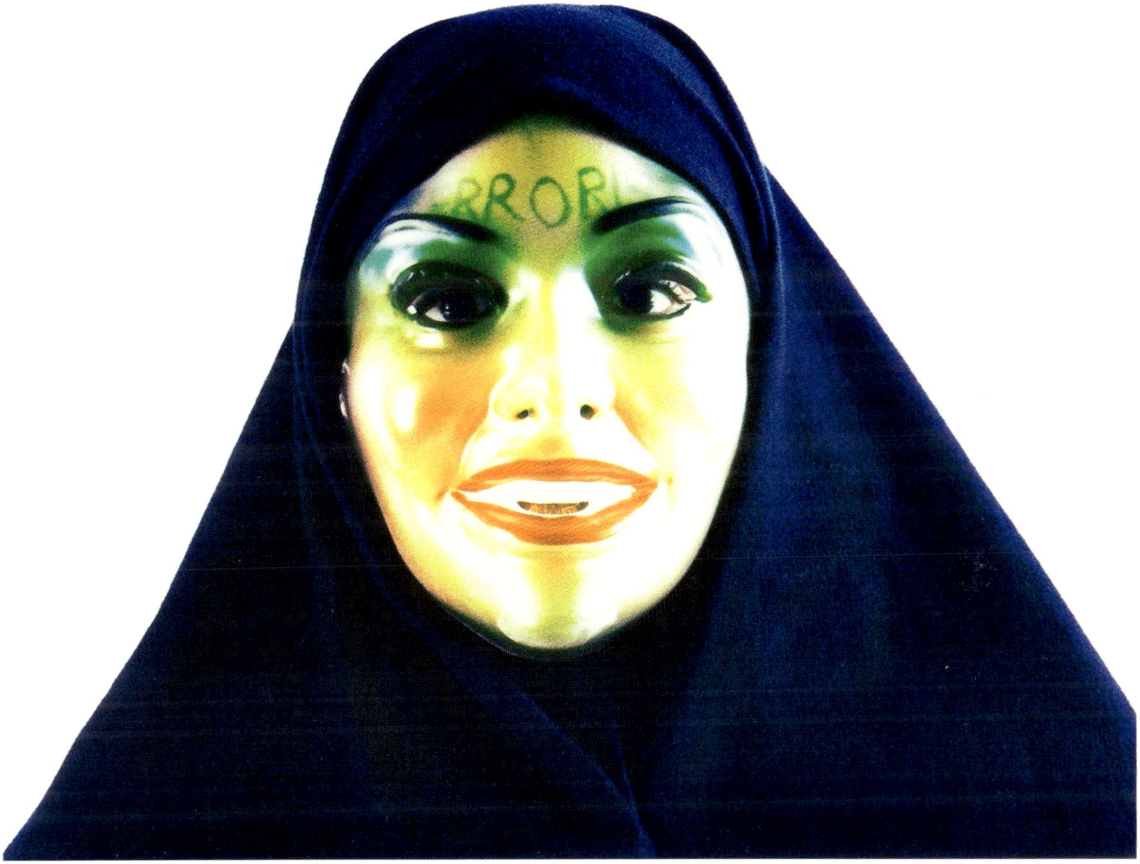

From *Mask* series, a series of 3 images. By Sara Rahbar, Iran, 2005.

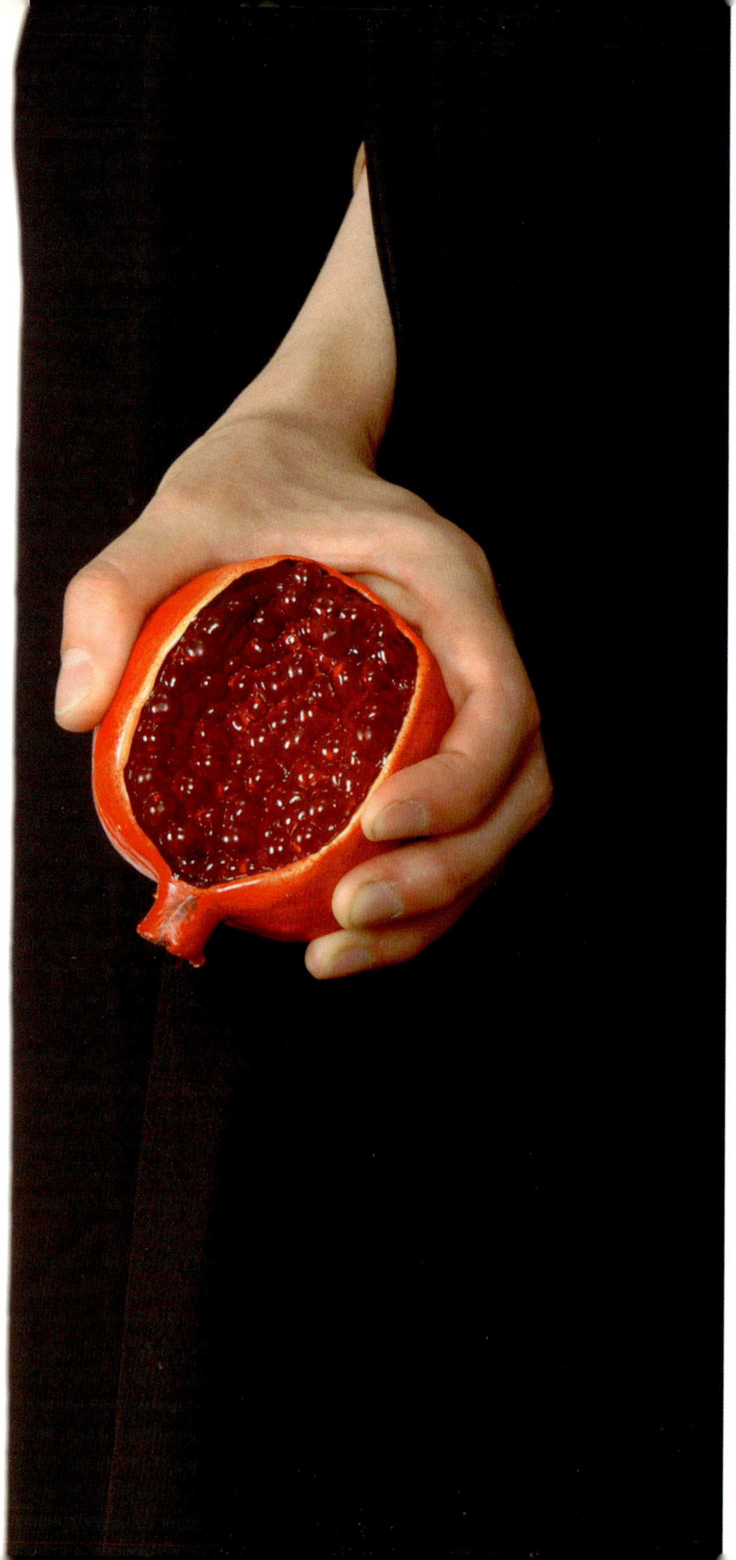

From *Oppression* series 2,
a series of 12 images.
By Sara Rahbar, Iran, 2007.

Behind Bars

The Colour of Khaki

Lipton Bhau

Gore hakim gaye re bhaiya,
aagaye hakim kale
pehle ek lathi khate the,
ab khate hain chaar

(The white bosses have gone my brother,
the darker one has come
then we used to get one strike with the lathi,
now we get four)

The Indian state has always been violent, but the rapidity with which its capacity for violence and its tendency to use violence are increasing, is quite remarkable. In the last few years, the profile of the state in its violent aspect has undergone a sharp quantitative change. There was a time when the image of the policeman could and did include, as one of its dimensions, the fat stupid blundering cop. Our films made use of this image with unfailing success to raise a laugh. Today that possibility is quite dead. The only dimension that remains is that of violence, and a vicious variety of violence at that. – K. Balagopal

Dr Binayak Sen has been languishing in jail in Chhattisgarh for the past one year even as false and fabricated charges of sedition have been mounted against him. Given this, it feels a little undeserved for me to be asked to write about my experiences with the police and jail. But Binayak Sen is just another in a long list of activists who have been at the receiving end of police atrocities, brutalities and excesses. Keeping in mind that my experiences are negligible compared to the experiences of these brave visionaries and fighters, I humbly recall some of my experiences with the police and reflect on how these have shaped my understanding of the same.

Thinking back to the days when I was a full-time activist with the Narmada Bachao Andolan (NBA), there are several memories about 'encounters' with the police that have failed to dim with time. In early 1999, along with a group of students and social activists, I had gone to the NBA to experience, first-hand, the struggle that has inspired so many other movements and peoples. After a few days in the Adivasi villages of Maharashtra, Madhya Pradesh and Gujarat, we set out to return and had to go to Baroda to catch our train. From the Adivasi villages the only route out then was through Hapeshwar, then Kadipani, then Kawat and a bus to Baroda. We reached Kadipani, a small mining town, late in the night and decided to spend the night at the bus-stand itself since there were no buses leaving Kadipani. As the rain fell, the police also descended upon us and began roughing us up. They then bundled us into police vans and jeeps and took us to the Kawat police station where we spent the night. We were released the next day, after they had taken down all our names and addresses.

In a way, this encounter with the police made firm my decision to return and become a full-time activist with the NBA. That was my first face-off with the police where the only crime committed was visiting the NBA. I will not go into the manner in which the entire bureaucracy, the police machinery, the politicians and even most of the civil society have internalized the flawed discourse of the Sardar Sarovar project – but suffice it to say that for the police, being a part of the NBA, or even being sympathetic to it, was a crime for which we as a group faced their wrath that night. My visit to the NBA and meeting with such articulate adivasis and farmers made me question the kind of work I wanted to do in life. The force of organized struggle and its passion captivated me entirely, so much so that I wanted to be part of the struggle immediately. In fact, while in the village Domkhedi, I remember conversations with my friends as to why we were not able to do this kind of work, and why could we not drop everything and become full-time activists. This question haunted me throughout my stay in the Adivasi villages for those few days. Then Kadipani happened and everything became clear. I had to come back and join the struggle. But I wondered how. Actually I have never quite been able to fully explain this, but I suppose the indignation suffered at the hands of the police made me realize that when we, the so-called middle-class supporters of the movement, were being treated in this manner, what then would be the fate of the Adivasis and farmers.

Eventually, along with several others I returned to Bangalore, quit my job as a civil engineer in an NGO and came back to join the NBA. I look back on that as one of the best decisions of my life. Sometimes it is ironic, the kind of response police brutality can produce. In fact, at that time, many of my friends in the NBA wanted to thank the Kawat police station for helping them recruit another full-time activist!

So I joined the NBA and began life as an activist, working with the Adivasis and farmers from the Narmada valley in the struggle against the Sardar Sarovar dam. Or, actually, a struggle for justice and a questioning of the dominant development paradigms that operate. For almost the whole of my first year there I was in Adivasi villages in the Satpudas in Maharashtra. It was here that I was initiated into regular confrontations with the police, even as we sat in peaceful satyagrahas or held peaceful rallies and demonstrations. The fearlessness of the Adivasis and farmers taught me to be less fearful and with every confrontation my fear diminished. The reverence and fear with which I, an English-speaking, urban, middle-class person, viewed the police began to rapidly evaporate. Every *dharna* and every roughing up that one received from the police accelerated this process.

So, by the time I went to jail for the first time in late 1999, I was free. We were roughed up, thrown into lorries and police vans, and transported to Dhule Jail from our *dharna* at a small town, Dhadgaon. We were kept in jail for about 15 days, during which time we sang and danced, played *kabaddi*, smoked tobacco rolled in newspapers, cleaned toilets, and held discussions on various issues. When we were finally released, my transformation into an activist was complete. For some of the NBA veterans at that time, it was just another jailing. For some others who had gone to jail for the first time, it was not such a pleasant experience. But for me it was actually exhilarating.

After this, during the many years that I have been associated with the NBA, going to jail or being beaten up became a regular feature. My partners in this were mostly Ashish Mandloi, a full-time activist whose land and house is to be submerged by the dam, and, sometimes, Sukumar, another full-time activist from Gudalur in Tamil Nadu. Once Sukumar and I were thrashed by about a dozen cops in Badwani; Sukumar ended up with a cheek torn open and me with a broken head. This was a day after we had had a long discussion with the Chief Minister of Madhya Pradesh, Digvijay Singh, on various issues. By sheer coincidence, the following day, Digvijay Singh flew to Badwani to visit Baba Amte, and, apparently having heard that we were injured, insisted on meeting us. Thus, from our beds in the Badwani Government Hospital, we were carted into police jeeps and taken to meet the Chief Minister who acted pained that we were beaten up so badly. He ordered an enquiry into the police brutality. Incidentally, the enquiry report and the subsequent police cases framed against us suggest that we were guilty of damaging government property and causing grievous injuries to government officials!

One question, in this context, continues to haunt me: where does the bounden duty of police constables and inspectors to obey and carry out the orders of their superiors overlap with, or probably get taken over by, the personal biases of the police officials themselves? For instance, when the order to lathi-charge a demonstration is taken by senior police officials in consultation with the district administration and ministers, and is communicated to the police constables and inspectors at the demonstration spot, to what extent may the lathi-charge be attributed to their obeying orders and to what extent is it because of their personal biases? My understanding is that the force of the lathi coming down on demonstrators is not just a factor of obedience to orders or even personal biases, but also owes to the sadistic pleasure derived from this violence and the arrogance of wearing the khaki uniform. To some extent this conclusion derives substance from

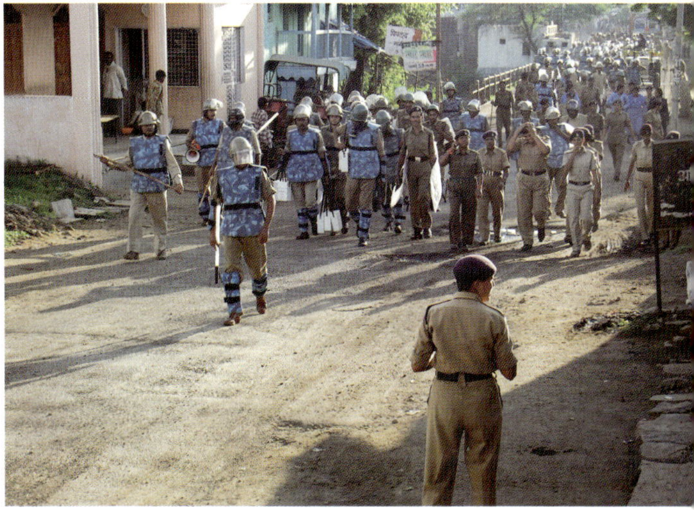

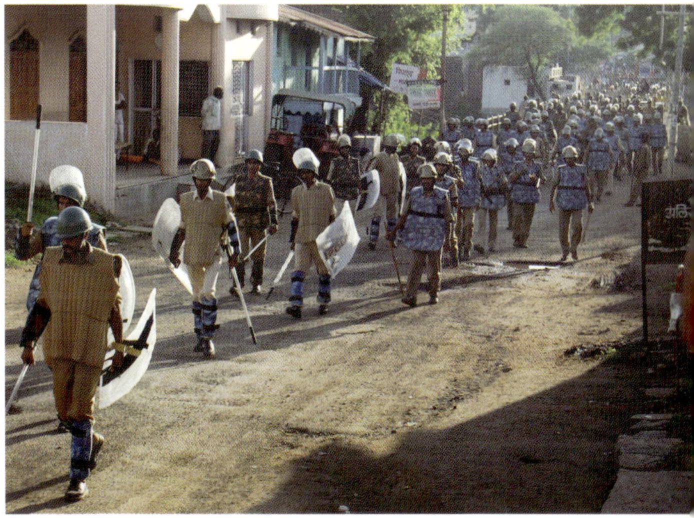

Security forces in their hundreds march into Alirajpur town in Madhya Pradesh, to suppress a protest by villagers against the Sardar Sarovar project.

instances where police officials have stood up to the bureaucracy and the executive, and refused to implement such orders.

R.B. Sreekumar, Additional Director-General of Police in Gujarat during the genocide of 2002, is one such police official. At the invitation of the Nanavati Commission, set up to probe the Gujarat genocide, he filed four affidavits along with a diary, a speech of Chief Minister Narendra Modi, and taped conversations with two bureaucrats who asked him not to offer testimony before the Commission. The gist of his testimony was that Narendra Modi had explicitly asked the police chiefs not to take action against Hindus who had needed to vent their anger. According to the reported statement of Sreekumar:

> When senior officials, political leaders, including the honourable Chief Minister, though hierarchically superior to me, were unabashedly going contrary to the provisions of the Constitution, I thought that my intrinsic duty is to resist such a trend and initiate possible and feasible remedial measures.
>
> My register recorded illegal directives from authorities.

While not complying with these orders of Narendra Modi, Sreekumar maintained a diary as proof of the same.

The last incident that I would like to relate concerns the general treatment we received at the hands of the Gujarat police. I remember once we had organized a huge rally in this town called Rajpipla in Narmada district in Gujarat. I went, along with several Adivasis, to the *dharna* from the Adivasi villages by boat. We got off at Kewadia Colony, just behind the dam wall, and began walking towards the bus-stand to go to Rajpipla. Suddenly more than 200 police officers came screaming towards us in vans and jeeps. We were beaten up and thrown into the police vans, and taken to the Kewadia police station. We demanded throughout that the police tell us what the charges against us were. I guess they did not like my voice or the fact that I was 'not from Gujarat'. So I was taken inside and made to sit on a stool next to the door of the sub-inspector's room. Thereafter, for the next two hours, every police constable or officer who entered took it upon himself to verbally abuse me and then slap me to their hearts' content. I remember that my face went numb after a point, but it was the verbal abuses that hurt the most.

I could go on like this, relating innumerable experiences of my confrontations with the police – in Bombay or Dhule or Bhopal or Badwani or Delhi, or every other place where the NBA held *dharnas*, protests, rallies, or engaged in any other perfectly democratic expression of dissent. I could also relate incidents of how government officials, along with hundreds of police, entered villages to carry out surveys for land acquisition and, in the bargain, thrashed people mercilessly when they opposed this forced survey. And these are just 'my' experiences. The movement has been going on for more than 25 years now, and its supporters have faced relentless and merciless beatings and imprisonment. In fact, village activists tell me that the police brutality meted out now is nothing when compared to what happened in the formative stages of the movement.

At some point in the early 1990s, the police force stormed into the village Anjanwara in Madhya Pradesh, and mercilessly thrashed every person upon whom it could lay its hands. As if breaking the bones of Adivasi men, women and children was not enough, they then began to systematically damage their houses, throw grinding stones into the river, confiscate foodgrains, and, of course, kill chickens and goats, as is done by police forces marauding Adivasi villages anywhere. In fact, years later, in March–April 2001, a police operation was carried out in which the police raided five tribal villages in Bagli tehsil in Dewas district of Madhya Pradesh on consecutive days, not only demolishing houses, but also poisoning foodgrains and wells, and assaulting Adivasis, besides misbehaving with the Adivasi women. As news spread of the rampaging police force – all in the name of confiscating illegally felled timber – entire Adivasi populations from more than 16 villages were forced to abandon their homes and seek refuge in the nearby forests, fearing police brutality. This expedition of the police force culminated on 2 April 2001 at the village Mehednikheda, where six Adivasis, including a 12-year-old girl, were killed in police firing.

These are not isolated incidents where police parties, with the agenda to terrorize people and plunder, have rampaged through villages, reminding one of the marauding armies of kings and queens of the pre-colonial and colonial eras. This has been going on in Adivasi areas for centuries and it continues well into the so-called post-independence era. Thus even today in the Narmada valley, though it would appear inconceivable that such police raids continue to take place, this is the reality in most of the Adivasi areas struggling for justice and the right to a peaceful and undisturbed life.

I remember that on 9 August 2000, the NBA celebrated *Kranti Din* (Martyrs' Day) at a small village called Chinchkhedi in Maharashtra, to pay homage and respects to Rehmal Punya Vasave, a 15-year-old Adivasi boy who was shot dead by the police in 1994, when it opened fire indiscriminately on a group of Adivasis who were attempting to stop the police from forcibly entering their villages. In a subsequent protest against the proposed dam and this killing that was held at Dhule, more than 1000 policemen and women broke the skulls, legs and hands of peaceful protestors, sending hundreds to the hospital. When I heard the full details of the manner in which Rehmal Vasave had been killed in cold blood, it put into perspective the struggle of Adivasis against forcible evictions and pauperization, and the police brutality they faced due to this resistance. Protestors being shot to death by the police, again, is news that does not surprise anyone. In the past one year, in Rajasthan alone, there have been 22 incidents of police firing in which scores of people have been killed.

During my years as a full-time activist, there were several incidents of extreme police brutality and murders around the country. The reality and reasons behind such police action were brilliantly captured on video by two filmmakers, Biju Toppo and Meghnath, in their documentary *Vikas Bandook ke Nal Se Behti Hai* ('Development Flows from the Barrel of the Gun'). This documentary addresses the issue of state violence against Adivasis and farmers protecting their lands and forests, and preventing forcible alienation in the name of 'developmental' projects including mining, dams and ports. In more ways than one, it completely exposes, through moving interviews with Adivasis and farmers affected by various projects in Kashipur (Orissa), Koel-Karo (Jharkhand), Mahendikheda (Madhya Pradesh), Umbergaon (Gujarat) and Nagarner (Chhattisgarh), the lopsided development paradigm of the state and the repressive role of the police in protecting the state's agenda. It also captures the detrimental impact of globalization and the neoliberal policies of the state on Adivasis and farmers, and the protection given by the police force to these destructive policies.

From a socio-economic point of view, in a country experiencing increasing turmoil and discontent, it comes to be even more visibly expressed in the form of the thousands of collectives, movements, unions and other social formations – whether they are Adivasi struggles against dams or mining projects in the central and northeastern states, farmers' movements across the country, the emerging urban poor movements in urban centres, the Maoist struggles across more than ten states, or the numerous Dalit struggles across the country. The police, as it exists today, has retained all the principal characteristics of its previous *avatar* constituted by the British under the Indian Police Act, 1861, passed subsequent to the 1857 struggle for independence. If, at that time, the police was just an arm of the state which ensured that 'law and order' was maintained (read: no struggle for independence), then today, the police is used as the law-enforcing machinery meant to maintain 'law and order' (read: no questioning the implementation of anti-people economic policies).

Clearly, the police as an armed extension of the state is meant to mercilessly suppress any voice that is raised against the state and

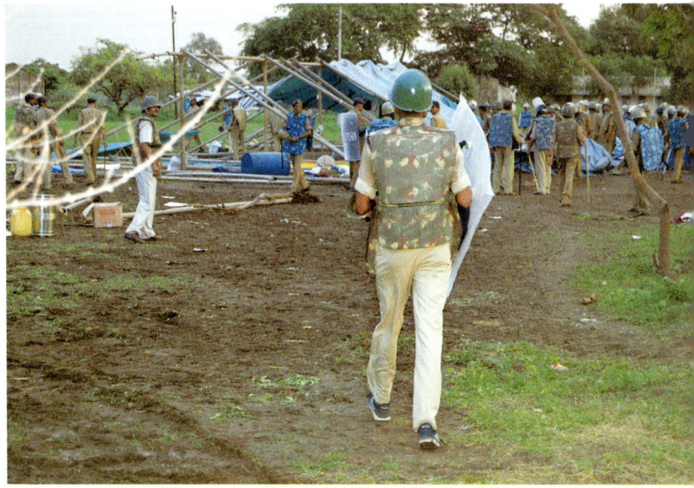

Security forces set up camp in Alirajpur, Madhya Pradesh, as they prepare for a long siege.

its oppressive policies. On numerous occasions, during protests and *dharnas*, we have screamed at the police, demanding that they get out of the way and bring the officials and ministers before us. But the job of the police is to be a barrier, a 'wall' that protects the bureaucracy and the executive. And they do this job remarkably well. The recent Gujjar protests and the manner in which this was dealt with exemplifies this. While Vasundhara Raje Scindia spoke aggressively before the full glare of the media, threatening, 'We will not let them hold us hostage', the police fired at will and shot to death 43 agitating Gujjars even as scores were injured. The rage of the agitators is the mirror reflecting the evil face of the state. This, the state cannot handle and, like the mafia, it lets loose its paid henchmen.

Still, all this police repression and violence does not dampen the voices of the dissenting masses. If anything, the struggles only multiply. The people have also learnt this. Just take a look at some of the popular activist slogans:

> *Sarkar humse darti hai …*
> *police ko aage karti hai.*
>
> (The government is scared of us / which is why it forces the police forward.)
>
> *Police teri taanashaahi …*
> *nahin chalegi nahin chalegi*
> *Police teri goondagardhi …*
> *nahin chalegi nahin chalegi.*
>
> (The dictatorship of the police will not be allowed.)
>
> *Bade sharam ki baat hai …*
> *police unke saath hai.*
>
> (It's such a shame / the police is also with the state.)
>
> *Satpuda mein kaun charta …*
> *gai nahin, police charta.*
>
> (Who grazes in the Satpudas / the police, and not the cows.)

The slogans that the people chant in the Narmada valley encapsulate the lessons learnt. The character of the police force and what it symbolizes are captured best by these slogans. Thus, while recognizing the character and role of the police, the people and movements continue to agitate and struggle, and to assert their rights. Gross inequality increases even as the rich get richer and the middle class gets more comfortable in their consumerist lives. However, for the majority of the citizens of this country, every day is a struggle, either in an organized or a disorganized manner. It is these struggles that give us the hope for a better future and a more equal society. And no police force or its firings or jailings, or whatever new methods of social control it can create, can stop this.

'May I take a book with me?'

Kian Tajbakhsh

Kian Tajbakhsh spent four months in Evin Prison in Tehran, from May to September 2007, making him the fourth Iranian-American to be arrested, detained and held without charge. This piece was written following this prison experience. Since then he has been arrested again in 2009, and has been one of the defendants of a mass trial along with hundreds of others arrested following the protests after the presidential election. As of April 2010, Tajbakhsh has been granted 'temporary release' from prison, but is prohibited from leaving Iran.

'May I take a book with me?' The arresting officer, probably amused by my assumption that the detention would last no more than one book, nodded his assent.

The solitary cell was empty except for a blanket on the floor and a copy of the Quran. But I was allowed my one book and my glasses. Huddled in the blanket, angled to catch the fluorescent light coming through the small barred window of the thick metal door, I read. Sometimes it was hard to sleep. With the dim light-bulb high above always on, night and day became indistinct. So I read slowly, stretching out the only source of distraction which was a link to home. But it was a bitter source of comfort, for the book I had brought with me was *The Kite Runner*, a sad and painful story of our part of the world, which I would rather have finished and put aside quickly.

As it became clear that my stay in Evin prison would not be over soon, a sense of panic gradually came over me. I struggled to imagine what I would do once my book was finished. I began to dread the prospect of a vast, empty time stretching out towards apparent infinity. The stress of solitary cell confinement is a mental roller-coaster as the mind waxes, desperate with imagination, in a space that is contracted but in a span of time that is frighteningly expanded – hope, panic, optimism, fear, resignation,

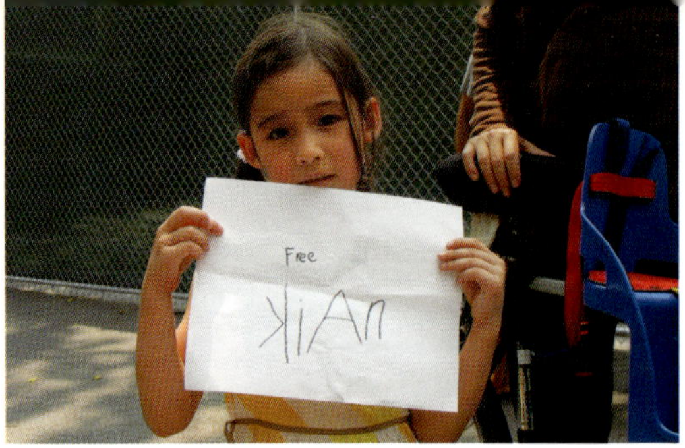

A young protestor joins the demonstration demanding the release of Kian Tajbakhsh from Evin Prison, located in northwestern Tehran. It is noted for its political prisoners' wing where prisoners have been held both before and after the 1979 Iranian revolution.

trepidation, equanimity, compete and repeat, on and on.

There were other distractions. Several times a day I would stand submerged under the rushing water of the shower, my eyes closed, to become lost in the roaring echo around my skull. I washed my few items of clothing. I cleaned the rough carpeting. I paced to tire myself out. I squashed mosquitoes. After some physical exercise, I felt more resolved and calm. But once it was over, it was again me and the walls. I tried sitting calmly and meditating as I had been taught to do – seeking to 'empty the mind' – but in a particularly maudlin moment, hazy images of saints with tranquil countenance being burnt at the stake would arise. After a while I would think, 'This is a waste of time! I can't keep dread at bay this way, and even if I could, I don't want to empty my mind – I'd rather fill it!' It soon became clear that the best way to focus my mind and emotions was to read, to think. I began taking notes and making a list of books that I would like to read. So I requested other books from home. Bahar sent me four or five: history and non-fiction as well as novels, mostly in English. They were inspected. They were all allowed. Even a history of the French Revolution called *The New Regime*.

I began to stack my books in a row on the floor against the far wall – 3 metres is farther than 2! Quietly, they began to take on the familiar quality of a bookshelf – the various sizes, colours, subjects. I started looking forward to the next book I had yet to read. And as I stared at the little library, I began to experience a most remarkable change in my perception of time. The more books there were facing me, the more the time ahead of me began to take on a palpable, comprehensible texture. The panic of an immeasurable span of time seemed to reverse itself. Rather than too much, there was too little time ahead. The vast, unfathomable expanse stretching to the horizon began to contract.

As the line of books waiting to be read lengthened before me, every day, every minute became too short. The worst moment of each day – the moment of opening my eyes after waking – was relieved by my eagerness to read. Reacting to my request for a dozen more books, Bahar asked, 'How long do you expect to stay in there? Will you really read all these books?' I realized then that the more unread books I had in my library, the better equipped I was to overcome the helplessness, to manage the passing of each day. I began taking notes and making a long list of books to read. I began to sense that fiction was not always suitable. Reading fiction requires keeping one part of the mind free and relaxed, to be able to experience the associations alluded to by the narrative. But that open door was also the way in for dread.

Books also helped open my cell to the world outside. I must have seemed mad to request deliveries from Amazon, shipped to Paris, couriered to Bahar, then relayed to me through the prison system. But imagining a worldwide network of booksellers, all in motion to bring a book to me, was exhilarating and reassuring. I ordered a book by a French writer I had met at the New School years before, and felt in touch with my former colleagues there. In a footnote I saw the name of a Polish intellectual I knew, and again felt less anonymous. The pencilled margin notes in a book given to me by a friend took me to a cool hill-station in Pakistan. If I was thinking of all of them, maybe they were thinking of me. Simply being able to have these unread books appear in my little cell in a growing row expanded space and contracted time.

What did I read? Friends sent me Simenon, Hesse, Kazantzakis, Shakespeare, *The Mysteries of Udolpho*, Dostoevsky's *The Gambler*, Graham Greene's *Our Man in Havana*, *Human Factor*, Le Carre, among others. After many years on my bookshelf, I finally finished Vikram Seth's *A Suitable Boy* – a gently running book the length of the Nile. His description of the *zenana* (harem) as 'a limited but complete world' has stuck in my mind. I did read the Quran, a taxing book to read, to say the least, especially in one sitting. The writings and speeches of Ayatollah Khomeini over a 40-year period was an eye-opener. I also read, believe it or not, books by Fromm and Reich, to learn about the authoritarian personality and the fear of freedom. A disappointing history of life in Mussolini's Italy at least showed how banal, inefficient and rustic fascism could

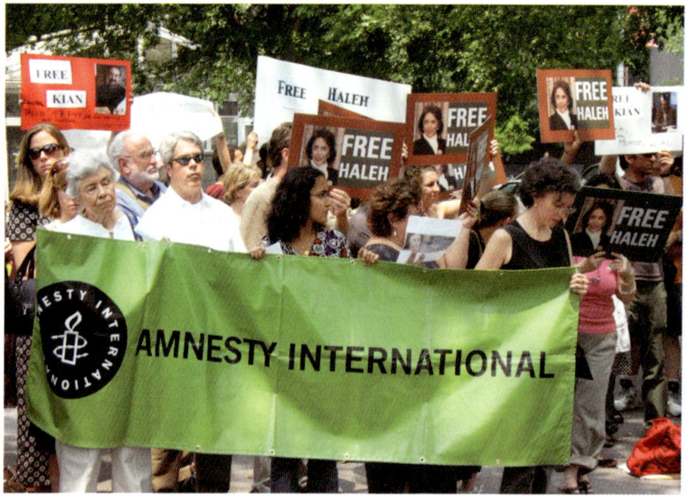

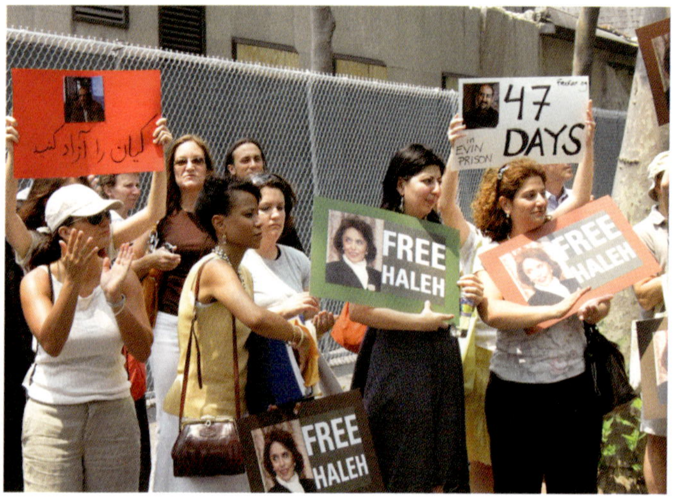

Amnesty International and members of other human rights organizations stage a demonstration demanding that Kian and Haleh be freed.

be. Ken Pollack's *The Persian Puzzle* was especially surreal when he compliments the Iranian Security Services for their effectiveness. The book on the history of the French Revolution had been recommended by a former professor in New York only a few months earlier – simply following up on the suggestion made me feel less isolated. On the other hand, it was less than heartening to learn that Napoleon was able to create, in less than a decade, an authoritarian system that coerced and rather efficiently administered a nation the size of France. The moral I drew from that? *It can be done.*

When possible, I asked that some of the books be sent over to Dr Haleh Esfandiary, a fellow-traveller. I think she found solace in them too.

Unread books are a familiar burden to most in academia, which is my own background. In the cell, I rediscovered the joy, as opposed to the chore, of reading. Over the course of the four-and-a-half months I spent in solitary confinement, I read almost everything I had, cover to cover, slowly, with care. I used the practice of meditation to help me read as an art or a calling, with focus – not as a means of mining for information. I have come to realize how poorly and how little most people read, and am shocked by the number of intellectuals and academics who complain that 'we don't have time to read', and consequently read superficially, skimming more often than they would like, or care, to admit.

My greatest regret is that Bahar had to endure those 140 days pregnant with our baby girl, Hasti. I now know that it can be harder for those who are outside, and that by imprisoning one person, many others might also be shackled with the bonds of their affection. But I don't regret the time that I spent in there – just one of the thousand natural shocks that flesh is heir to. Good books – those who write them, publish them, sell them – are a precious resource for each person to try and 'become who they are'. For the primary value of the attentive reading of the best books is to nourish the source of one's own thoughts, to help these ideas emerge and develop, have them challenged, so as to be able to put together a view of life that could then be embraced.

It is one of the best things we can do with our solitude.

(*Dedicated to the memory of Richard Rorty*)

When Prisoners Reform

Sunil Batra and Charles Sobhraj, two notorious criminals, have ironically been responsible for crystallizing the legally enforceable rights of a prisoner in India. Writ petitions filed by them in the late 1970s led to some landmark judgements about the fundamental rights of a prisoner.

Batra had been sentenced to death in 1977 after being found guilty of a gruesome murder and massive bank robbery. Sobhraj was already infamous as the Bikini Killer, for a series of 12 murders of western tourists in Southeast Asia. He had been convicted in 1976 and would, towards the end of his first term, escape dramatically from Tihar to avoid being extradited to Thailand. As unusually 'empowered' prisoners, the two were inadvertently responsible for ensuring the humane treatment of many far less empowered prisoners in Indian jails.

Sunil Batra, a prisoner in Tihar Jail, filed a writ petition in 1978 challenging his incarceration in solitary confinement. In the same year Sobhraj, an undertrial in Tihar, challenged his confinement with bar-fetters. Batra's solitary confinement was quashed and the court called solitary confinement inhumane. In the case of Sobhraj, it was held that there was no arbitrary power to put an undertrial under bar-fetters. Further, a judicial hearing is essential before putting prisoners in fetters and no prisoner can be put in fetters at night.

In another instance, Batra sent a letter to one of the judges of the Supreme Court alleging that a jail warder had tortured his fellow-prisoner to extract money from his visiting relations. The letter was treated as a *habeas corpus* proceeding and led to the important principle of law that a writ of *habeas corpus* is available not only to secure the release of a prisoner illegally detained, but also to regulate the conditions of legal detention of a person.

The Supreme Court held that imprisonment cannot mean total deprivation of a person's right to life and liberty. It ruled that 'safe custody does not mean deprivations, violation, banishment from the lanter barguet of prison life and inflictions of travails as if guardianship were best fulfilled by making the ward suffer near insanity'.

The Costs of Proving One's Innocence

Nandita Haksar

Article 11. Everyone charged with a penal offence has the right to be presumed innocent until proved guilty according to law in a public trial at which they had all the guarantees necessary for their defence.
– *Universal Declaration of Human Rights*

The presumption of innocence in favour of the accused is the foundation of the administration of criminal law and a fundamental human right in democratic countries. Yet thousands of men and women languish in jails all around our country because the state looks upon them as guilty even before they have been formally charged, and sometimes even without any charges at all. The social and political costs of these illegal arrests and detentions have neither been documented nor quantified. You will get a glimpse of the problem from two illustrations here.

Four Years after Operation Bluestar

Balbir Kaur (name changed) had gone to the Golden Temple early that morning, after giving tea to the security forces camping on the roof of her home which was right next to the Golden Temple in Amritsar. She and her husband had not been comfortable with their guests nor did they support the Sikh militants holed in the temple.

Balbir had not yet completed her third circumambulation round the temple when the firing started and she was injured in one eye. She did not know then that she was in the middle of Operation Bluestar, an offensive carried out by the Indian army to flush out terrorists hiding in the Golden Temple. Before she could realize what was happening, someone forced her to put her hands behind and tied them up. Screaming in pain, she was dumped in a heavily guarded hospital. She could see her husband, a garage mechanic, from a distance but they would not let her speak to him.

And within a few days she was transported to Jodhpur, India's maximum security prison. She was charged with being a hard-core terrorist and kept in the company of three other women who were picked up at the temple, along with men who were kept in a separate ward.

Balbir Kaur's husband came to me to request me to file a *habeas corpus*, and I filed the case in the Supreme Court of India. I was happy that the petition came up before a judge known to be sympathetic to human rights. But he did not listen to me; he just said: 'Ms. Haksar, I cannot help in this case.'

Four years later, I received a phone call. It was Balbir Kaur from Amritsar. She had been released from Jodhpur and wanted to come to Delhi to meet me and thank me personally. She asked what I would like from Amritsar.

We met at Sri Ram Centre. She looked like any other ordinary, middle-aged Sikh woman. I immediately noticed that she had only one eye. I asked her breezily: 'So it must be good to be home again. Your children must be so happy to have you back?'

She was silent. Then she told me her story. She said that only the thought of her baby, who was barely six months at the time of her arrest, had sustained her through the hardships of life in prison. Day and night, she waited for the day she would hold her child in her arms again. Her husband visited her only once because it was difficult to leave their three young daughters; besides, it was very expensive to travel all the way to Jodhpur. Then, after four years, she was suddenly released and told to go home.

When she stepped into her home with arms stretched out to her baby daughter, the 4-year-old ran away, terrified of the stranger who had just walked into the house. The oldest daughter had given up school to look after her baby sister and she was the only mother the little girl knew. The second girl had had a severe shock and never recovered from it. The home that Balbir Kaur had dreamt of, while in prison, had been torn asunder.

A Doctor in Jail

There is no count of the number of people who have died of falciparam malaria in the villages of Dhamtari district of Chhattisgarh. By the time the patient could be taken for a blood test, the blood sample tested in a laboratory and the report

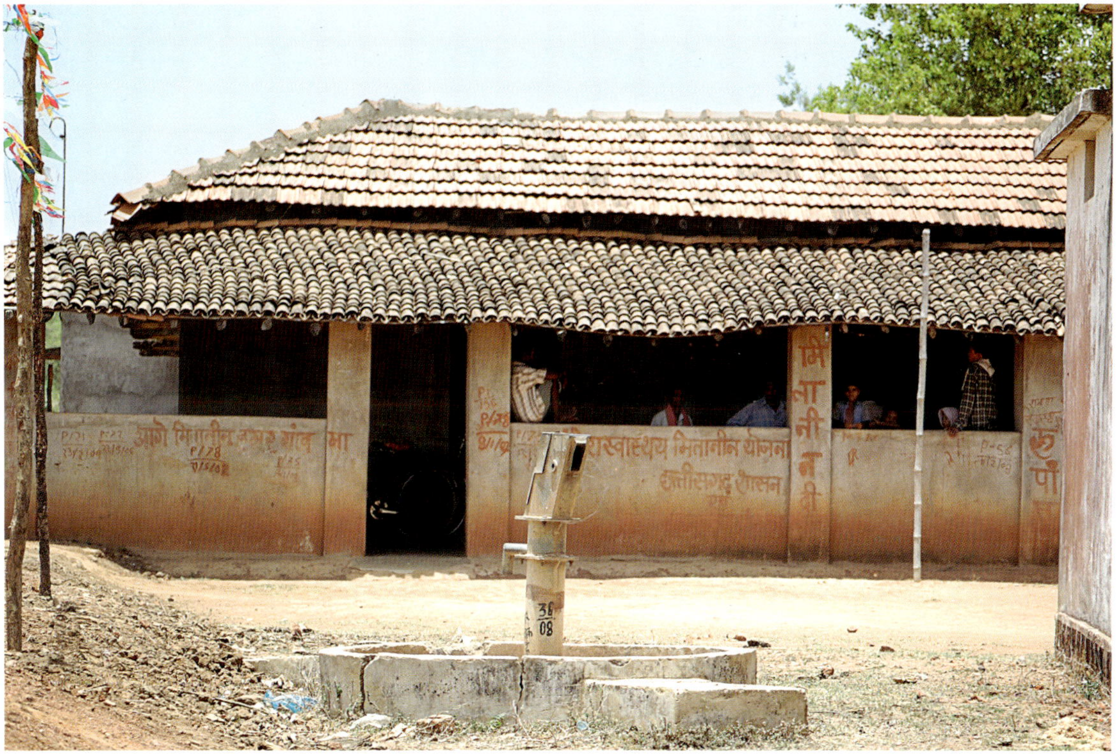

Adivasi hospital in Bagrumnala, Dhamtari district, Chhattisgarh – quiet while its driving force, Dr Binayak Sen, was in prison. Photo by Sebastian M. Hongray, a Supreme Court advocate from Manipur who in his student days filed the first case in the Supreme Court against the Armed Forces Special Powers Act.

reached to the patient, the patient would have died. Death came quickly.

Perhaps that was better than seeing your near and dear ones waste away slowly with tuberculosis. It was painful, it made you weak and there was nothing to be done because medicines were not available. And if they were, they were too expensive; and even if the family spent its entire savings and took loans the medicines were not regularly available, hence the treatment was incomplete. Besides, who could afford to have better food when there was no food available at all?

Most babies born were underweight. Mothers often suffered from malnutrition and their babies too did not have enough to eat. The most difficult part of being poor was to have to watch your children die because you could not afford to get them medical care.

There was a government primary health centre but the doctor was never available and the centre did not even have the basic medicines to treat snake-bites, let alone chloroquine for malaria. On the other hand, the primary health centres were being used to fulfil family planning targets or as instruments for population control through coercive methods.

For the people living in these villages medical care was not affordable, accessible or effective. It did not serve their needs, so they either tried local remedies or quacks, or just gave themselves up to fate.

But over the last fifteen years things had changed – ever since a dedicated doctor with kind eyes and a flowing beard had come into their lives. The doctor had opened a clinic which looked like any other village home, made of mud and tiles. The doctor's name was Binayak Sen.

Dr Binayak Sen had trained more than 25 villagers and they were now health workers who could look into microscopes and diagnose malaria. They also had other medical instruments based on appropriate technology that could help diagnose tuberculosis and diabetes, and these health workers lived among the people. Within the first year of the setting up of the clinic, the incidence of malaria in Bagrumnala village came down and now there were no deaths owing to malaria.

Often the patients needed treatment in a hospital, sometimes they needed surgery. The doctor would take the patients on his motorcycle; more recently he had acquired a car.

Then, one day in May 2007, while the patients were waiting for their doctor, he did not turn up. This was most unusual. It had never happened before. The next week too, he was missing. By now the people had found out that the police had arrested him. Everyone believed that it was a terrible mistake, but more than a year has passed and the doctor is still in jail.

There is nowhere the patients can go. The Chhattisgarh government says there is a severe shortage of doctors who are willing to work in rural or tribal areas. The Centre has already given the state Rs 4.57 crores under the National Rural Health Mission (2005–10) but the people do not know where the money has gone. Nor do they know when the doctor will be back.

The people are outraged. They collected money and took a bus all the way to Raipur to demonstrate their anger at the arrest of the doctor. On the first anniversary of the doctor's arrest, they gathered together at his clinic at Bagrumnala. The media, however, did not reach them.

The police say Dr Binayak Sen is a doctor only in name. They claim that he used his identity as a doctor to help the Maoists. The Supreme Court of India refused to grant him bail. Binayak Sen has been presumed guilty even before he was charge-sheeted. And now the charge-sheet states that he was not a real doctor. They want to wipe out the thirty-year history of his contribution to public health.

However, his work has won him national and international recognition. More than twenty Nobel laureates have appealed to the Indian government to release him, and he has been awarded the Jonathan Mann Award by the Global Health Council – the first South Asian to get the prestigious award for work in health and human rights.

The trial has begun, but it proceeds at a snail's pace with six witnesses in six months. The prosecution has cited 85 witnesses, so perhaps it will be another three to four years before the doctor can prove his innocence. Till then, the poorest and neediest citizens bear the cost.

Tales from Tihar

Iftikhar Gilani

During the last days of my imprisonment in Delhi's Tihar Central Jail, the semi-literate jail librarian, a man serving a life sentence, summoned me. He asked me to suggest names of books to be purchased, as the Delhi government had approved a budget of Rs 30,000 for the library.

From memory, I collated a list of books on law, some novels, the jail diaries of political leaders and some books for those pursuing courses from the Indira Gandhi National Open University (IGNOU). I included the jail manual, and a few books on civil liberties and the rights of prisoners. The librarian submitted the list without even glancing at it but claimed credit for it. Misfortune awaited him. A few days later he was summoned to the control room (the *chakkar*), and severely thrashed for the inclusion of books on prison laws and prisoners' rights in the list. He blamed me and I got a call from the *chakkar*. I explained that I did not know that books on prison laws were proscribed. The administration, expecting my imminent release, pardoned me with only a tongue-lashing. The poor librarian was condemned to work in the prison factory as a labourer for the rest of his term. None of the books ever reached the library. No one knows what happened to the library budget. This episode highlights the fate of our much-touted prison reforms. The relationship between an inmate and jail administrator continues to be that of a slave and master.

Fragments of Kiran Bedi's reforms, the ones she had tried to introduce in Tihar Jail a decade ago, are still visible. For instance, the Mulahiza ward had around 500 inmates when I joined it, when its capacity is less than 200. A decrepit signboard outside Barrack No. 10 in the ward indicates that it was once the Kiran Theatre. Similarly, the IGNOU ward was started in 1994 during Bedi's tenure as Inspector-General of Prisons. The IGNOU Study Centre had been started in a barrack of ward no. 11 in jail no. 3. However the overwhelming response of the inmates forced the authorities to expand it to the whole ward. Later, a study centre of the National Institute of Open Learning was also started for school-level education. An old inmate used to tell us how two former inmates, Shahabuddin Ghauri and Ghulam Nabi War, had nurtured the study centre with the active support of Bedi and the then superintendent, Tarsem Kumar. Ghauri, a former research scholar from Jawaharlal Nehru University (JNU), had tried his best to create the ambience of a JNU hostel in the ward with weekly debates.

One barrack has been turned into a library, another houses a computer lab, commercial art and typing classes, while two barracks are reserved for classrooms. During Bedi's tenure, the inmates managed the study centre and no official was allowed to interfere. Today, the ward is a hub of swindlers, some allegedly involved in enormous financial fraud. The computer lab has three obsolete machines, donated by a famous computer education company. An officer told me that the company had donated computers worth not more than Rs 50,000 but made the administration spend almost Rs 1,00,000 for publicizing their philanthropy.

Bedi's success in introducing reforms lay in the fact that she visited the wards and interacted with the inmates almost every day. But her experiments failed to address the social realities of an Indian prison. For example, she banned non-vegetarian food and smoking inside the prison. There are many Indian prisons where smoking is not prohibited but in Tihar the prisoners have to manufacture cigarettes secretly. I had to guard my English dictionary round the clock as its fine paper would have been perfect for making cigarettes. When some people donated copies of the English translation of the Holy Qur'an, the jail superintendent refused to distribute them, afraid that someone seen tearing the holy book could spark a bloody row.

Kiran Bedi had introduced petition boxes. No prisoner dares to post complaints in these boxes because the jail officers act against the complainant. The jail has its own intelligence system, reminiscent of the famous Hari Ram Nai, the mole planted among prisoners in the film *Sholay*. Our own Hari Ram Nai once told the warder that someone wearing spectacles had smuggled tobacco inside. All the inmates wearing glasses were given a thorough thrashing.

The presence of moles was not the only similarity between Tihar and the *Sholay* jail. Most of the jail staff mirrored the celluloid jailer's famous views: 'We are jailers of the British era. We are not the kind who try to reform the prisoners. We know you cannot be reformed.'

One night the sirens started wailing loudly. The officials descended on the Mulahiza ward, ordered the inmates out, and counted them again and again. We wondered whether someone had escaped. Instead, it turned out that the officials suspected there was an extra person in the prison. It was a terrible night. The officials were deeply angry and tense. The whole jail was kept awake and inmates were beaten up. Finally, around 4 am, the officials discovered that a new inmate had been inadvertently logged twice. They beat up the poor fellow severely, as if he was responsible for the error.

One very strict deputy superintendent, V.D. Pushkarna, had been nicknamed 'Punish-karna Saheb' by the inmates, but the work culture of the entire administration reflected the punitive theory of incarceration. For instance, frequent shifting of prisoners, originally meant to prevent the formation of gangs, has been perfected as a punishment. Jail authorities shuffle prisoners like cards. Shifting is always sudden, further punishing the inmates by not giving them a chance to even say goodbye to those they had been living with.

Likewise, the segregation of prisoners could be a legitimate practice aimed at separating first-time offenders from hardened criminals. However, the practice has degenerated into a punishment. Those charged with murders and robberies are spared; others charged with lighter offences like pickpocketing or offences such as espionage, which is considered anti-national by the 'super-patriotic' jail officials, are subjected to severe punishment.

Lodging prisoners in a so-called high-security ward, nicknamed the 'Highlight', is a serious punishment. The prisoner is kept in solitary confinement for at least 23 hours a day. Sometimes, prisoners who have been shifted back from the 'Highlight' after a considerable period of time are so psychologically damaged that they are unable to fit into a general ward again. They beg to be sent back. Then there are the *kasoori* cells where prisoners are provided meals only once a day, and no fan.

Jails outside Delhi allow relatives to meet their near-and-dear ones in a humane environment. But Tihar has continued the British practice where inmates and relatives have to meet in a dingy room separated by double-thick mesh and bars. It is almost impossible to see a person's face clearly through the mesh. The *mulaqat* (meeting) room is lucrative for jail officials. Taking home-cooked food into the jail could cost the relatives as much as Rs 500. During my stay in the jail, an honest assistant superintendent, Rajendra Kumar, was removed from his post in the *mulaqat* room as he was an obstacle to the money-making processes.

The jail administration has many prejudices. They treat foreigners better than the Indian prisoners, white-skinned Europeans better than the Africans, the powerful and the rich better than everyone else.

The religious lives of inmates too need urgent attention. I did not ever meet a Muslim jail official. While Muslims form around 12 per cent of India's population, they comprise more than 35 per cent of the jail's population. One afternoon, some of us were given orders to march towards the *chakkar*, the Control Room, where we would be transferred to the dreaded ward no. 5. Almost all of us were Muslim inmates. We begged in vain to stay in our ward, trying to justify it in terms of the IGNOU courses we were studying or teaching. In ward no. 5, the Mathematics teacher Badar Mohsin was given the task of 'Sumo driving' – a euphemism for the collection and disposal of garbage. Others were given the job of cleaning filthy toilets. Though I was later returned to the IGNOU ward, others continued there.

A few days later, the motive for this sudden move was revealed. One morning, we were not unlocked at 5.30 am. We remained locked for the entire day. The next day we found that the authorities had demolished the two small open mosques in ward no. 10 and 11. The Delhi Jail Manual expressly prohibits the gathering of prisoners for religious functions. However, Bedi had demarcated places for a *mandir* and mosque in every ward. The mosques had been open platforms without roofs and with a small almirah to keep copies of the Holy Qur'an. The authorities offered ingenious explanations for the demolition. They said they had found some improvised knives buried under the mosque. No one cared to explain how knives could have been buried there without breaking through the cement floors.

The prisoners despised the self-styled religious preachers visiting Tihar who treated us all as hardened criminals but exhorted us to join their groups if and when we were released. Even NGOs sometimes delivered religious harangues. Major (retd.) Dinesh, for instance, was to be visiting the jail as an expert in communication skills but was more interested in propagating his views on Islam. In his lecture, he claimed that the Holy Qur'an exhorts its followers to kill infidels. An inmate asked him to point out such a directive in a copy of the English translation of the Holy Qur'an. Dinesh could not find any examples but promised he would bring his own copy of the Holy Qur'an to show us. He was never seen thereafter.

Many of Tihar's unwritten rules have no logic except the perpetuation of a servile mentality. The unwritten code of conduct demands the following: prisoners shall not sit on chairs, only on stools; they shall stop whenever they see any official approaching and not resume walking till he goes away; while visiting any official's room, they shall leave their footwear outside. An inmate was severely beaten for drinking water in a cup instead of a steel glass. One absentminded inmate was thrashed ruthlessly for addressing an official as '*Chacha*' (uncle) instead of 'Sir'. Another was beaten up for remaining seated when a doctor passed by. During Bedi's tenure some of these rules had been discarded, but they returned soon enough.

If the jail is to be treated as a place of reform, we need to re-examine its practices. The Supreme Court has delivered many judgments emphasizing the rights of prisoners, but our jails are still run on the basis of outdated laws. Even the meagre rights available to prisoners under the old laws are not permitted by the jail authorities.

If Indian society wishes to have fewer criminals, it needs a three-pronged approach. First, we need to counter the socio-economic conditions that contribute to crime. Second, we need to strengthen the mechanisms enabling an offender to return to society as a normal citizen. Third, we need to detach the jail administration from a police set-up. What kind of a society are we if our conscience does not agitate against the ill-treatment of prisoners, an overwhelming majority of whom are incarcerated in jails without being convicted?

Two Sojourns in Prison

Saroj Mohanty

The first time I went to jail, I was sent to Bhabanipatna Jail, Orissa. I was not alone – I was with 14 friends. Leela, the wife of a well-known singer–activist in the Niyamgiri movement (the Adivasi movement against bauxite mining by the corporation called Vedanta), was one of only two women in the group. The other was my life-partner Aanchal.

All of us were arrested and detained by the police first in Ambadola police station. To begin with, the police seemed a little doubtful about whether they had arrested the right people. Then we began singing songs popular in the Niyamgiri valley. Listening to our songs, the police felt comforted that they had indeed arrested people who were involved with the Niyamgiri movement. The police then sent us to Bhabanipatna police station. They spent the whole night trying to frame us and to find 'eyewitnesses' to our 'anti-social activities'. They manufactured charges against us such as rioting, robbery, attempt to murder and arson. By the next morning we were all behind bars in Bhabanipatna Jail; Leela and Aanchal were shifted to the women's cells. Writing about all the experiences in Bhabanipatna Jail would require a long essay. So I am going to mention just a few things here.

Every morning we were given *chuda-gur* (flattened rice and jaggery) or *bhat-dal* (rice and dal) and made to exercise, but unfortunately could not be guaranteed any tea. Two days after we were imprisoned we started doing *baithakis* (group meetings) in the mornings and at night. In the *baithakis*, we sang songs from different peoples' movements. In a month-and-a-half we had discussed topics such as the problems of Dalits, women and Adivasis; the strengths and limitations of identity politics; the anti-displacement movement, the Maoist movement and issues specific to parts of Orissa; globalization and indiscriminate industrialization; Marx, Ambedkar, and so on. We discussed the life-histories of Birsa

Munda, Dharanidhar, Rindo Majhi and Surendra Sai, all of whom had fought against the British rule. On some days we recited poetry or narrated stories. Sometimes we tried to include other prisoners in our discussions and asked them to share their experiences. Seven to ten prisoners, mostly the younger ones, regularly took part in our discussions.

We were fortunate to have friends in Bhabanipatna who sent us books. The jailers were friendly and allowed us to read. We were even given pen and paper to write. My friend Hemant was in the same cell as I. Between us we translated more than 30 revolutionary poets from countries like Vietnam, Nigeria, Nepal and Chile. After the Gujarat riots I had decided to write some essays on communalism which could be understood by the lay reader. My long stay in jail helped me to complete this work. Despite the hot days and low-voltage electricity on most nights, all of us read and wrote alot.

The second time I was arrested, I was in Raygada Jail. This time I was alone. Fortunately, the Gandhian Bhagvat Path provided me with books with the permission of the jailor. The jail officials also provided me with pen and paper. I started writing articles on books which were published in *Samdrishti*, a fortnightly magazine, under the rubric 'Talk with Books'. I wrote about books such as *Silent Spring*, *Confessions of an Economic Hitman* and *Consumer Terrorism*.

Since 1997–98, I have had the opportunity to participate in the people's movement of Kashipur against the project of Utkal Alumina, the L&T project at Sunger and the Birla project at Laxmipur. A few years later I was also involved with the people of Niyamgiri against Vedanta. To ensure their livelihood, culture, ecology and the future of the next generation, the people who fight companies and the government which run terrorizing activities are swamped with criminal charges such as murder, attempt to murder, looting, theft, riot and conspiracy against the state. How could I have been left untouched by these? It is regretful that the response of the educated, urban middle class, and sometimes human rights organizations, is relatively muted when farmers, tribals and Dalits are being arrested, as compared to when activists known to them are. Most of the time, the person is more important than the cause.

The political economy and the process of development followed by the Indian state are fatal for those whose lives are closely tied to natural resources and labour-heavy arts and skills. For the survival of their socio-cultural identity, farmers, Adivasis and Dalits have to fight this process of development. The ruling class, mainstream political parties and, with the exception of a few newspapers and journalists, almost all the media houses, the upper-middle class and urban elite are diehard supporters of the path of development that our state follows. In such a situation, it is common and somehow natural for people spearheading and for those supporting movements against this inhumane process to be labelled anti-development, anti-national, even naxalite at times, and to be tortured. This has become the bitter truth not only in Orissa but in the whole country. In this brutal process, it was strange when my name got attached to the long list of tortured and betrayed farmers, Adivasis and Dalits, and associates of the movements.

The government and the police are indifferent while torturing children, women and aged people who are battling against these corporations. The Kashipur experience is not exceptional. Schoolgoing students, persons on their way to examination centres, women going to the market carrying cereals and vegetables, sympathizers such as post masters, teachers and government employees – none of them were rescued from police terror. They went to jail and lost their jobs. The Central Reserve Police Force (CRPF), Special Armed Force (SAF) and the Orissa State Armed Police (OSAP) marched from village to village to create panic among the people. They forced villagers to surrender to the police, and compelled them to either support the invading industry or go to jail. In fear, people stopped going to markets, hospitals, schools and colleges. Even farmlands were left unploughed.

Once, Latara Majhi and Mukundi Majhi, the cashiers of our organization, were arrested while withdrawing money from the bank and were charged with robbery. They suffered in jail for about nine months. I remember Jira Majhi shedding tears in jail when she heard the news of her daughter who had been burnt to death. Makari Majhi, in her old age, was sent to jail for months without knowing the charges against her. She was surprised and was always asking the jail officials what her crime had been. There were a large number of cases against hundreds of people. Those who were arrested did not get bail in the lower courts. Even the judges questioned the movement and asked our lawyer why he was working on behalf of people who were against development.

In the year 2000, three Adivasis, Abhilash Jhodia, Raghunath Jhodia and Damodara Jhodia, were gunned down by the police at Maikanch, and more than 50 people were injured. The P.K. Mishra Judicial Commission, instead of identifying the guilty, made comments beyond its ambit such as announcing that the region was unproductive and thus an industry should be established there. Charges have been filed against so many people and, in the process of getting bail for them, all the *pattas* (traditional land title deeds) have been exhausted. It is near-impossible to get the *pattas* back.

Kashipur–Laxmipur is an area of bauxite-rich mountains and springs. For the companies, these mountains are depots of bauxite, whereas for the people, they are the sources and natural store-houses of water, their lifeline, and also their god. Their culture, their festivals, songs and dances are centred around these mountains and rivers. The mining projects will affect more than 200 villages and the livelihood of 1 lakh people, directly and indirectly. The life-span of these projects is not more than 25 to 30 years and the local people have no employment opportunities. Mass displacement and mass destruction will be the sole results – and all to serve the interests of private companies.

The people of this area have formed local *samitis* (committees) and have been battling these corporations for the last 15 years. They have faced police firing and dozens of lathi-charges during these years of struggle. They faced an undeclared emergency at one point. The Congress, Bharatiya Janata Party and Biju Janata Dal formed an all-party committee to help establish these companies. Where hospitals and schools are needed, the government set up new police stations instead, and started camping at different places to terrorize the masses who are fighting for their mere existence.

When I went to jail with the people of these regions, I very often sang with others:

I am an insect of this earth,
I have lived here,
eating this earth.
Go back, go back,
I won't let you make business
of my dear mother.

To some extent, the relationship, dialogue and solidarity among these movements have already started. It has to be strengthened more and more. I must thank all those friends, writers, journalists, human rights activists and organizations, peoples' organizations and trade unions, who have extended their solidarity during my arrest and to the cause.

From my experiences so far, I have come to believe that jails are only for the poor, especially Dalits, Adivasis, small and marginal farmers, and all those unable to evade the law by virtue of their class identity or relationship with the ruling elite, or simply by possessing a lot of money. Being poor is a crime in itself. Thus the jails are crowded with the poor.

Life in jail would be interesting, if only it were for a short while.

A Fraudulent Matter

Lachit Bordolai

Assam witnessed one of the worst massacres in its history at the hands of the security forces at Kakopathar of Tinsukia district, on 10 February 2006. At that time, negotiations were going on between the Indian government and the People's Consultative Group (PCG), appointed by the United Liberation Front of Assam (ULFA), for a peaceful solution of the conflict. The first and second rounds of the talks took place at the prime ministerial level on 2 October 2006 and 7 February 2006, respectively. In these rounds, the Indian government expressed its desire to undertake confidence-building measures (CBMs), and emphasized that both the Indian army and the ULFA should exercise restraint. The background to this was that on 5 February 2006, before the end of the talks, the Indian army had killed Ajit Mahanta, a daily wage-earner, in a so-called 'encounter'. The local people blocked the national highway from 6 February 2006 onwards, demanding justice. As the government paid no heed to public sentiment, thousands of people marched towards Kakopathar town. The police opened fire on the procession and nine people were killed. Ever since then, the first week of February has been a time for the people of Kakopathar to remember their martyred comrades.

On 9 February 2008, some of my colleagues and I went to Tinsukia in Upper Assam to attend the Martyrs' Day ceremony. Just after midnight, while I was on my way, I received a call from my wife who, along with my daughter, was in Guwahati because of my daughter's forthcoming examinations. She told me that the police from the Chandmari police station in Guwahati had searched my home and taken away some documents, CDs and the laptop I had borrowed from a friend. Although the police had taken my number from my wife, they did not contact me that night.

We reached Tinsukia in the morning. It is a two-hour journey from Tinsukia to

Kakopathar. We were stopped and searched several times on our way by the police, and they took down our addresses. After taking part in the Martyrs' Day ceremony at Kakopathar, we came back to our hotel in Tinsukia at night. By that time, we sensed that some conspiracy was being hatched against me. The police had cordoned off the area around the hotel, though no policeman approached me. Rather, they sent an elderly journalist to meet me. The next day, 10 February 2008, news of my possible arrest was published in all the newspapers of Assam.

As I was returning to Guwahati with these newspapers in hand, the bus stopped at Moran so that the passengers could drink tea. It was here and at that time that a top police officer, accompanied by a magistrate, arrived. They arrested me and took me to the Moran police station. My mobile phone had already been seized. As local journalists came to know of my arrest, they thronged the police station. I was taken to Guwahati in a jeep in great haste, and jailed in Chandmari police station at around 8 pm.

The next afternoon, I was presented before the magistrate. The police wanted to place me in custody for ten days. However, after the court heard my advocate's plea, it granted permission only for a seven-day custody. It must be mentioned here that I was arrested on the basis of a confession made by Manoj Tamuli, a surrendered ULFA militant, in a case filed at Noonmati police station. Tamuli had already surrendered twice earlier and was under police protection at the time. He had been helping the police in their various counter-insurgency operations against ULFA. According to the police, he was arrested with arms and ammunitions three days before my arrest. He had confessed to them that as an active member of the ULFA, he had conspired to hijack a plane from Guwahati airport. The police alleged that I had helped him in the 'hijacking' plan. This pernicious bit of 'information' was dutifully reproduced in the print and electronic media as part of the security establishment's disinformation campaign.

However, Tamuli was also detained in the Chandmari police station for some days, and when we met, he told me he had not made any such statement to the police. I asked him whether he had ever met me earlier. He told me that he had seen me at some public meetings and on television, but we had never met in person. He said as much to the journalists when he was being taken to appear before the court. The dossier produced for my arrest under the National Security Act (NSA) stated that Manoj Tamuli knew of my connections with the top leadership of the ULFA. My so-called 'connection' with the planning of the hijacking of the plane was mysteriously left out of the dossier.

Why was I arrested at that particular time? The police had arrested me on two charges lodged at Rangia and Nagaon police stations that were at least a year old. Why had they not arrested me a year earlier, then?

As I mentioned earlier, as part of the People's Consultative Group (PCG), we had taken part in three rounds of talks with the Central government. According to us, the talks were successful. The government had given their word that it would set free five of the top ULFA leaders, after which it would sit down directly for talks with the ULFA. But after the last round of talks on 22 June 2006, the government's tone began to change. Instead of keeping to their promise, they started placing new conditions before us. Not surprisingly, the peace process was stalled. The PCG wanted to withdraw from the negotiation as a mark of protest and requested the ULFA to dismantle it. But the ULFA, in a display of goodwill, did not dismantle the body. So we decided to restart the negotiations and, along with advocate Arup Borbarah and journalist Ajit Kumar Bhuyan, I went to Delhi. Although we had insisted on keeping the state government involved in the process in 2005–06, we observed that rather than facilitating dialogue, the state government and sections of the entrenched counter-insurgency agencies had begun to spoil the chances of direct talks between ULFA and the Indian government. Seeing their negative role, we decided to keep them away from the talks and requested Veerappa Moily, the Congress observer, to restart the process. A new strategy was also decided upon. A fresh round of talks took place in the month of January 2008 which only a select few knew of. My assumption is that the conspiracy to arrest me was hatched by the state government to stop the possibility of a new political negotiation. I was arrested ten days after my return from Delhi. For this reason, the chances of negotiation also failed.

After putting me in police custody, the police concentrated on holding press conferences to explain the reason for my arrest. Considering the gravity of the charges against me, the interrogation did not last long. A team of top police officials, including the DIG, the SSP and the SP, interrogated me for two days. But most of the time the police did not visit me. After ten days, I was again brought before the magistrate for extension of my police custody. This time, Manoj Tamuli, the SULFA (surrendered ULFA) man was also brought to the court. There was an attempt to keep us away from the journalists, but they managed to reach us, helped by the heavy crowds. Tamuli told the journalists categorically that he had nothing to do with me and that he had not told the police anything about my involvement in the supposed plane hijacking. Unfazed, the police took me into custody again for two days. Once again, there was no interrogation. However, they took my personal e-mail identity and password along with that of my organization, Manab Adhikar Sangram Samiti (MASS), for examination. They tried to malign me by creating a concerted campaign that I worked on behalf of the ULFA. During this period, the irregularity of meals and lack of sleep saw me suffering from severe gastritis, and I had to be hospitalized in Guwahati Medical College. After seven days in the hospital, I was again sent to Guwahati Jail for further treatment. During my treatment in jail, pressure was mounted on the doctor for my release, but the Nagaon police intervened. They arrested and took me to Nagaon Jail on the basis of the one-year-old case, No. 103/07, filed in Raha police station. Once again I was produced before the Nagaon court and the police took me into custody for three days. There was no interrogation at the Nagaon police station either.

Three days later I was produced before the magistrate of Kamrup district, and this time another case lodged in Rangiya police station was invoked. I was sent to Nalbari Jail. The ambience and the food there was better than in Guwahati Jail, and I was kept with some ULFA detainees. When my bail was granted for the Rangiya case, I was again incarcerated in Guwahati Jail under the NSA, invoked for the same charges.

I found myself lodged with Pradip Gogoi, the vice-president of ULFA, who had been imprisoned for the last ten years, and Bhimkanta Buragohain, advisor to ULFA, imprisoned for the last five years following the Indo–Bhutan operations in 2003. Along with them were other mid-level ULFA cadres and twelve detainees suspected of having Inter-Services Intelligence (ISI) links. These detainees were kept separately from others, and there was also a separate arrangement for their meals.

I came to know that the case lodged in Raha police station was based on the arrest of a vice-president of MASS from Karbi Anglong district the previous year. The police had recovered a small switch, which they claimed to be one used in programmed time-delay (PTD) bombs. According to a testimony, I had directed him to collect the switch and give it to a Hiranya Saikia of Nagaon. There was no explanation for why the police had not arrested me earlier, and despite trying very hard, I have not been able to recall knowing any Hiranya Saikia of Nagaon.

In the same manner, the case lodged in Rangiya police station was also a year old. A MASS member from Darrang district had been caught transporting explosives. According to the police, I had given directions to another MASS member to help him. This person, who was out on bail, had arranged a press meet and told journalists that I had no involvement in this case. He had given a written testimony to me in this regard, which I had shown to the advisors of National Security Council.

Another incident took place during my custody which exposed the conspiracy hatched by the police against me. A young man was brought by the commandos of the sub-divisional police officer (SDPO) and put in the same lock-up where I was lodged in Rangiya. He started talking to me as soon as he entered. Introducing himself as the bodyguard of Akash Thapa, a wanted ULFA leader, he informed me that he had been arrested along with Akash Thapa. He even mentioned that he had spoken with me earlier and that his leader Akash Thapa had also kept close contact with me. As I could not remember anything to that effect, he changed the topic and asked my opinion about the issue of sovereign Assam and the future of ULFA. When I told him I was involved only with the human rights of the people and the peace process, he seemed disheartened. After some time he was removed from the lock-up. Later on, I learnt that neither Akash Thapa nor any of his bodyguards had been caught by the police during that period. I could well surmise that it was a ploy to extract information from me.

According to the directives, I was produced for five days before the 'advisory council' of NSA. Though the police tried to keep me away from the media, on one of the occasions when I was produced before the court, I had the opportunity to clarify my stand and to expose the conspiracy of a young minister in the whole episode. As my interview was telecast in the evening bulletin, the sub-inspector accompanying me, along with five other policemen, became the scapegoats and were suspended from duty. This gave me great mental agony. Furthermore, it became very difficult for my family members to meet me after this.

The NSA advisory panel put its seal on the conspiracy hatched by the police and the state government. I had already received bail on the other four charges against me, and my advocate Bijan Mahajan swiftly moved the high court against the possible invocation of NSA. Accordingly, the court gave its verdict against my detention under NSA, and I was finally released from jail on 26 June 2008.

From the Underbelly of the Beast

Kanak Mani Dixit

Kanak Mani Dixit was arrested in Kathmandu on 8 April 2006 with other professionals for defying curfew to press for democratic rights in Nepal. This column was smuggled out of jail.

All over the subcontinent, every day, the most disadvantaged fall through the cracks. They are pummelled by the forces of the state, of the market or feudalism. For the middle class, the political parties, or those linked to the state, there is some recourse to justice, although it may not be always available or efficiently delivered.

The tragedy of South Asia is that those who are left out are not the exception but the rule. Abuse of power in South Asia can cover a whole spectrum of activities, from the displacement of the tribals from the forest reserves which have been their traditional homes, to trans-boundary missiles that land in the shanties of the North-West Frontier Province in Pakistan, to young people on the streets of Nepal devoured by the security machinery of an autocratic state bent on repression.

When two dozen other protestors and I were imprisoned by Kathmandu's royal regime for wilfully (and with prior announcement) breaking the curfew order, I had the opportunity to see how the 'militarist' state machinery can ride roughshod over some of the weakest members of society. It was an opportunity to take a look at the underbelly of the monster the government can be. What we have seen during our incarceration are spaces and events that the privileged, with contacts in high places or the money to buy themselves safe passage, rarely care to see or understand.

There are three types of inmates in this makeshift detention centre at the Duwakot Armed Police Force barracks in the north-east of Kathmandu Valley. The relatively well-known human rights activists and members of 'civil society' have little fear of violence once they are taken in. Then there are the political activists, both young and old, who receive some protection from party affiliations and links. But there is a third category, of true innocents.

Most of these young adults, some of whom are mere boys, are migrants who have left their families in faraway hills and plains to work in menial jobs in urban Kathmandu. They represent the rural poor of all ethnicities and castes, but they are united in their lack of influence anywhere in the state structure. This lack of agency is only matched by their absolute poverty. The trauma that these boys of Duwakot face exists at several levels. First, it is the chase on the streets, attacks by batons and staffs, abuse, and the bundling into the back of trucks.

There is no one in the detention centre to plead innocence with. Toilet facilities are non-existent. Then they are transported from one detention centre to another, given no information whatsoever. Food is provided only once a day and, when it is, it is rice and some tepid *dal* of the lowest grade imaginable.

There is fear that authorities in need of proof of Maoist 'infiltration' within the democratic 'people's movement' can cast a dark shadow on these young lives. With the flick of a pen they can declare you insurgent, and do away with your life and prospects.

Who will tell your family? Who will inform your employer? Who is the lawyer or activist who will speak for you? Who will seek a writ of *habeas corpus*, defend you, charge the regime with wrongful imprisonment, and demand release and reparation?

Dambar Nepali, 14, is from Udayapur in thc hills of the east. He works as a construction labourer. On his way home from work he was taken in by the police and beaten up.

Ramesh Basnet, 23, from Dhading, was returning from the printing press where he works.

Ram Kumar Tamang drives a microbus, license plate no. 4266, and was crossing the road during a curfew when he was taken in.

Biraj Sharma, 18, was hanging about near a shop in an area outside curfew limits. 'The policemen were like demons,' he recalls, 'they kicked my head as if it was a football.'

Four boys were resting inside a bus at a bus depot, where they work as cleaners, when they were dragged out: *Dhruba Timilsina*, 17, of Hetuada; *Buddha Lama*, 16, of Sindhupalchok; *Ramesh Thapa Magar*, 17, and *Ram Lama*, 20, both from Chapagaon. They were brought in to Duwakot together with our civil rights group. They have all now been moved elsewhere. It will be important for the International Committee of the Red Cross to determine their fate and whereabouts.

Some policemen can be fine, sensitive individuals. But they take orders from an insensitive state run by a ruler who has sought, time and again, to prove his contempt for the people of Nepal. When autocracy and militarization are combined with contempt for the masses, those without recourse suffer unseen and unheard. This is one more reason for the urgent need to return to democracy, pluralism and peace in Nepal.

Ramesh Basnet, the boy from the printing press, told me the day before yesterday, before he was taken away:

Is this the kind of country I was born into? I love my country, but I hate the government. I have not picked up a stone, I have not burnt a tyre in protest. Why am I here, and where will they take me?

In-Security

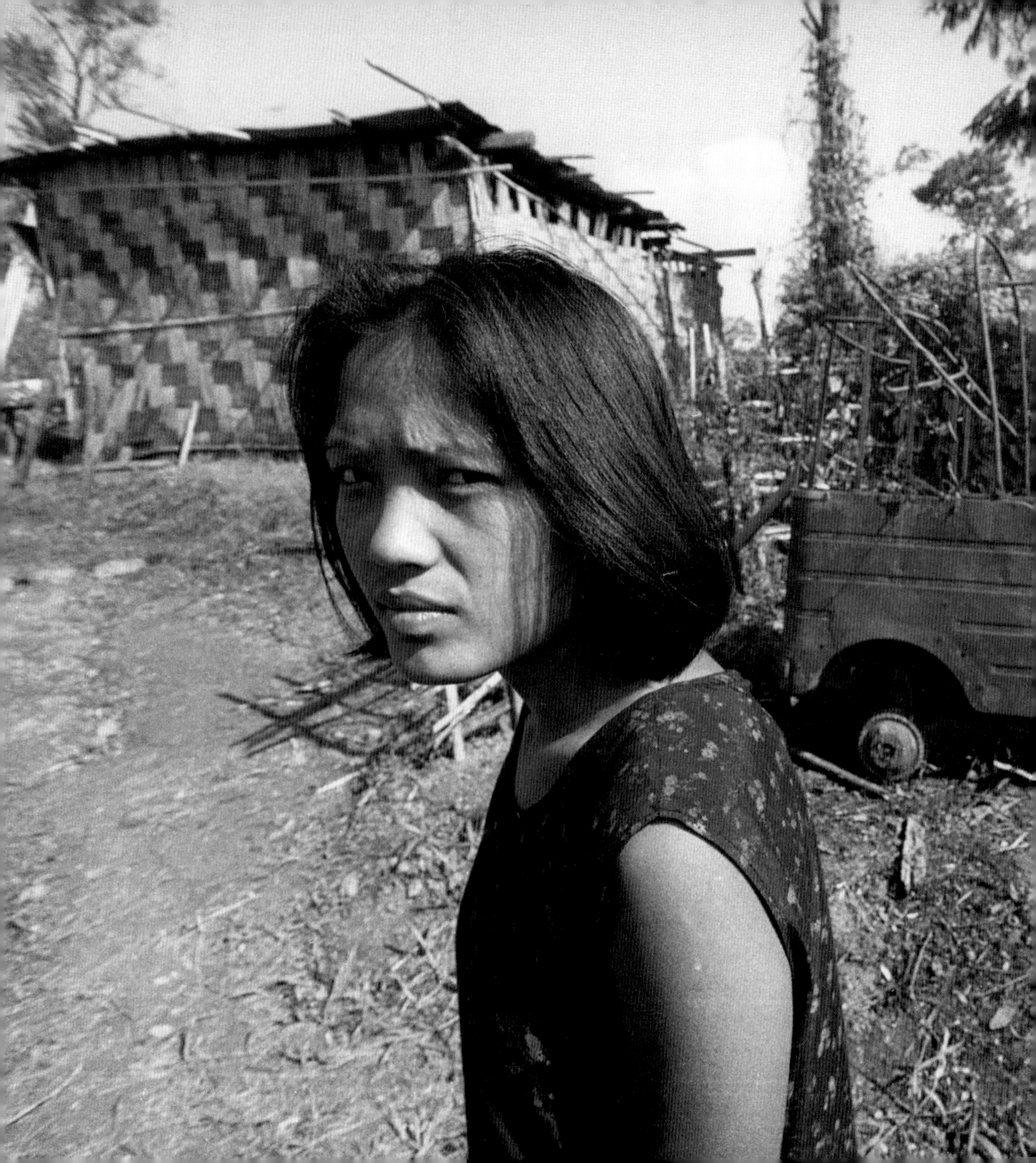

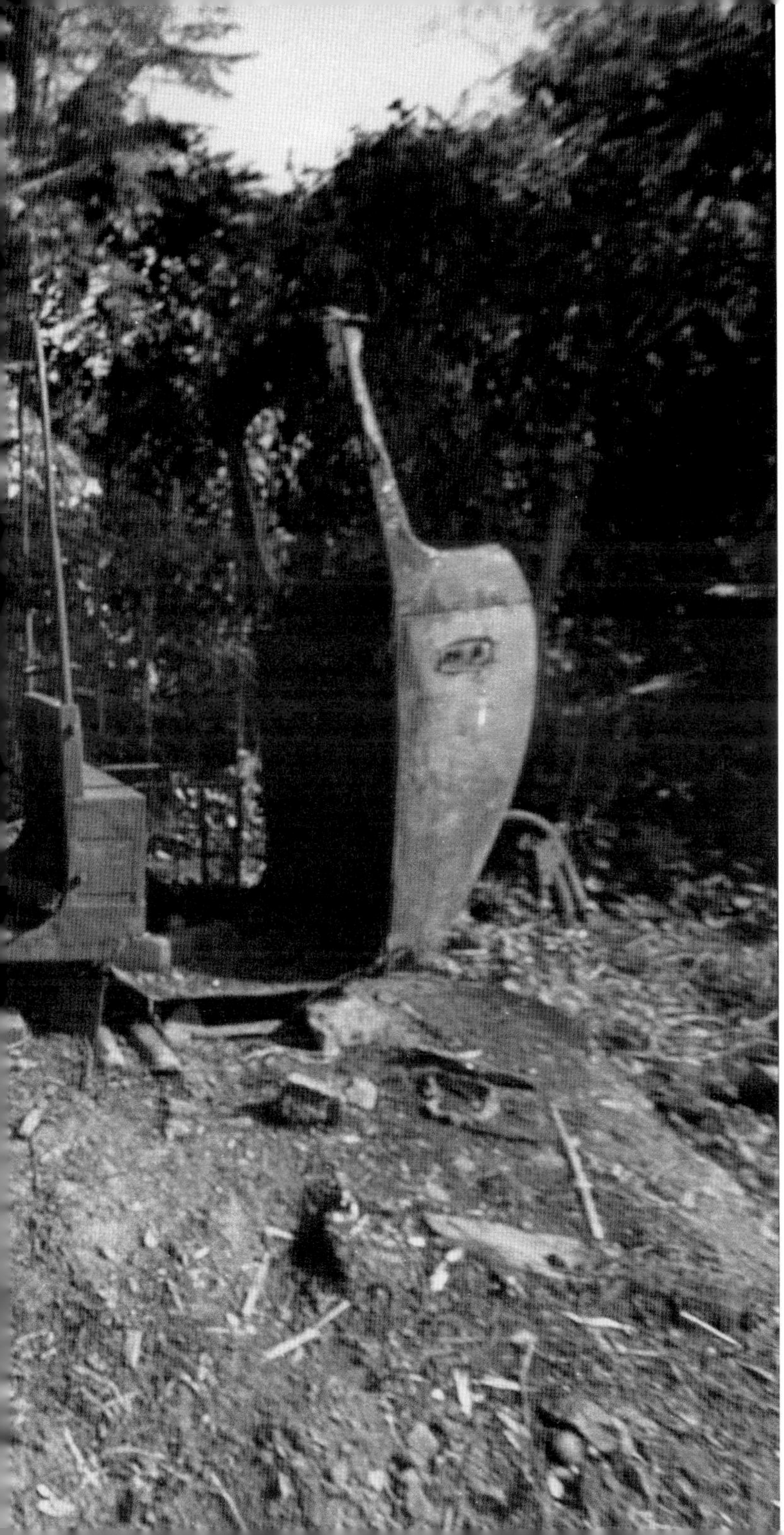

Gaze

Swapan Nayak • Parthiv Shah

Sampoi Nungtau of the Hamar tribe lost everything, even her primary means of livelihood. Her autorickshaw was set on fire on 10 June 2003 in a sudden attack by members of the rival Dimasa tribe in North Kachar Hills, Assam. By Swapan Nayak, India.

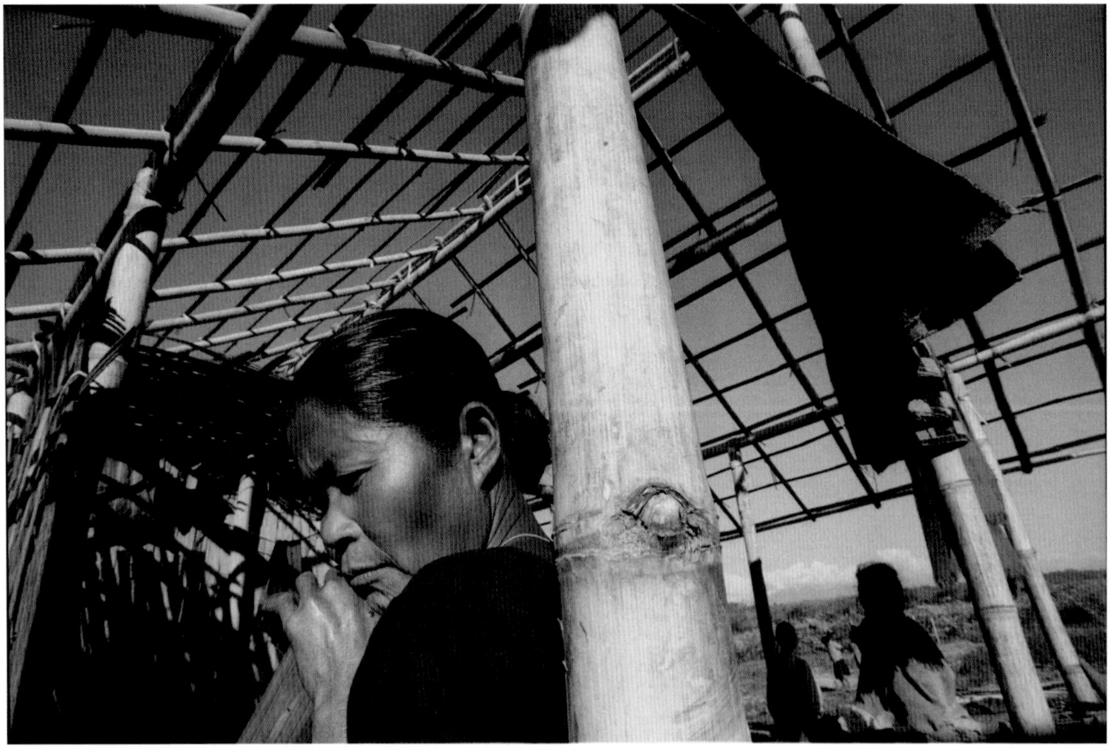

Shakka Devi Chakma at Daiyun, Arunachal Pradesh, since 1965. The Chakma tribe has been fighting with the Arunachali tribe for not having received Indian citizenship during their resettlement in Arunachal Pradesh. By Swapan Nayak, India.

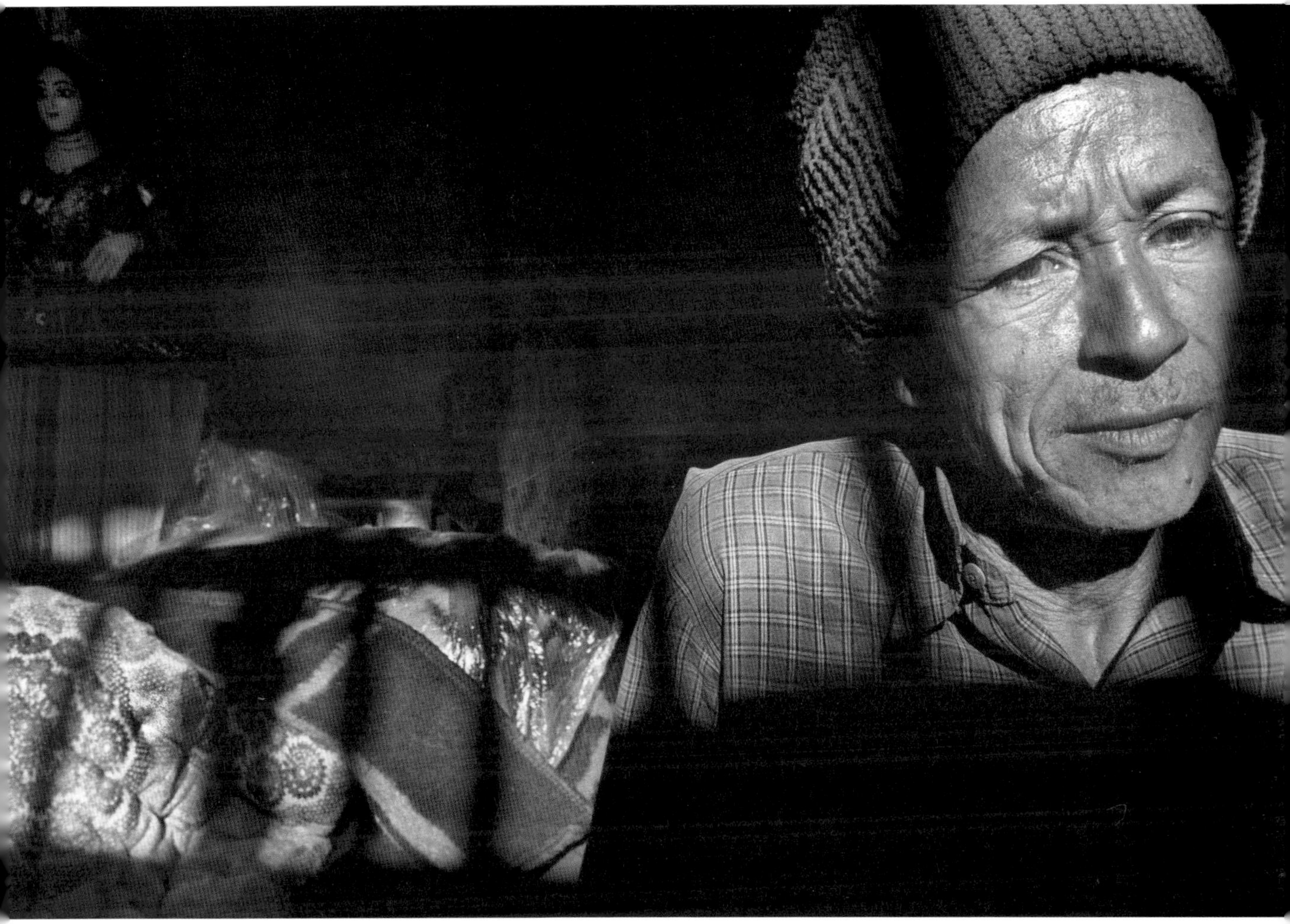

Lalringthng Hekte, head of Newzoar village, at the Mahu Soil Conservation Department hostel camp. They left their village during a conflict between the Hamar and Dimasa tribes in June 2003. By Swapan Nayak, India.

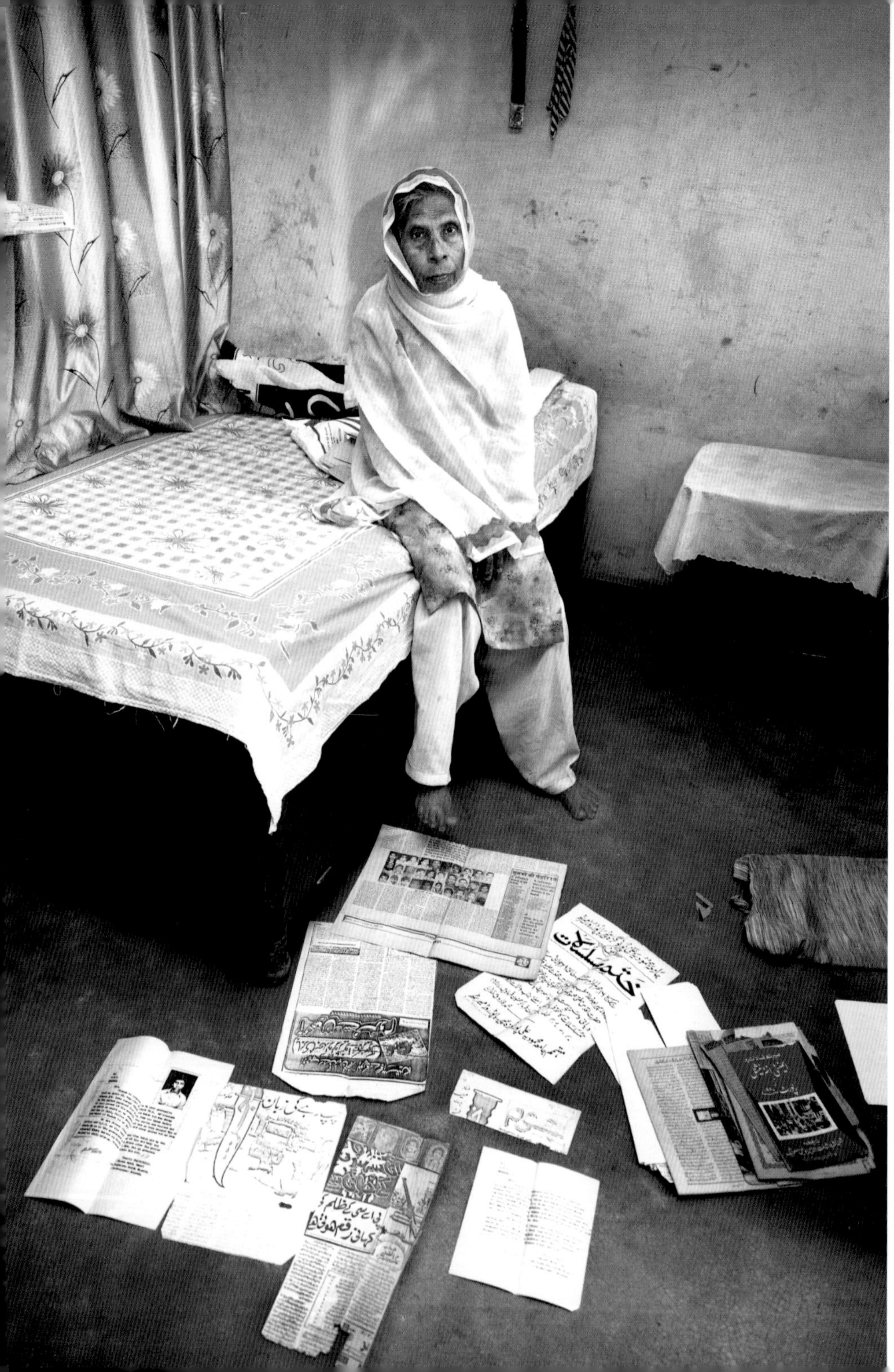

Naseeban, who lost both her husband Jameel and her son Naseem in the Hashimpura massacre, sits surrounded by paper-memories. From the *Hashimpura* series by Parthiv Shah, India, 2008.

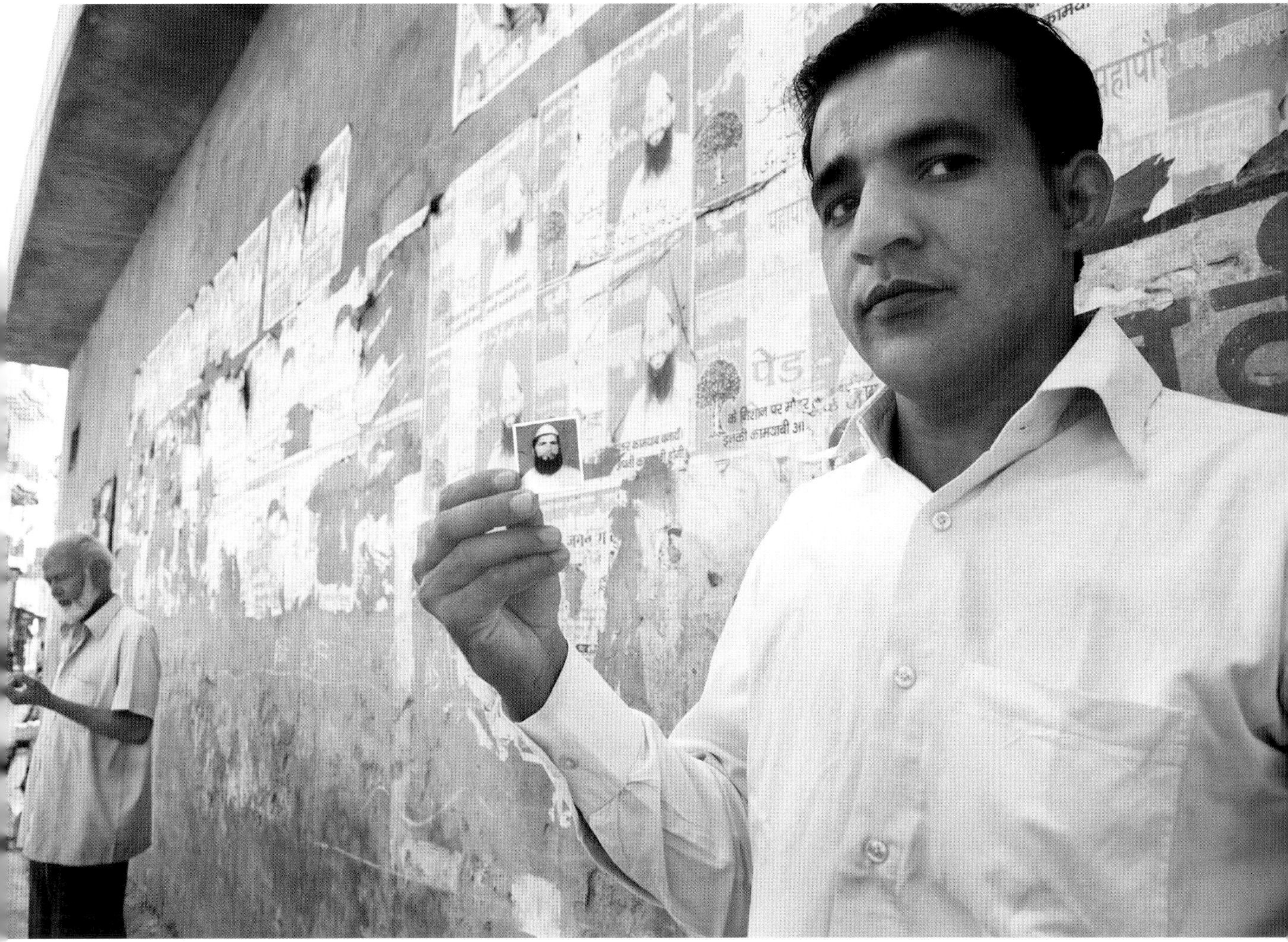

Fathers and Sons: Rasheed holds up his father Haji Shamim's photograph to the camera. Haji Shamim was killed in the Hashimpura massacre. From the *Hashimpura* series by Parthiv Shah, India, 2008.

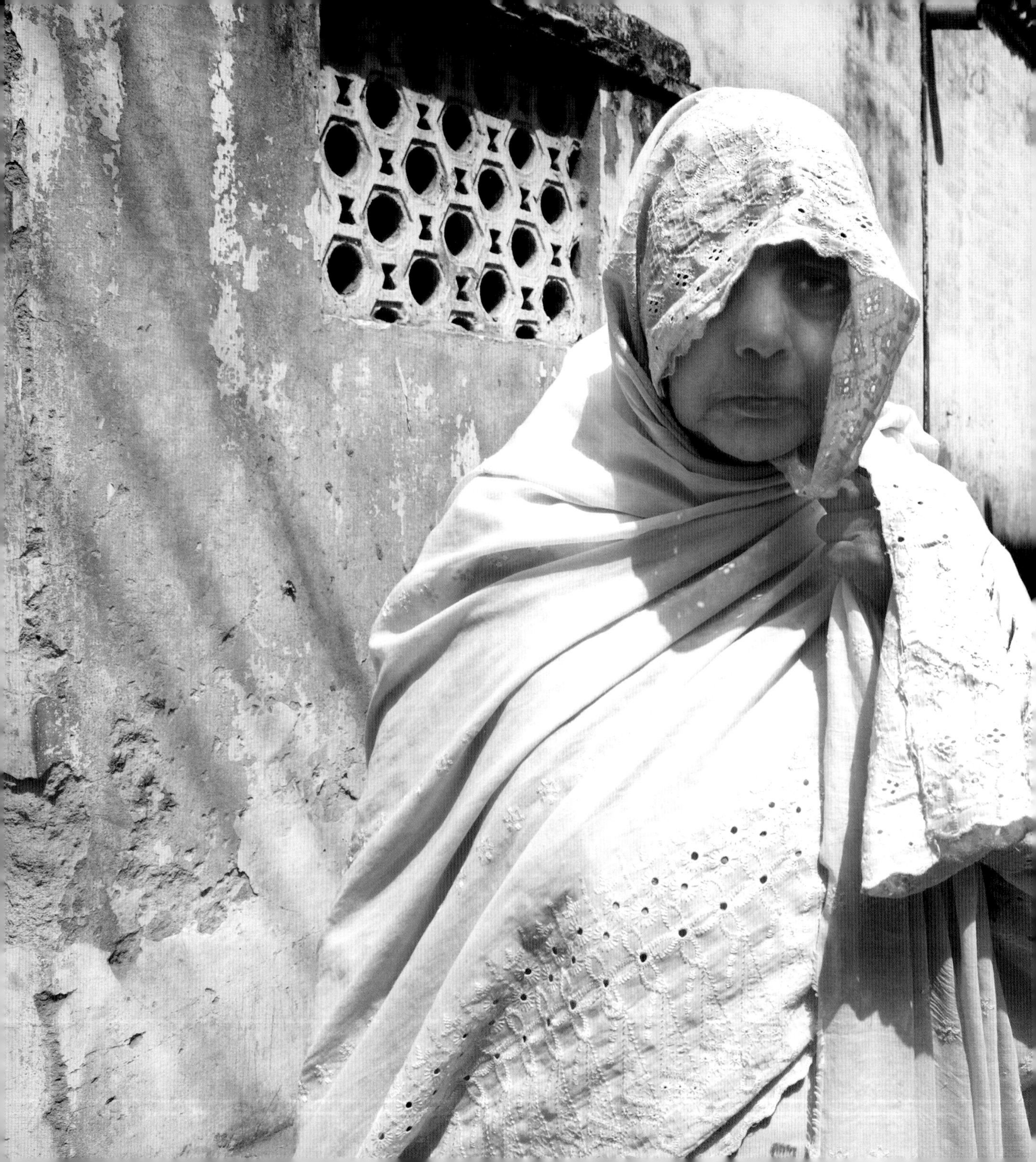

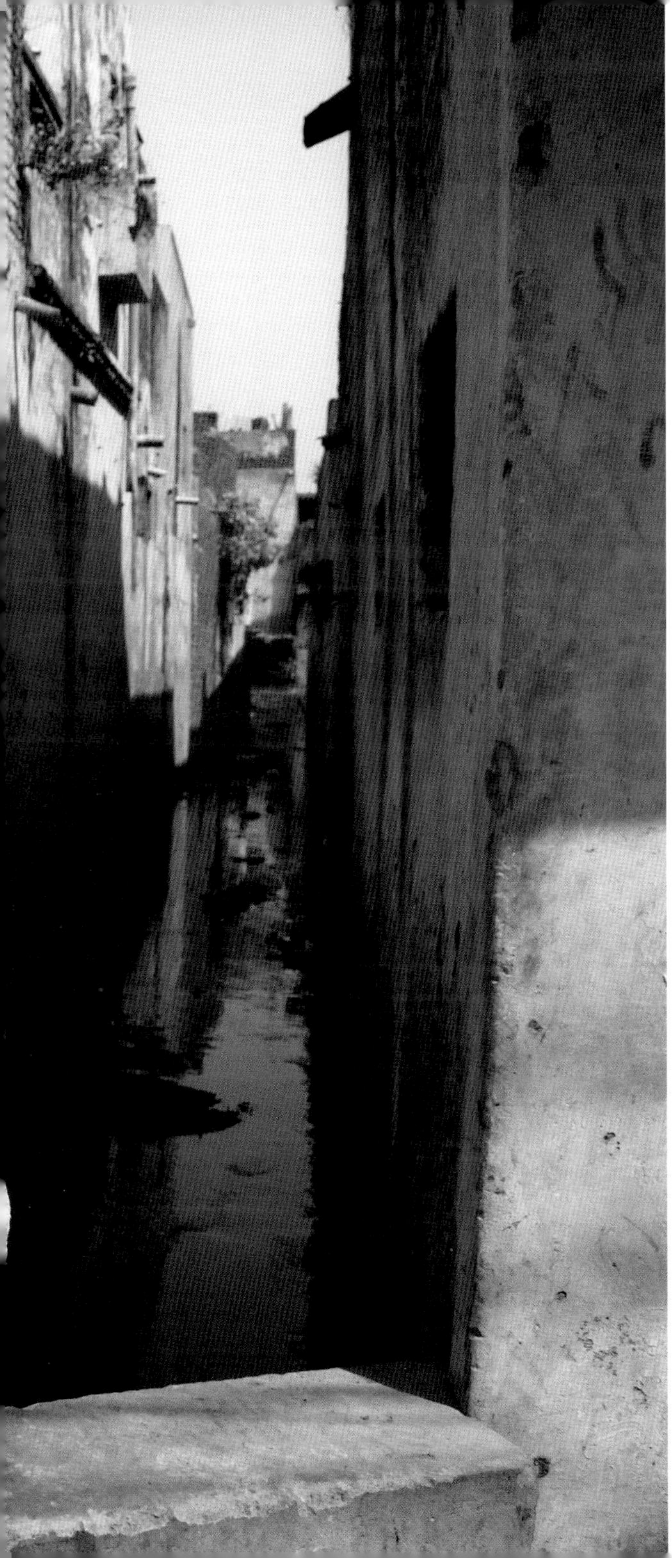

Returning the gaze – is there any hope? Zarina, whose husband Zaheer and son Javed were killed in Hashimpura, stares vacantly into the camera. From the *Hashimpura* series by Parthiv Shah, India, 2008.

The Knock from the Attic

Vibhuti Narain Rai

Some experiences stick with you throughout your life, like a nightmare or a burden on your shoulders. The experience at Hashimpura was one such for me.

The night of 22 May 1987 that I spent in the wild undergrowth along the stream flowing through Makanpur village in Hashimpura, situated on the Delhi–Ghaziabad border, looking for living souls amidst the dead bodies covered with blood under the dim light of my torch, is engraved in my memory like a horror movie.

That night I had returned to Ghaziabad from Hapur at around 10.30 pm. District Magistrate Nasim Zaidi was with me and I dropped him off at his house before arriving at the residence of the in-charge at Link Road police station at that time. The moment the headlights of my car fell upon the gates of the residence I encountered a shocked Sub-Inspector, B.B. Singh.

I could tell from experience that something serious had happened in that area. I instructed my driver to stop the car and leave. B.B. Singh was so horrified that he was incoherent and unable to explain things. But whatever he could stammeringly convey about the events was enough to shock me. I understood that somewhere in his station area, the Police Armed Constabulary (PAC) had killed some Muslims. Why? How many? And from where? It was not clear. After asking him to repeat his facts again and again, I tried putting together a narrative of the events, piece by piece.

According to the picture so drawn, B.B. Singh was sitting in his office when, at around 9 o'clock at night, he heard the sound of firing from the direction of Makanpur. He and everyone else at the station assumed it to be a robbery in progress in the village. Today, Makanpur's name can only be found in the revenue records. It has tall magnificent buildings, but in 1987 it was all just barren land. Through this barren land ran a check road on which B.B. Singh raced his motorcycle towards the village. Behind him sat the station officer and a constable. They had barely covered a hundred yards on the check road when they saw a truck racing towards them from the opposite direction. If they had not driven the motorcycle off the road the truck would have run them over. What they saw, while trying to maintain their balance, was that the truck was yellow in colour and had the number '41' printed at the back. They even saw people in khaki clothes sitting in the rear of the van. It was not difficult for a police officer to understand that this was a truck belonging to the 41st battalion of the PAC carrying some of their officers. But this made the situation more complicated. Why would a PAC truck be coming from Makanpur at this hour? What was the mystery behind the firing? B.B. Singh got the motorcycle back on the check road and proceeded towards the village.

The scene that he and his officers saw, not more than a mile down the road, gave them goosebumps. Before reaching the inhabited part of the village, the check road goes past a stream at a bridge, which flows across into the Delhi border. As B.B. Singh reached the bridge, the headlight of his motorcycle fell on the undergrowth along the stream, and he understood the mystery behind the firing. There were bloodstains all over the place. Along the stream, in the undergrowth and in the water, there were bodies with fresh wounds. B.B. Singh and his men inspected the scene and tried to guess what had happened there. All that they could make out was that there must be a connection between the bodies and the PAC truck they had seen on the way. Leaving the constable at the scene, B.B. Singh and his fellow officer turned back to the main road. The headquarters of the 41st battalion of the PAC were situated on the Delhi–Ghaziabad road, near the police station, and both headed there.

The main gate was closed when they arrived. Despite lengthy arguments with the sentry, they did not receive permission to enter. B.B. Singh then decided to come to the zonal headquarters and tell me about the events.

From the narration it was clear to me that a horrifying event had occurred and that Ghaziabad could go up in flames the next day. Since the past few weeks the neighbouring district of Meerut had been witnessing communal riots and these riots could now move to Ghaziabad as well.

I first called the District Magistrate, Nasim Zaidi. He was about to retire to bed. After that I called the Additional Superintendant of Police (ASP) at the district headquarters, a few Deputy

Superintendants of Police (DSPs) and Magistrates, and asked them all to get ready. In the next 45 minutes we were all heading towards Makanpur village in seven or eight vehicles.

We parked a little distance away from the bridge on the stream. No one had come out of the village, which was situated on the other side of the stream. It seemed that terror had forced them all to go into hiding in their homes. However, there were some police officers from the Link Road police station. The weak beams of their torches fell on the thick shrubs beside the stream but it was difficult to see anything in that dim light. I told the drivers to turn the vehicles towards the stream and turn their headlights on. An area of around 100 yards width was illuminated. What I saw in that light was the nightmare I referred to earlier.

Even the light from the headlights was insufficient to fully illuminate the horror and all the men used their torches as well. The blood on the bodies had not yet dried and continued to drip from them. The bodies of the dead were piled up all around and some were wedged in the bushes, while others lay half-submerged in the water. To check if anyone was still alive among the scores of bodies seemed more important to me than to count and remove the dead.

We were about 20 of us and everybody started looking in different directions to check if anyone was still alive. Hoping that someone would respond, we started calling

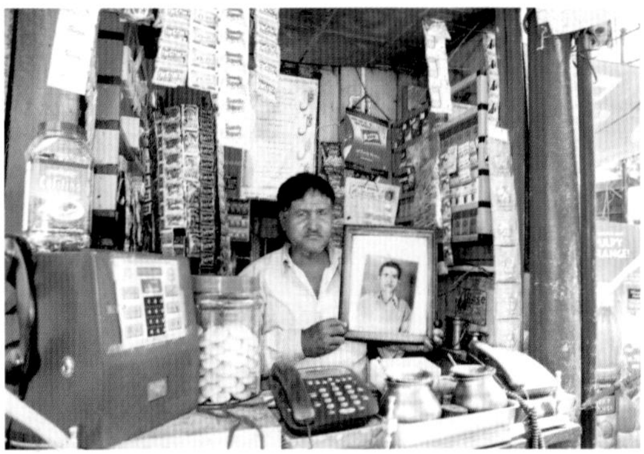

Jameel shows an old photograph of his father, Abdul Qadeer, who was killed in the massacre. From the *Hashimpura* series by Parthiv Shah, India, 2008.

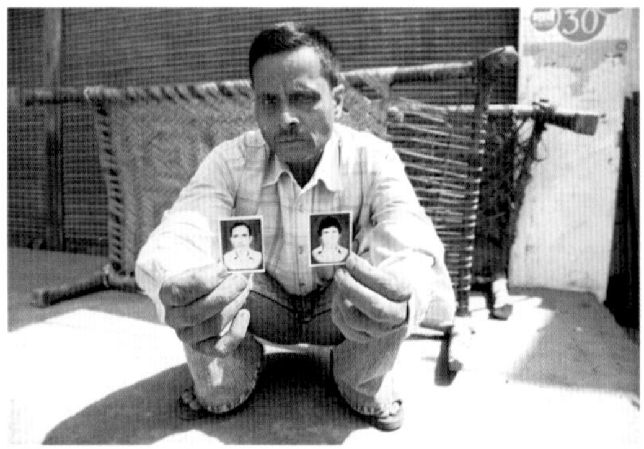

Salim holds up photographs of his father Jameel and brother Naseem, both of whom he lost in the massacre. From the *Hashimpura* series by Parthiv Shah, India, 2008.

out even while trying to tell them that we were not foes but friends, and that the injured would be taken to hospital. But we received no reply. Disappointed, some of us sat down on the bridge. The district in-charge and I decided that there was nothing to be gained by wasting more time. We had to devise our strategies for the next day and we decided to defer the task of removing the bodies and completing the necessary paper work.

We were about to proceed towards the Link Road station when we heard the sound of a cough from near the stream. Everyone froze. I leapt towards the stream. Silence fell over the place again. It was clear that there was a survivor, but he did not believe that the people looking for him were friends. We called out loudly again and shone light on each individual body until our eyes fell on a body that was moving. Someone was hanging by both hands from a bush with half his body in the stream in such a way that it was difficult, without paying careful attention, to tell if he was dead or alive. Trembling with terror and believing only after repeated assurances that we were there not to hurt but to save, the person who would later tell us about this horrifying event emerged from the stream. His name was Babuddin. The bullet had just missed him, leaving behind a mild scratch. He had fallen into the shrubs unconscious, and in the stampede the killers had forgotten to check if he was dead or alive. Holding his breath, he lay there half in the water and half in the bushes, and in this way managed to cheat death. He was not seriously hurt and was able to walk from the stream to the cars. He even rested on the bridge for some time.

When I met him 21 years later at the same place, while collecting material for the book I was writing on Hashimpura, he remembered that I had offered him a *beedi* after taking one from one of the constables. According to what Babuddin told us that very day on being rescued: after a routine check at Makanpur in Hashimpura, around 50 Muslims from the village were rounded up and forced into a PAC truck. All of them thought they were being taken to a police station or a jail. However, the truck turned off the main road about 45 minutes from Makanpur and stopped at a distance down the road. The PAC stepped out of the truck and ordered them to get down as well. Hardly half the people had gotten off when the PAC started firing on them. The people still on the truck took cover. Babuddin was

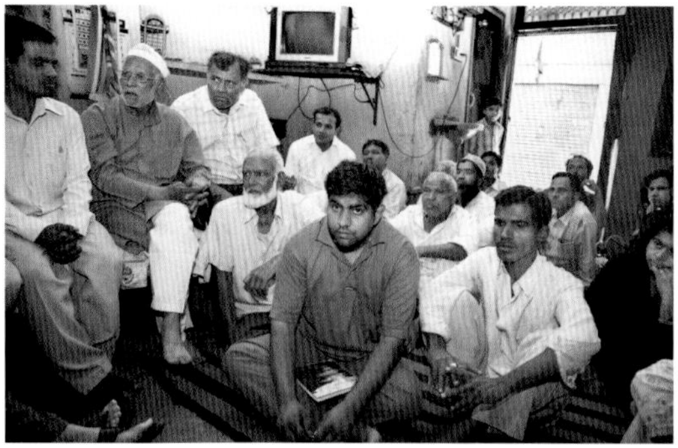

Survivors and relatives of the deceased recall the massacre. From the *Hashimpura* series by Parthiv Shah, India, 2008.

one of them. He could only guess what had happened to the others. The sound of the firing probably reached the neighbouring villages, as a result of which noises began to emerge from them. The members of the PAC got into the truck again, reversed and sped off towards Ghaziabad. Here, it came to the Makanpur stream and the PAC ordered the remaining people to get off. This time the horrified prisoners refused to do so; they were then pulled and dragged out of the truck. Those who stepped out were shot and thrown into the stream; those who did not were shot inside the truck and thrown out.

While Babuddin was relating the entire incident to us, we tried to assess the location of the first scene of crime. Someone suggested that it could be the stream that flows near the Muradnagar police station, which is situated on the road from Meerut to Ghaziabad. I called the Muradnagar

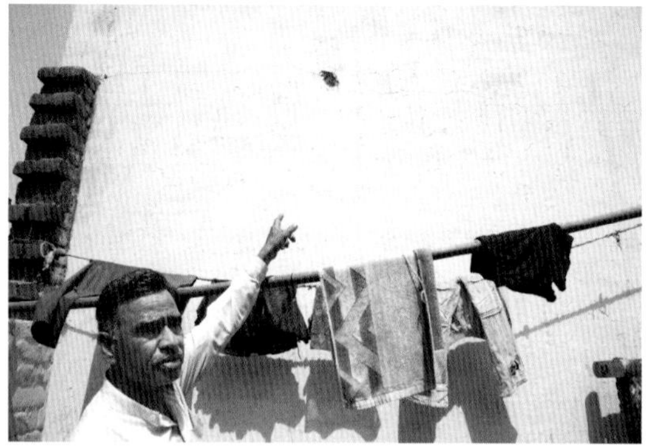

Mohd. Abid shows the bullet marks in his house, House No. 59. He was jailed and beaten up, like other men of Hashimpura who were carted away in trucks. From the *Hashimpura* series by Parthiv Shah, India, 2008.

police station using the wireless at the Link Road police station, and found that we were right. The Muradnagar police station had been facing a similar situation. Some bodies had been found dead in the stream and some were brought back to the police station alive.

What followed was a narrative of a long and torturous wait which involved issues of the relations between the Indian state and the minorities, the unprofessional attitude of the police, and the sluggish pace of a frustrating judicial system. The cases I had filed at the police stations at Ghaziabad Link Road and Muradnagar have faced various roadblocks over the last 21 years, and a logical judgement from the courts is still pending.

(Translated from Hindi)

Battling Impunity

Vrinda Grover

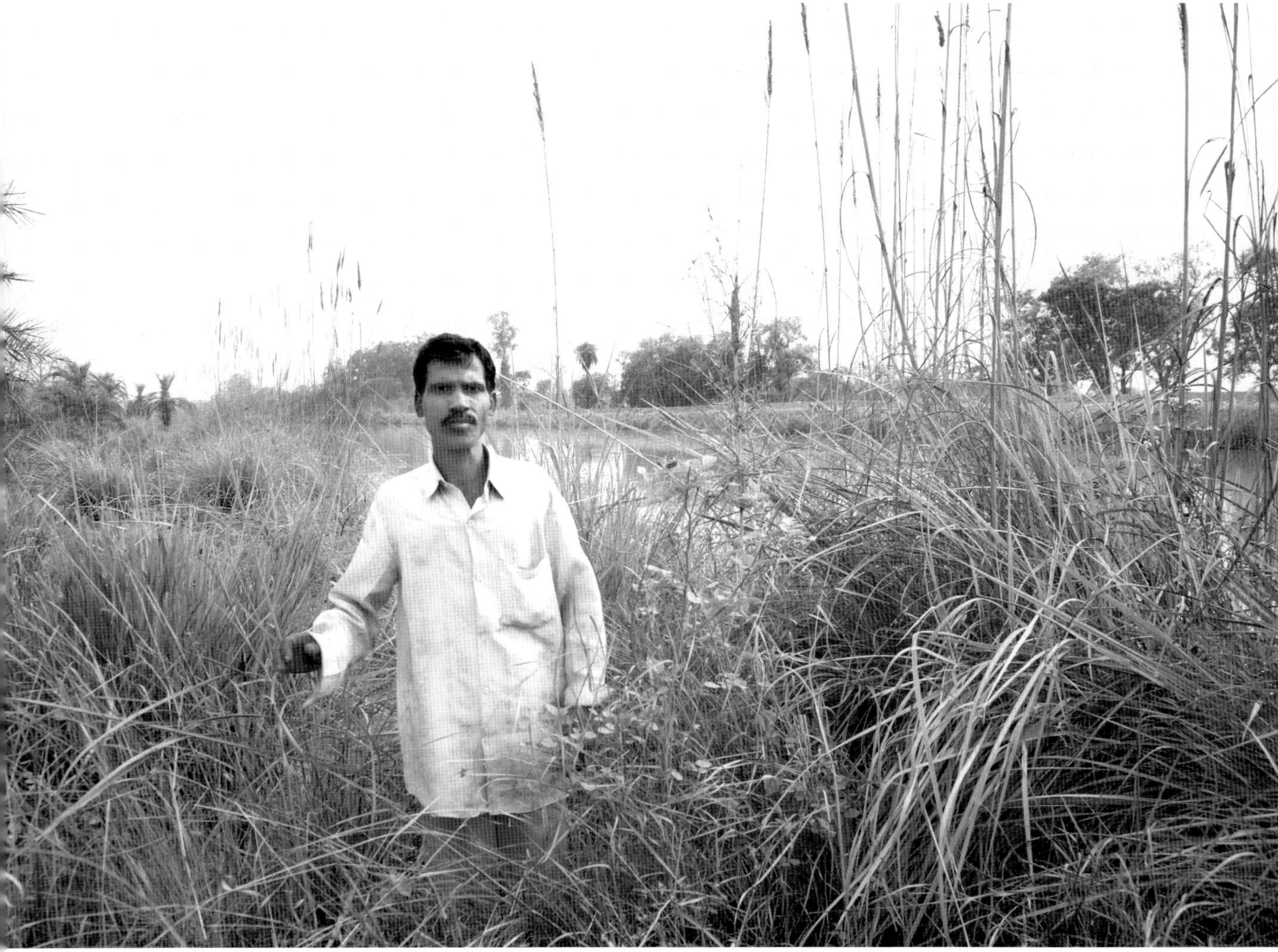

Mujibur Rehman, a survivor with bullet injuries, shows the spot of the massacre in the fields near the Muran Nagar canal. From the *Hashimpura* series by Parthiv Shah, India, 2008.

Twenty-one years is indeed a long time. Particularly in a country where mass human rights violations occur with alarming regularity, both temporally and spatially.

I have been asked by friends, lawyers and activists: Is there any point in pursuing the Hashimpura case in the court after so many years? Will the evidence still be intact? Are the witnesses still alive? Will they be able to recall accurately and depose before the court? What if the trial concludes in an acquittal?

In sharp contrast to this scepticism is the determination and perseverance of the survivors and families of the victims of the Hashimpura killings. They have doggedly pursued the prosecution of the accused PAC men, year after year, for over two decades.

The massacre of 43 Muslim men from Mohalla Hashimpura, Meerut, by members of the PAC had shocked the nation twenty one years ago. Soon it was overlaid in our memory with other egregious killings by the state. But in the homes and by-lanes of Mohalla Hashimpura, everyone knows the next date fixed by the trial court for recording prosecution evidence. In 1987, many of them were too young to comprehend why their fathers or brothers had never returned home after being arrested and taken away by the PAC on a hot summer's evening in May. Today, these young boys and girls accompany their mothers from Meerut to Delhi to attend each date of the hearing in the trial court. The next generation is getting ready to continue the vigil. The legacy of determination and an unyielding struggle for justice has been passed on.

As a human rights lawyer, it is the resilience of the Hashimpura community that gave me the strength and the inspiration to relentlessly pursue the case in court. Perhaps the way to combat the pervasive culture of impunity is to steadfastly prosecute and punish human rights violators who continue to hold public office. An effective counter to impunity is the yearning for justice among the affected community.

The Hashimpura struggle for justice is unique in myriad ways: first, in the horror and brutality unleashed by the 41st battalion of the PAC, led by Surendra Pal Singh, called in to contain a communal riot in Meerut. On 22 May 1987, the PAC took about 150 men into custody from Mohalla Hashimpura, as part of a search-and-arrest operation. Of these, around 50 were taken in a yellow PAC truck, driven to the Upper Ganga and Hindon canals, where, under the cover of darkness, these innocent and unarmed men were shot dead with 0.303 rifles. Their bullet-ridden corpses were then thrown into the canal. The Hashimpura case is thus unique in the horror and brutality unleashed by the agents of the state.

The victims included 17 boys under the age of 20 years. Two of them were as young as 13 years. More than 42 men aged between 13 to 70 years were taken into custody and executed in cold blood.

It ranks as perhaps the worst case of custodial killings in independent India – 43 men were shot dead in a span of two–three hours by the PAC.

These macabre killings were motivated by communal bias. Of the 644 men arrested that night by the security forces to quell the rioting, all were Muslim. For its deliberate targeting of Muslims, the case is a glaring instance of an institutional bias in law enforcement.

Persons in uniform, entrusted by law with the safety and security of citizens, mutated into mass murderers and executed innocent citizens, in gross abuse of their office and authority.

Despite the lethal firing by the PAC, a few survivors emerged from the canal. They still bear the scars of that fateful night and some suffer from disabilities caused by the bullet injuries inflicted by the PAC.

Rarely has an investigation into a crime been so protracted. The CB-CID Uttar Pradesh took an inexplicable six years to submit its inquiry report. It was only in May 1996, nine years after the massacre, that the charge-sheet was filed by the state.

Despite the Ghaziabad Court issuing 23 warrants against the 19 PAC accused, they did not appear before the court. The accused were in service and their addresses were known, yet they successfully thwarted the judicial process, finally surrendering to the court only after thirteen long years.

In September 2002, responding to a petition filed by the victim families, the Supreme Court transferred the case against the PAC from Uttar Pradesh to Delhi for trial. This was a tacit admission that the judicial machinery was unable to exact accountability when those charged with crime were themselves agents of the state.

Despite the transfer to Delhi, the state of Uttar Pradesh continued to procrastinate, and another three years elapsed before an SPP was appointed to prosecute the PAC.

A full ninteen years after the incident, the Delhi Court framed charges against 19 PAC officers. The charges included murder, conspiracy to murder, attempt to murder and the destruction of evidence, under sections 302/307/120B/201/147 of the Indian Penal Code.

Astonishingly, despite the trial court having found *prima facie* evidence of cold-blooded custodial killings against all the 19 accused, they continue to be in the service of the PAC. It is alarming that those charged with mass murder on duty continue to wield arms, and function as guardians of law and order.

It took twenty years for the Uttar Pradesh government to fulfil its constitutional obligation and award compensation. On the eve of the 2007 state elections, in January 2007, Rs 4,60,000 was given in compensation to the families of the deceased.

On the occasion of the twentieth anniversary of the Hashimpura killings, the families of the victims and survivors filed 615 applications under the Right to Information Act. Expanding the ambit of the RTI to issues of human rights and justice, these applications ask for the Annual Confidential Reports (ACR) of the accused PAC men who continue to enjoy state office and power. These RTI applications expose the farcical nature of the departmental enquiries and disciplinary action that the state has conducted. They seek to unmask the truth by demanding that the CB-CID inquiry report, marked 'Confidential', be disclosed, and that the collusion and complicity of the state apparatus in delaying justice be laid bare.

Those guiding this epic struggle for justice are Mohammad Yamin and Dr Harpal Singh. They have both lost young sons to communal violence in Meerut. Their unremitting commitment to secular values has inspired this quest for justice, and steered it away from communal vendetta and retribution.

Against the might of the state, the survivors of the Hashimpura killings have deposed courageously. The eyewitnesses – Zulfikar Nasir, Mohammad Naeem,

Mohammad Usman, Mujibbur Rehman and Babuddin – have each narrated the macabre sequence of killings by the PAC before the court. They have fearlessly and at grave risk to their lives, voiced the truth and not turned hostile in court. The hurdles on the path to justice have fatigued but not broken the spirit of the community.

Though, for twenty one years, the criminal justice system has failed to punish the guilty, the families of the victims continue to rest their faith in the judiciary. On many occasions they have felt exhausted and frustrated, but their spirit remains unbroken.

Indeed, Hashimpura today represents a community's unique struggle against impunity. But will the faith of the people of Hashimpura in the rule of law be vindicated? Will India prove itself to be a truly secular and constitutional democracy? Or, will we live to witness yet another instance of the guardians of law getting away with murder? Will the legal system punish the accused, break the continuum of impunity and enshrine the case as unique in India's legal history?

While time alone will answer these questions, the abiding injustice of the Hashimpura killings raises some pertinent legal issues. If the tide of impunity is to be reversed, there is an urgent need to delete Section 197 Cr.P.C. from the statute book. It requires that prior sanction be obtained from the government before prosecuting a public servant and thereby institutionalizes interference by the executive in the judicial process. Also, as recommended by the 113th and 185th Law Commission Reports and reiterated by the Supreme Court, Section 114B must be added to the Indian Evidence Act so that in cases of custodial crimes a presumption is raised that the bodily injury was caused while in the custody of the accused. Significantly, neither the Malimath Report nor the Madhava Menon Report on reform of the criminal justice system addresses the issue of impunity and custodial crimes. While the government ponders over the crisis in the criminal justice system and invests in managerial exercises to make it more 'efficient', it may be helpful to pay some attention to the lived experiences of impunity and injustice of large sections of the Indian citizenry.

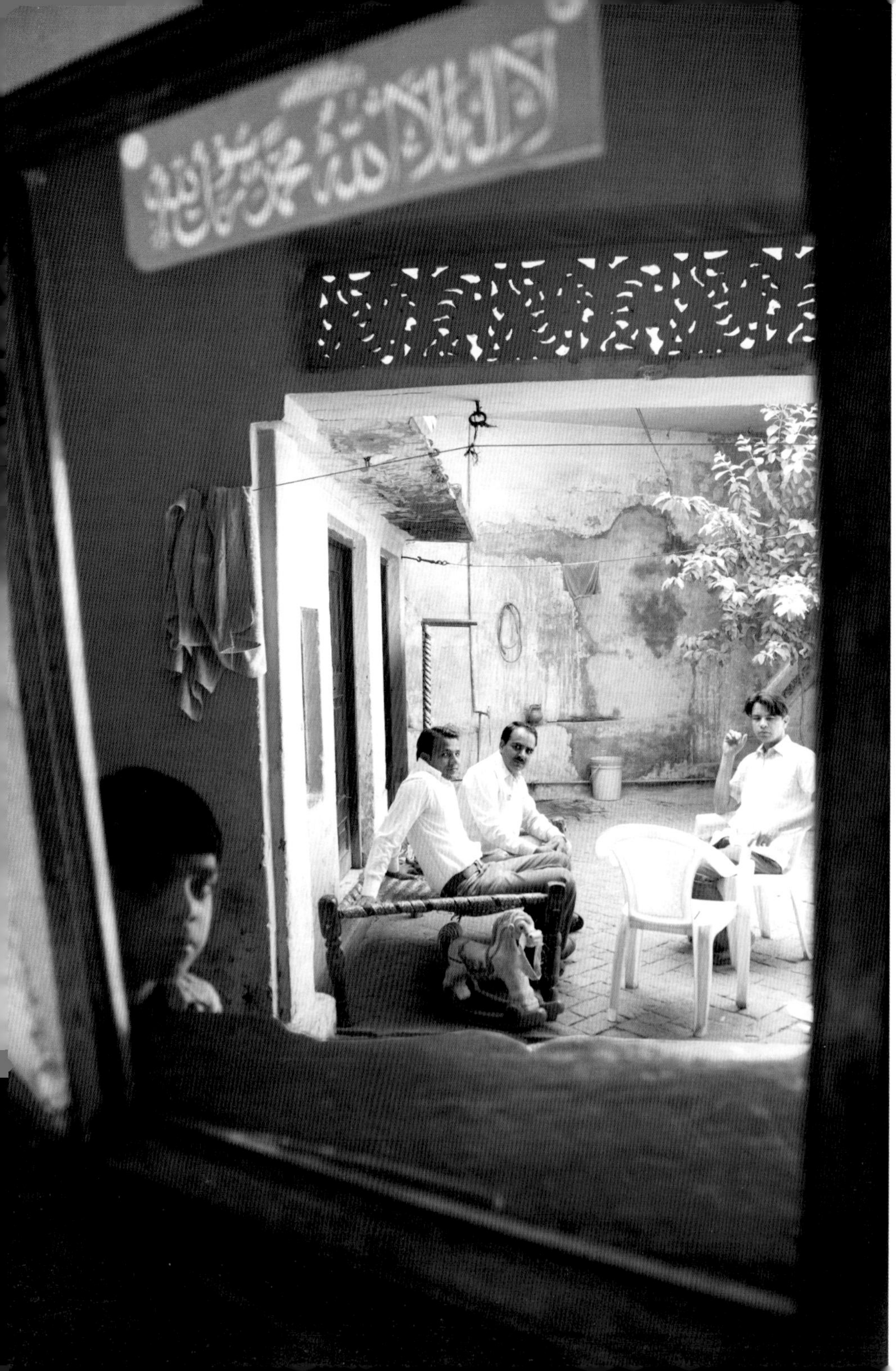

Growing up in Hashimpura – Zulfikar Nasir, a survivor with a bullet injury, looks into the mirror and gazes at relatives of the deceased. From the *Hashimpura* series by Parthiv Shah, India, 2008.

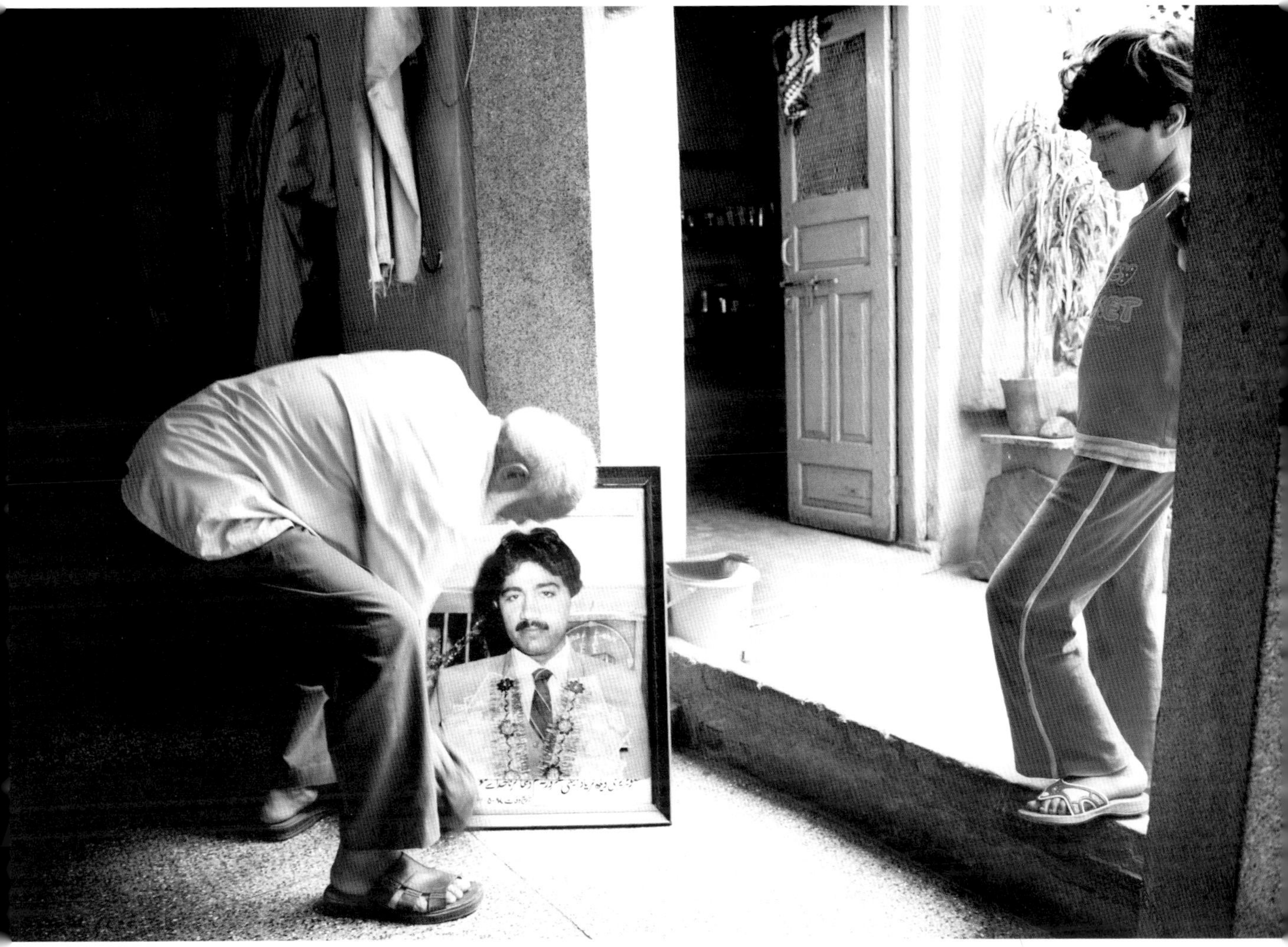

Old Jamaluddin cleans the framed photo of his son, Qamruddin, who was killed in the massacre.
From the *Hashimpura* series by Parthiv Shah, India, 2008.

Stitching up the pieces of her life – Zaibun, whose husband was killed and daughter born the same night as the massacre. From the *Hashimpura* series by Parthiv Shah, India, 2008.

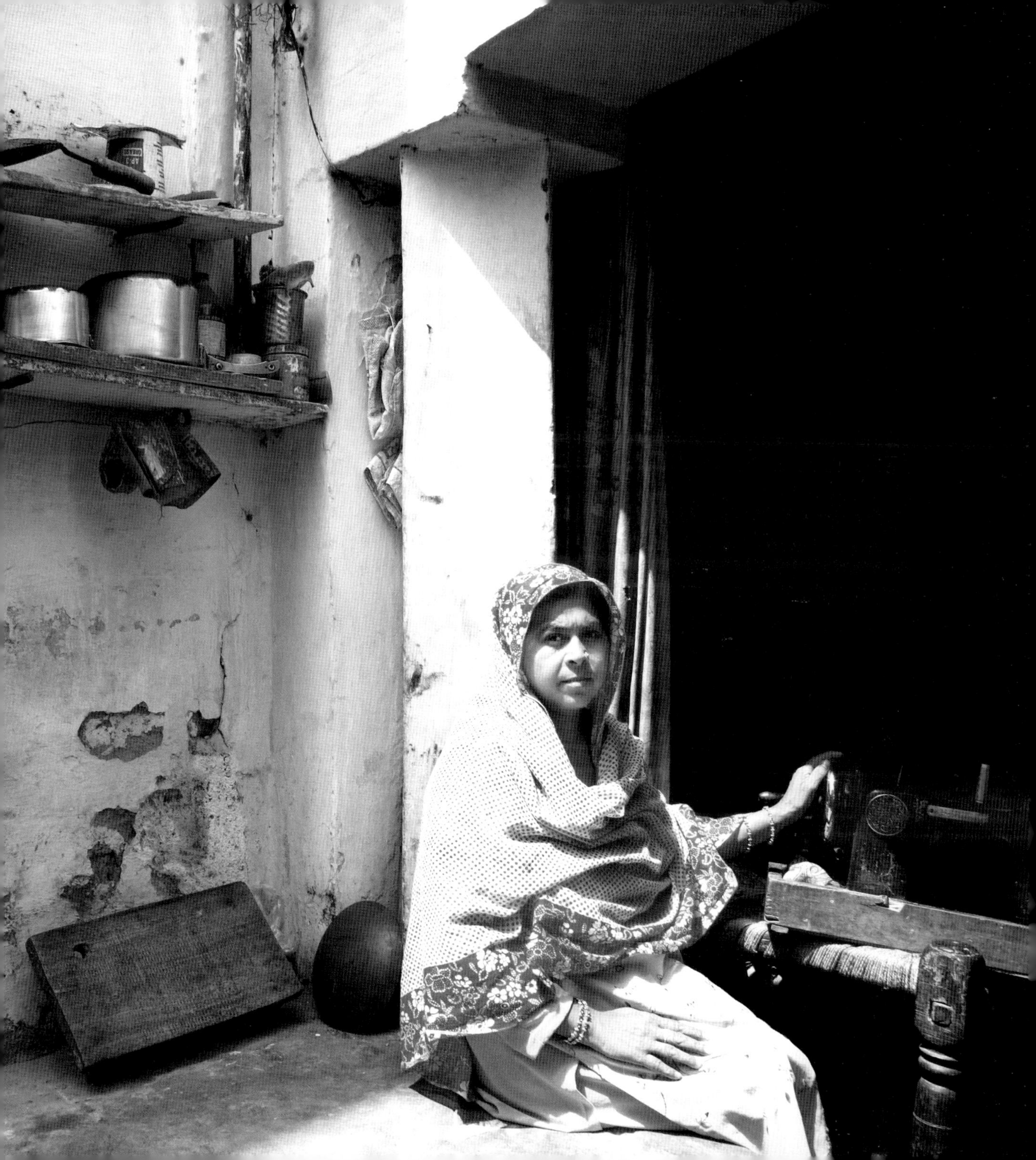

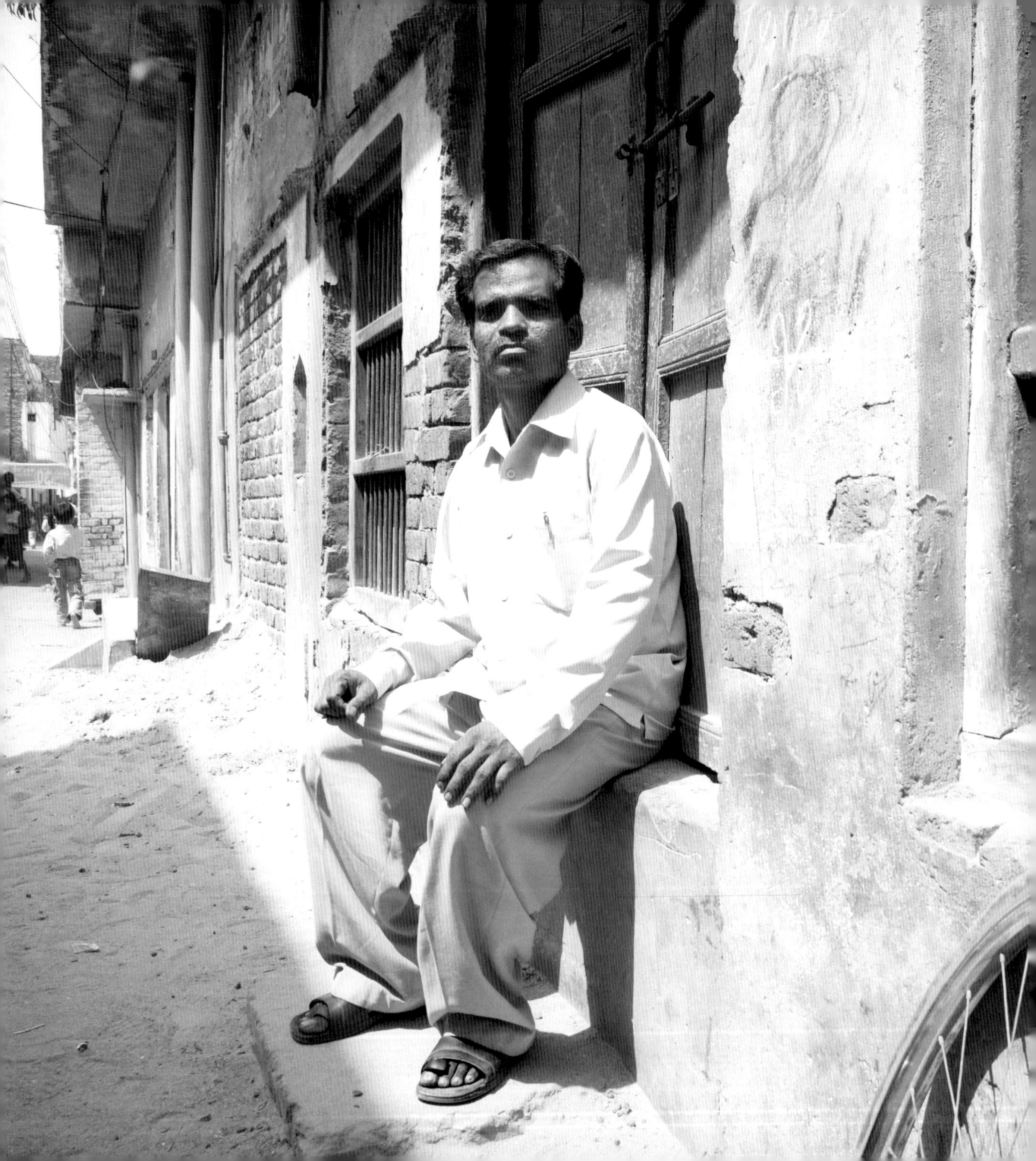

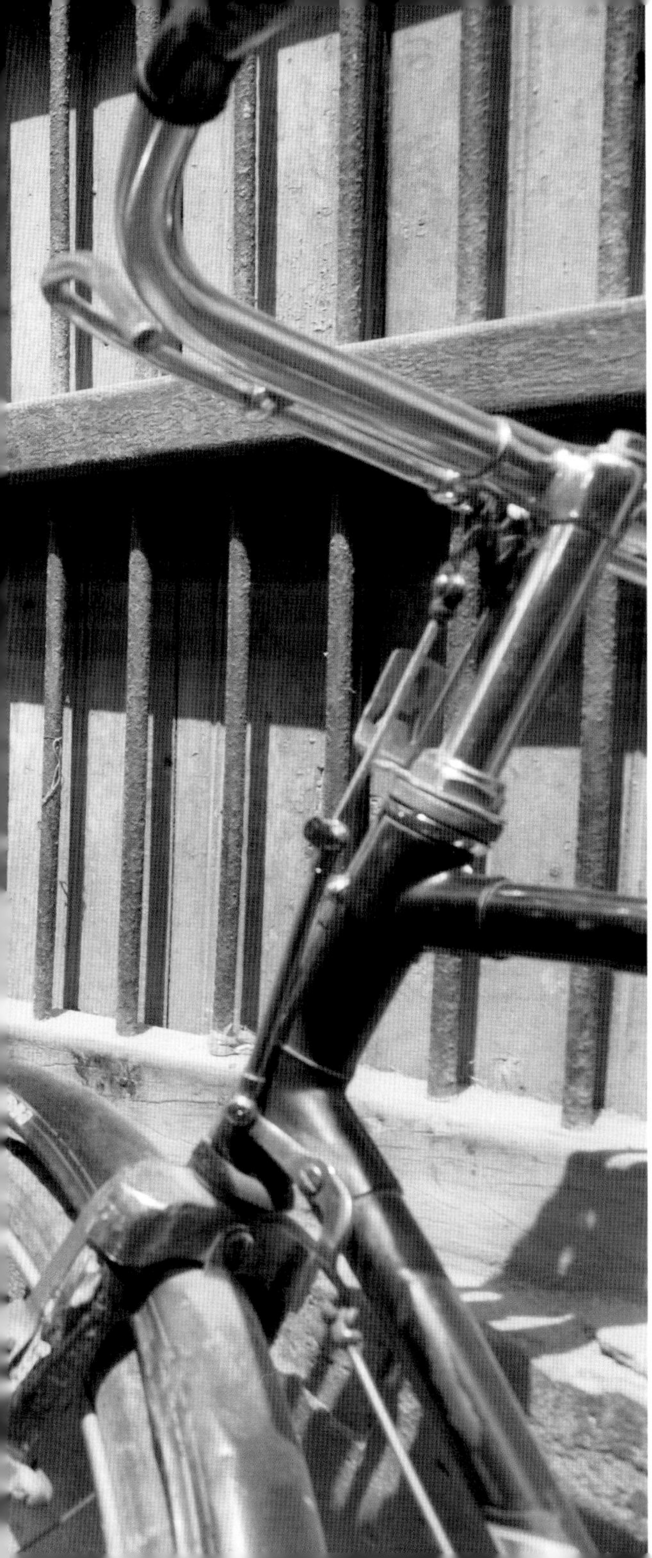

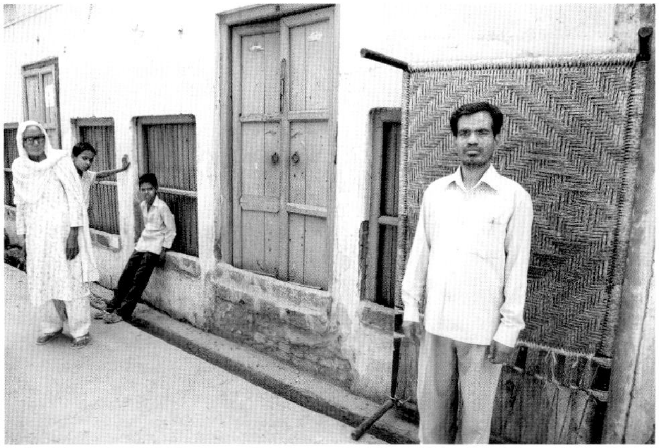

Babuddin, the first informant of the Hashimpura massacre case, who was also injured in the incident. From the *Hashimpura* series by Parthiv Shah, India, 2008.

Who Was HE?

Inder Salim

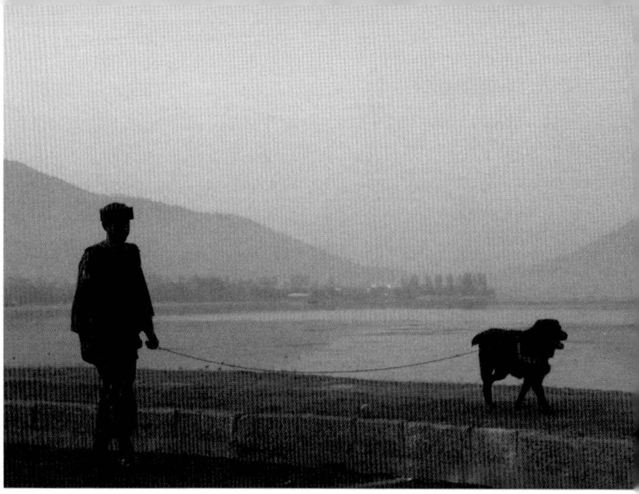

What does it take to make the army feel safe? Photo by Inder Salim, India.

varray chivah
(How are you ?),
He said to me, suddenly, in the higgledy
piggledy of jammu city,
He was not alone, he was not powerless
either,
He was in 'pheran' (kashmiri overcoat)
He was laced with a gun, which I felt the
moment he hugged me.

His hair was red, exceptionally red,
His eyes were friendly, he smelt of alcohol,
His memory was sharp, he knew me so well.
His father was a butcher, and mine a
Kashmiri pandit,
His education was nil, while mine was
complete.

He was in the city of temples, but it was 1990
He was fighting for the Azadi of Kashmir
He was a 'mujaheedeen', and me a 'migrant'
He was theoretically not my friend.
His name was Ali, and my name Abhinav
His religion was Islam, and mine Hinduism.

His hug was quite unexpected, but
His offer of a bundle of currency notes was
too unexpected.
His offer was too humble and disarming.

He said to me, accept this little help.
He asked me if Hindus of jammu give me
troubles?
He was not mincing his words, but meant
some actual help to me.

He said to me, innocently, that he is going
to cinema this evening,
He disappeared in the twilight of that
evening, after I refused money.

But who was He? I heard he died fighting
Indian security forces in Kashmir.

Despair

Sohrab Hura
Shahidul Alam
Parthiv Shah

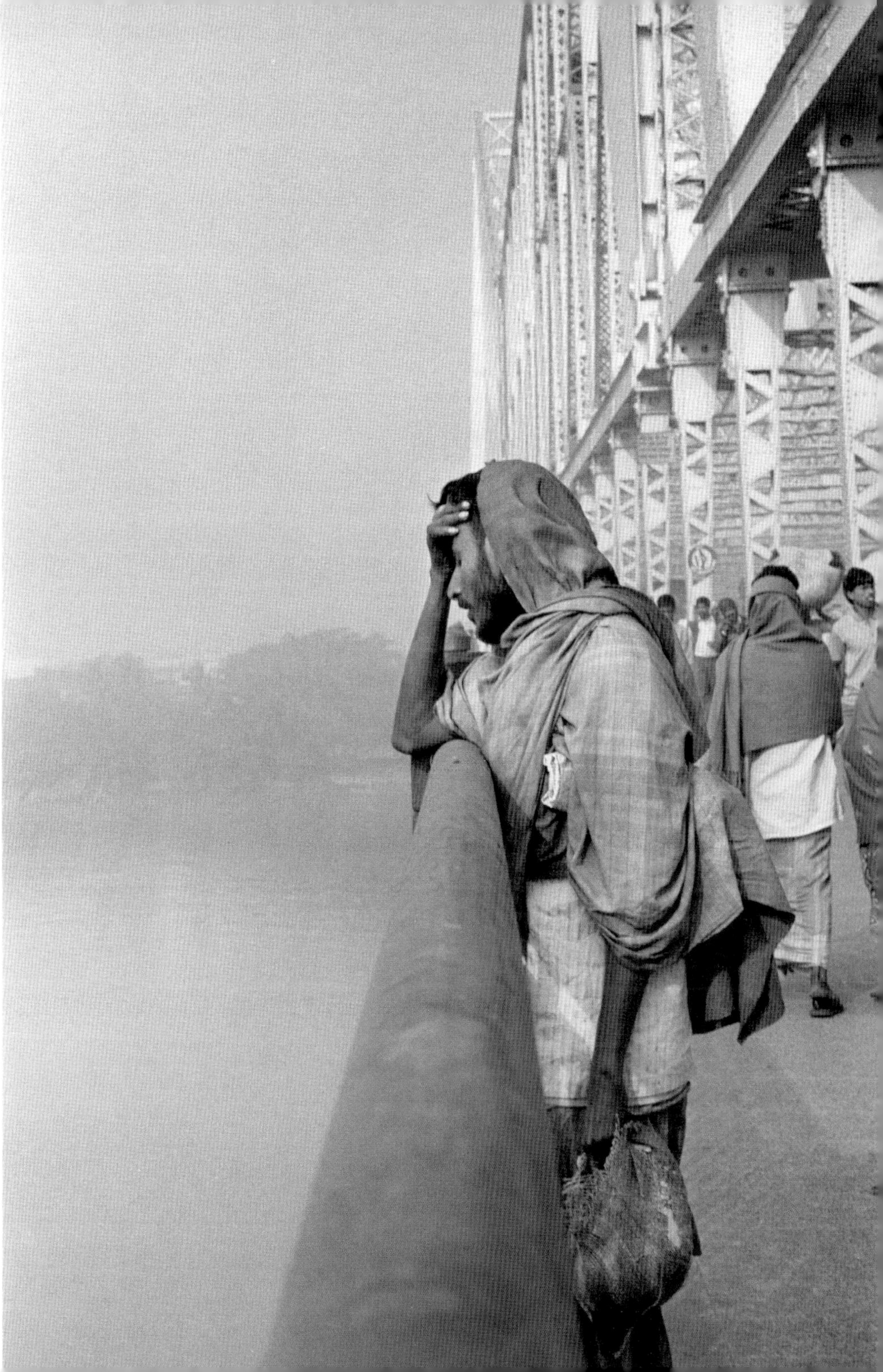

Lack of employment and livelihood opportunities in the villages force many to migrate to the cities with dreams of a better life. But only a few manage to survive. By Sohrab Hura, India.

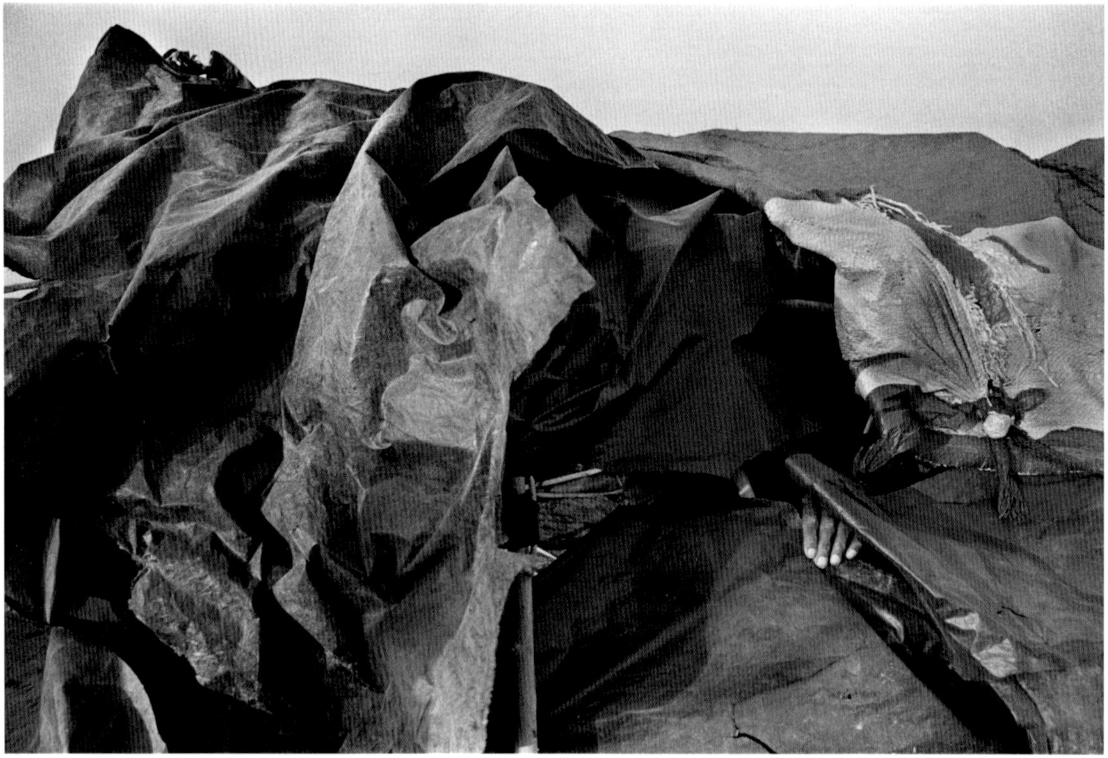

Plastic life: a woman tries to mend her makeshift home in Shivpuri, Madhya Pradesh. She, along her relatives, has migrated from the neighbouring districts of Sheopur and Baran in Rajasthan to come here to break stones for road construction. By Sohrab Hura, India.

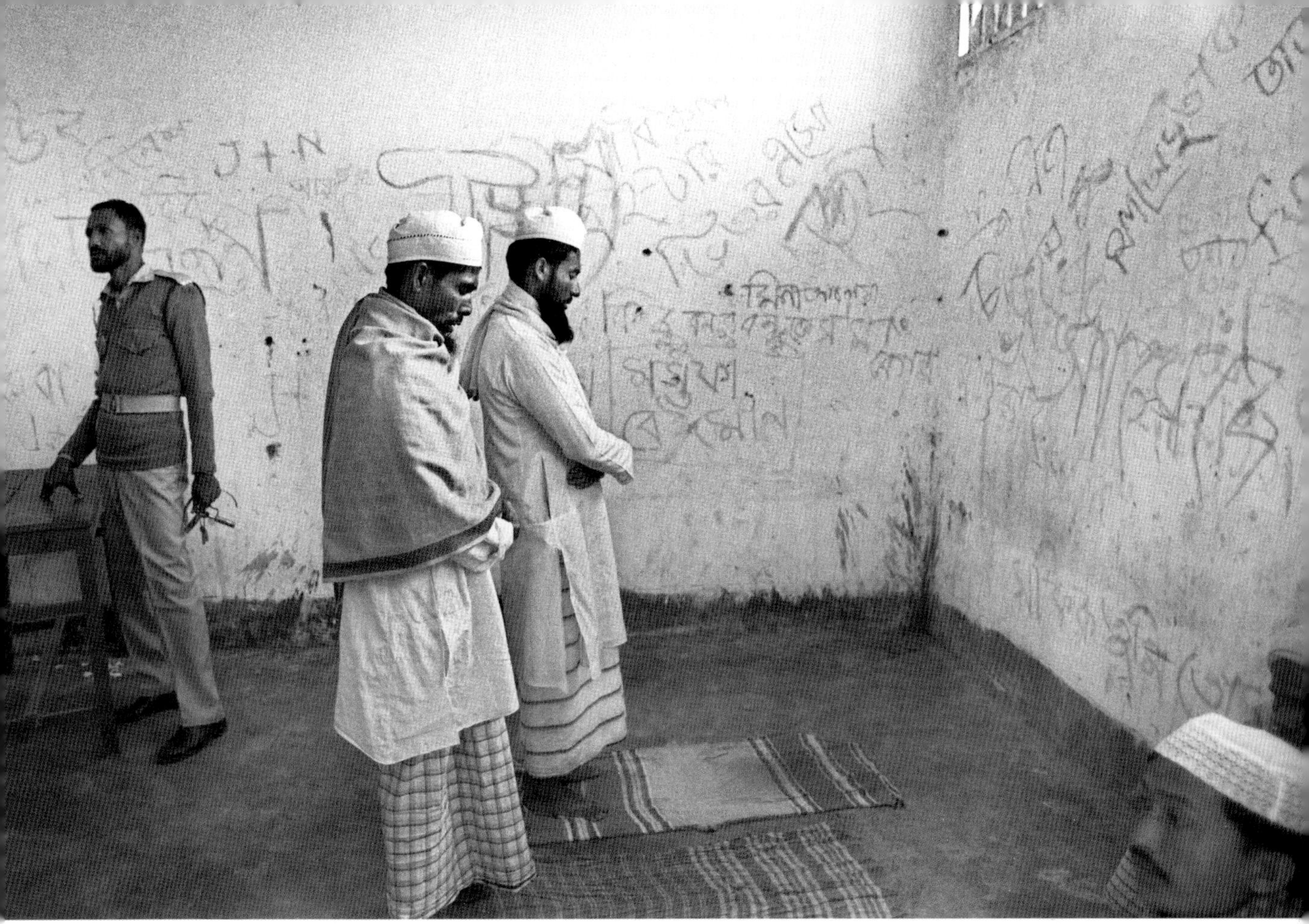

The imam leads prayers in the court jail. Nurjahan's father believes that his family was made to suffer because of long-standing enmity between him and the *shordar* (head of the *shalish*). A female relative of the *shordar* spoke ill of Nurjahan. 'She was a bad woman,' she said. 'She would be seen working outside her home.' A rickshaw-puller from Chattokchara came to her defence. 'Yes, she worked outside her home. But what other choice did they have?' he argued. 'The family is poor.' But he did harbour some doubts. 'Why was the wedding held secretly? Why were we not invited?' Nurjahan's death has raised many issues for the Bangladeshi women's movement. Her tragedy has highlighted the manifold forms of women's subordination within marriage, the family and the community. First, Nurjahan was abandoned by her husband. Then it was the imam who withheld the knowledge from her about whether she was free to marry or not, and misled her. Finally, it was the members of the *shalish*, all men, who judged and punished her. *Shalishes* have been known to fine and discipline members of the community; at the same time, there are also instances of women disobeying, ignoring or, in some cases, challenging *shalish* pronouncements. Nurjahan's death has given rise to questions about the sphere of jurisdiction of the *shalish*, which is a community body with no legal status. By Shahidul Alam, Bangladesh, DRIK.

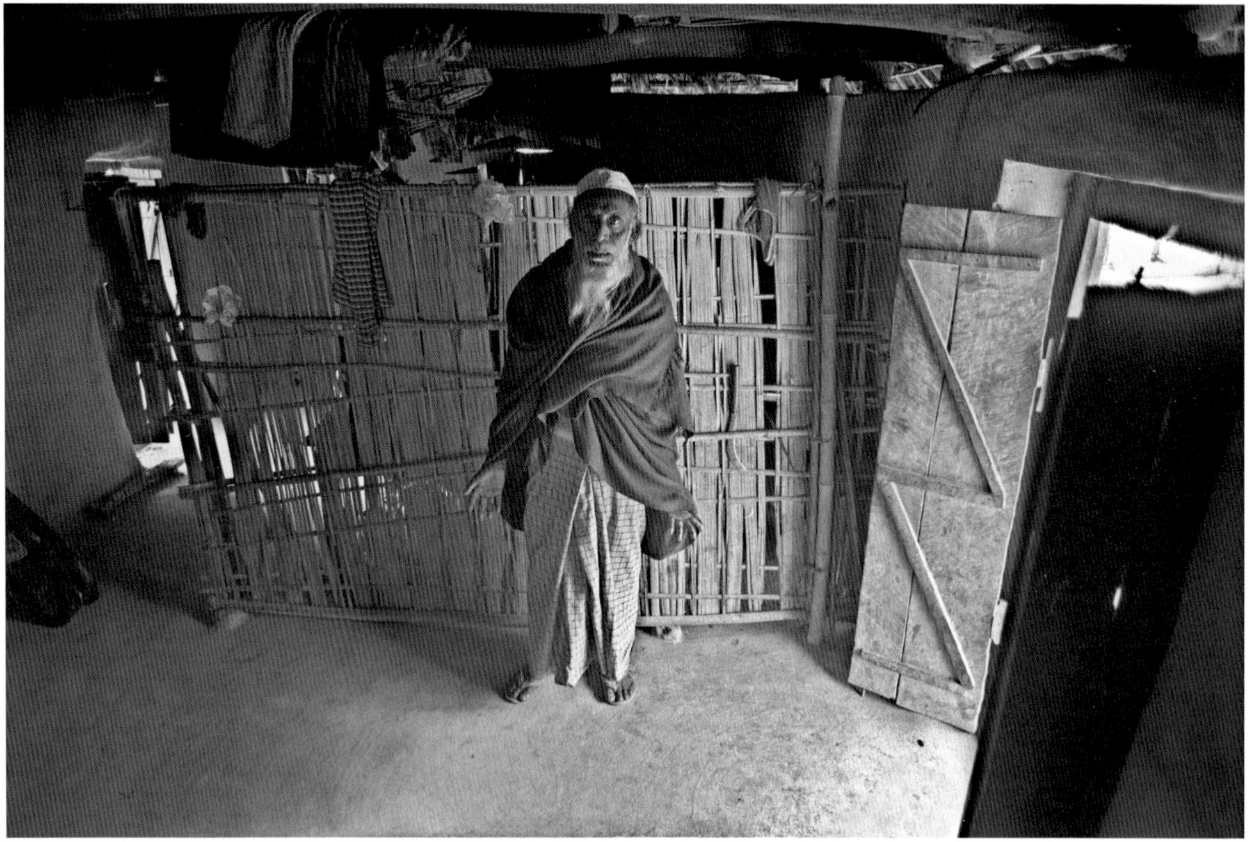

Nurjahan's father: 'This is where I found my daughter's body.' The affair was reported in a local newspaper. A campaign was launched by women's groups to demand a criminal investigation into the circumstances of her death. Public outrage and the success of the campaign turned it into a landmark case. By Shahidul Alam, Bangladesh, DRIK.

Working in the Mill No More

Working in the Mill No More: A selection of photographs from the series which narrates the story of the rise and decline of Ahmedabad's 1,20,000 textile mill workers. They highlight the mill owners' non-compliance with standard labour rights, and their greed and high-handedness, in the now-defunct textile industry; and emphasize the plight of workers mauled by the onset of global capitalism. Pictures of not only lock-outs, but also rioting and arson testify to the divisions among mill workers along caste and religious lines, that added to the disadvantageous employment conditions and intensified community divisions and violence. By Parthiv Shah, India, 1983-2003.

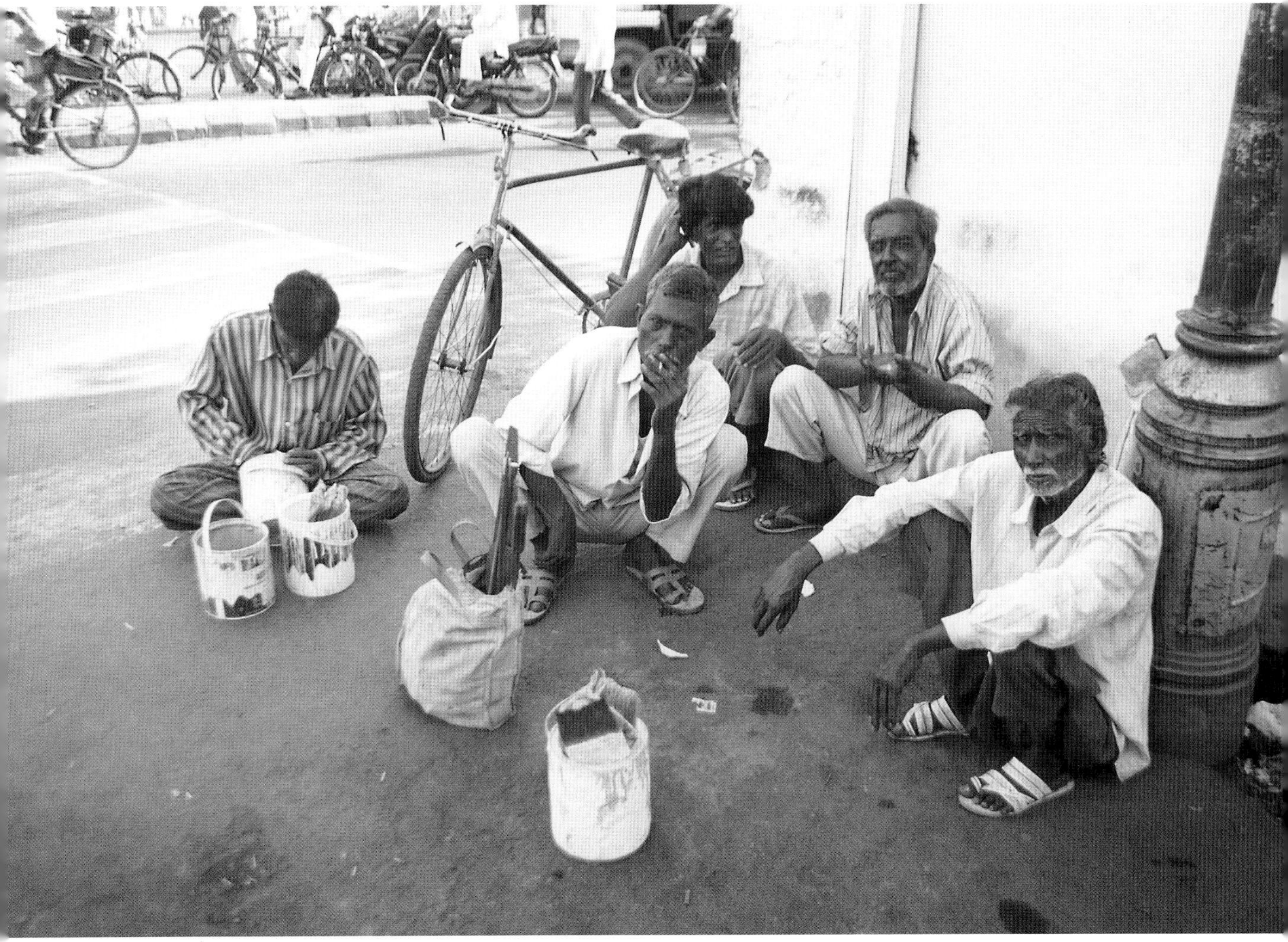

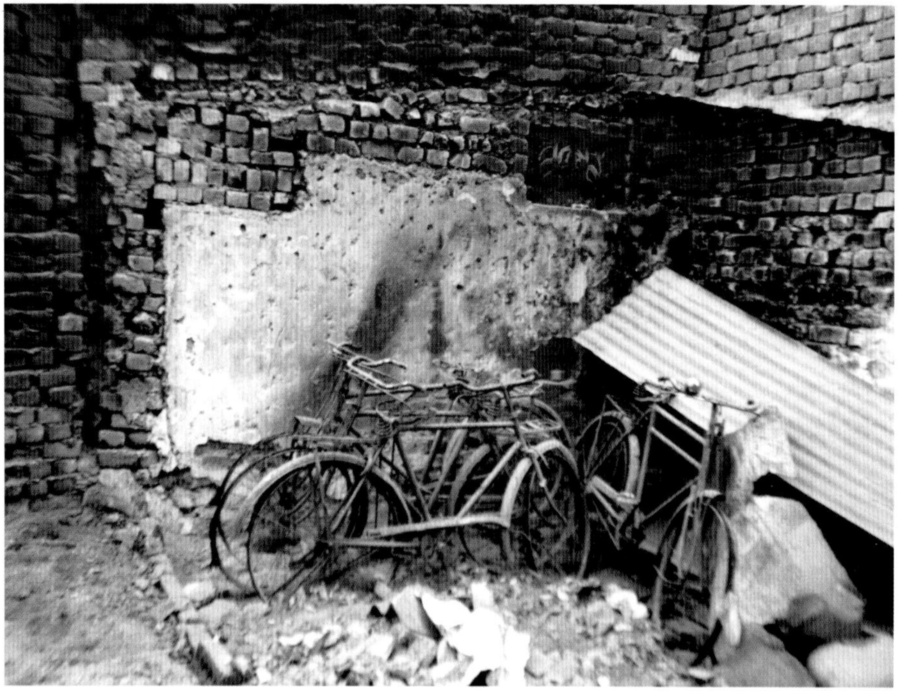

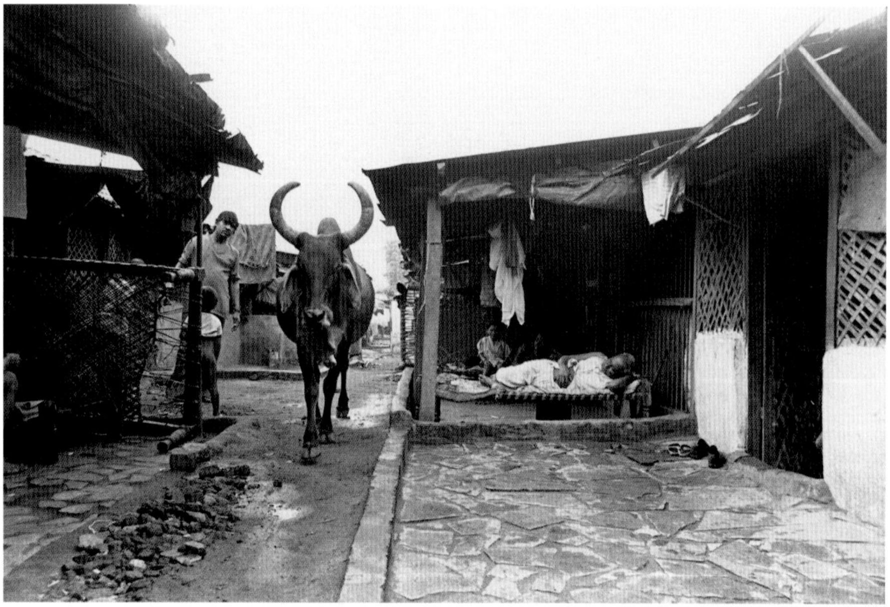

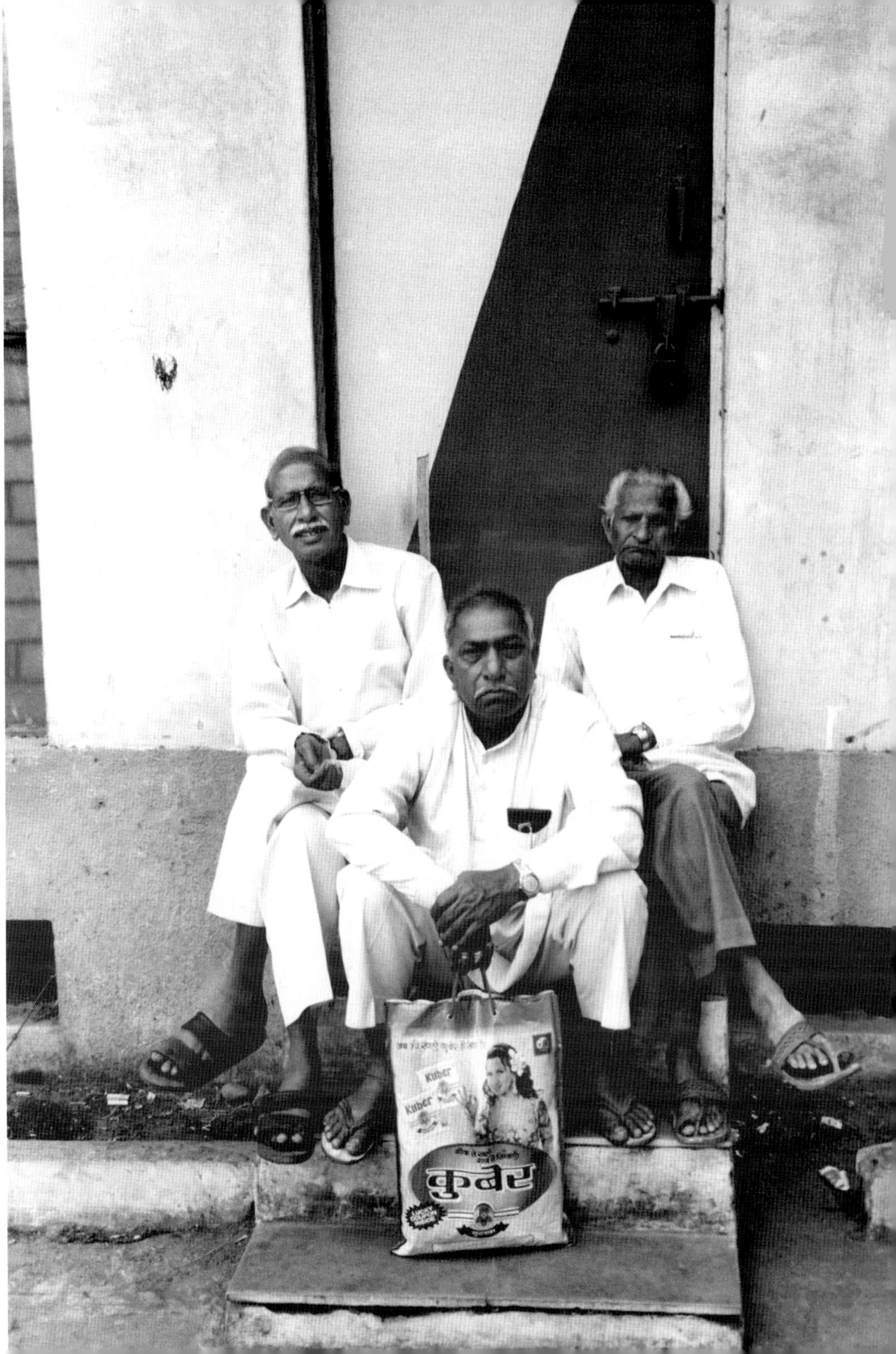
Kuber
Kuber
कुबेर

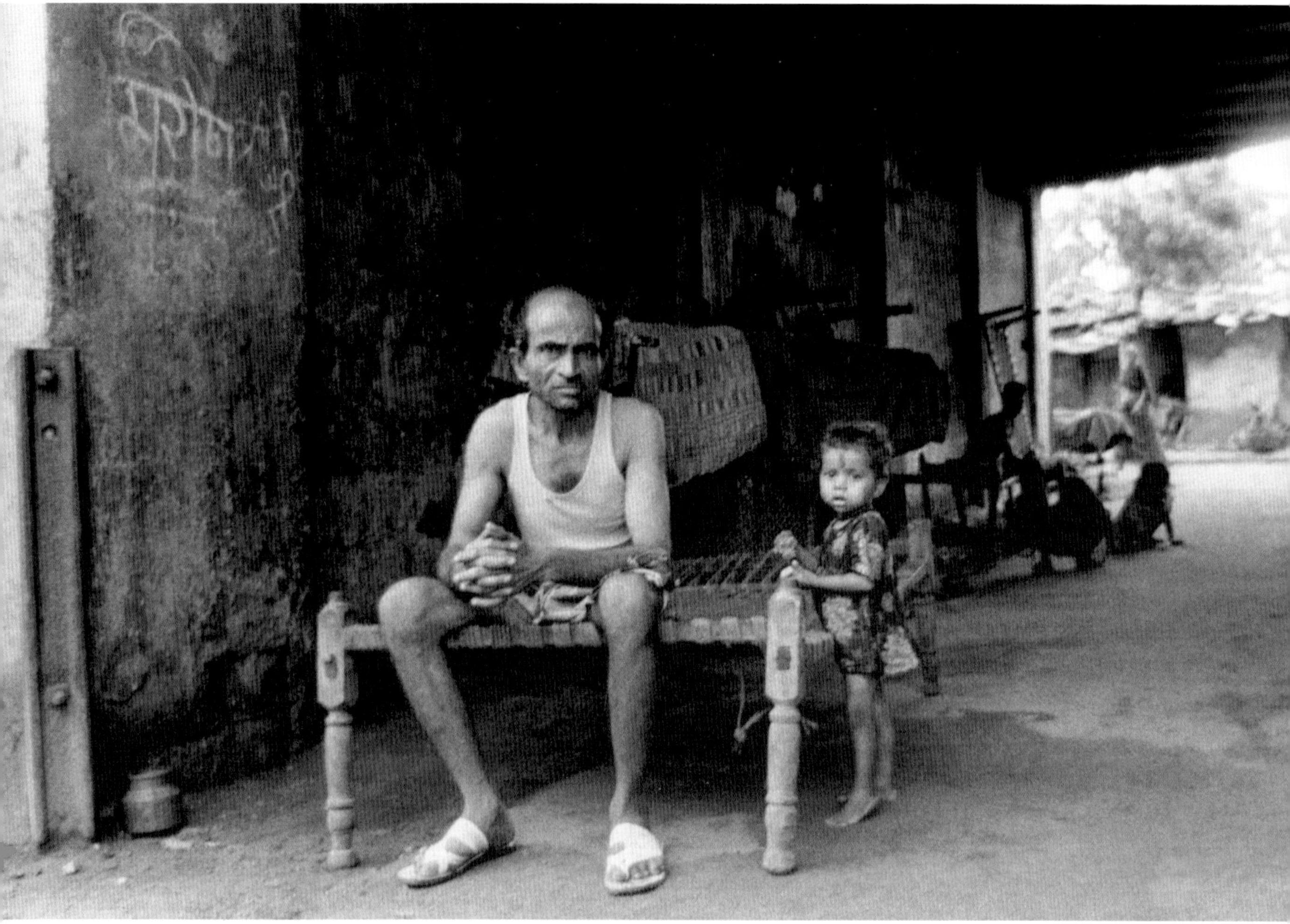

A Simple Question

Temsula Ao

Imdongla woke up that morning with an uneasy feeling; she was sure that she had had a bad dream but could not remember what it was all about. During her morning chores she tried to recollect it but without success, so she turned to her husband and told him of her foreboding. 'Listen, I've had a very bad dream, something bad will happen today. So don't shoot your mouth off like you always do and stay at home.' He simply grunted at her and muttered, 'You and your dreams!' But Imdongla insisted, 'Just be careful, today is not a good day,' and then she left for the far-off field.

Imdongla was barely literate, able to read only the Bible and the Hymn book, but otherwise a worldly-wise woman and knowledgeable about the history and politics of the village. She had grown up in a household where discussions on these were a daily fare because her father was a *gaonbura* (village headman). Her husband, Tekaba, was also a *gaonbura* and they had four healthy children. The *gaonburas* were appointed by the government from the major clans as their agents to help maintain order in the villages, and were issued a kind of uniform: red and black jackets, and red blankets as symbols of their status. They worked in tandem with the traditional village council, also founded on the principle of clan representation. Set up during the British days, the system continued even after India gained independence.

If during peacetime these elders enjoyed a privileged status, they were the most vulnerable during hostilities between the Nagas and the Indian state. They were held responsible by the government if young men from their village were reported to have joined the rebel forces. On the other hand, the underground forces ordered them to identify young men representing each clan to join the underground army, failing which they threatened to burn down the village granaries. The forced 'conscription' was soon followed by 'demands' for material support like money, grains and livestock. Whereas the *gaonburas* were supposed to inform the government about the activities of the rebels, they were under tremendous pressure from the underground forces who monitored every move of theirs at close quarters. There were instances when certain elders suspected of being 'with' the government were summarily executed. For the *gaonburas* it was an extremely untenable situation.

The demand for 'taxes', as they were termed by the underground, started innocuously enough. First, it was Re 1 collected from every household to pay for the travel expenses of the rebel leader going to foreign lands to plead for Naga independence from India. At that time Imdongla, though reluctant to part with hard-earned cash, however small the denomination, used to give in without much protest. But as the years went by the demands grew, and reluctance or protest was met with severe beating – not only of the person involved, but of the *gaonburas* and elders as well.

On several occasions it was Imdongla's presence of mind that saved Tekaba from being beaten. Once the 'tax' collectors had gathered in front of her house and were berating a villager for bringing less rice than he was supposed to, asking him why he had dared to disobey the command. The petrified villager could not say anything in his defence. Imdongla was watching the unfolding scenario from her house. Then the leader turned to her husband and said, 'What do you have to say about this?' At this point Imdongla decided that if she did not do something both the men would be beaten mercilessly. Dashing inside, she grabbed a basket of freshly husked rice and came out shouting, 'Hey, Toshi, why don't you tell this man that I could not return this rice to you this morning as promised. Remember, you lent it to my son for their age-set feast? Here it is.' She set the basket on the ground and turned to the collector, 'You can see, brother, this is more than what he has to give. Please take the lot and go, otherwise you will be caught in the rain.' The sky was indeed turning dark with rain-clouds. The man looked at her for some time, then gestured to his soldiers to gather the rice and left the village at a running pace, leaving both her husband and the villager dumbstruck.

Very soon, the entire land was gripped with terror, and within two or three years of the commencement of hostilities, the army had established camps in strategic villages with regular patrols mounted every day for the safe passage of more soldiers into the interiors. An army camp was built in their village too, on a hillock, and ironically, it was Tekaba and the elders of the council who accompanied the Deputy Commissioner of Mokokchung to officially hand over the site for the soldiers to set up their camp.

As soon as the soldiers moved into their camp, a new sense of foreboding fell upon the village. Whichever village allowed the setting up of army camps became a prime suspect in the eyes of the underground, and, as punishment, the taxes were doubled. Averting the arrival of the army, on the other hand, was not an option because then the government would take action against the uncooperative village: all the able-bodied men would be forced to work (without wages or food) in government projects like clearing up to 200 metres on both sides of the highway so that the rebels would not be able to ambush army convoys – a regular occurrence. Villagers who persistently resisted the setting up of army camps were forced out of their villages, and their houses and granaries burnt. They would then be relocated along with other recalcitrant villagers in a 'grouping' zone and kept in fenced-in areas, with their movements under constant surveillance and no freedom to cultivate their fields.

The situation was steadily growing worse; from their meagre harvest the villagers had to meet the demands of the belligerent underground 'collectors'. Now the 'taxes' were collected in all three forms: rice, livestock and money. Sometimes all three would be demanded at the same time. Imdongla could see the effects of the terrible pressure on her husband. His hair had turned white, his face was gaunt with hunger and apprehension, and his eyes always had a furtive look. He spoke little and tossed on his hard bed by the fireside all night. He even thought of resigning but Imdongla pointed out that if he so much as mentioned it to anyone, the government would suspect him of being a sympathizer of the rebels and arrest him. Besides, she pointed out, everyone would call him a coward; how would he like that?

The demand for a double 'tax' of rice from the underground 'brothers' came during a particularly bad year; they had already collected the 'tax' from the first harvest in August and now demanded another 'tax' from the winter crop. After the earlier lot had been paid, armymen, led by a fierce-looking *havildar*, had come round asking all sorts of questions. The villagers pleaded ignorance and managed to get away lightly with only some choice words of abuse. The second demand coming so close after the first put the elders in a quandary. They met in Tekaba's house and debated long into the night. Imdongla forcefully butted in to advise resisting the 'so-and-sos' from the jungle. Tekaba tried to hush her up, 'Keep quiet, woman, you know nothing.' At this she flared up: 'Know nothing? Well, who saved you the last time while you stood there like a statue about to wet its loincloth? Just think how our daughter will feed her children if they take away what's left after paying their debt to the uncle?' Turning to the other men, she continued: 'And you, venerable elders, where is your wisdom? Your courage? Can't some of you go to the jungle and talk to the leaders? Plead with them? Haven't we always given them what they wanted? Ask them for time; instead of rice offer them some pigs and chickens. We can do without meat but cannot live without rice. Don't you see

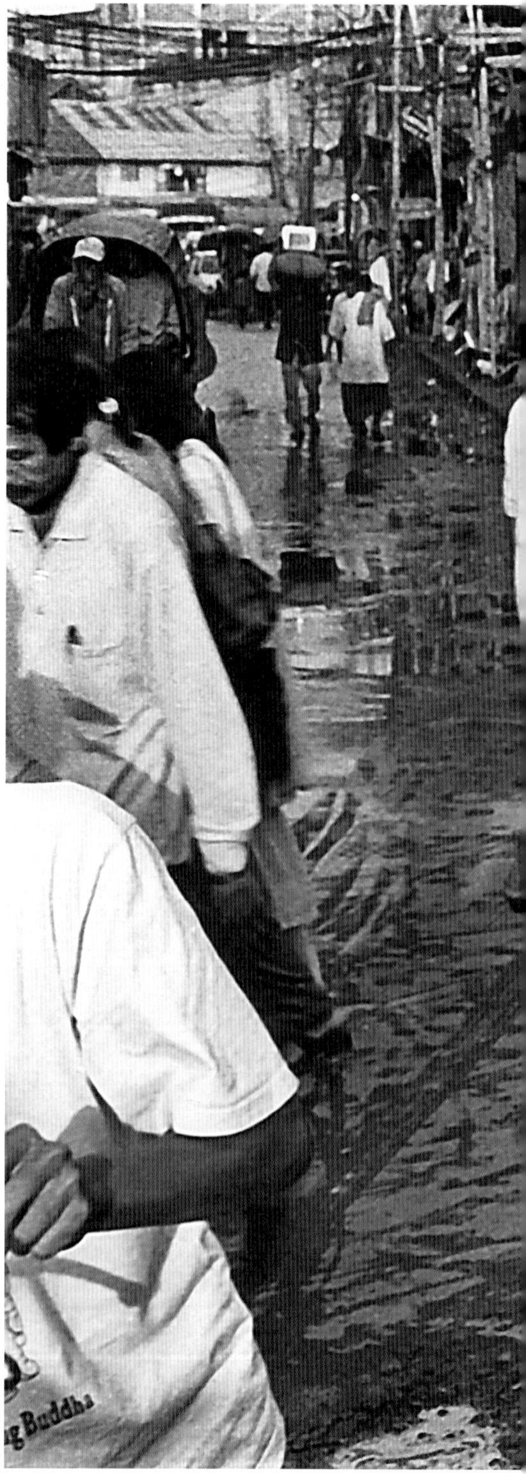

Anyone can be harassed any time in the name of security in the North East: this is in Imphal. By Suvendu Chatterjee, India, DRIK.

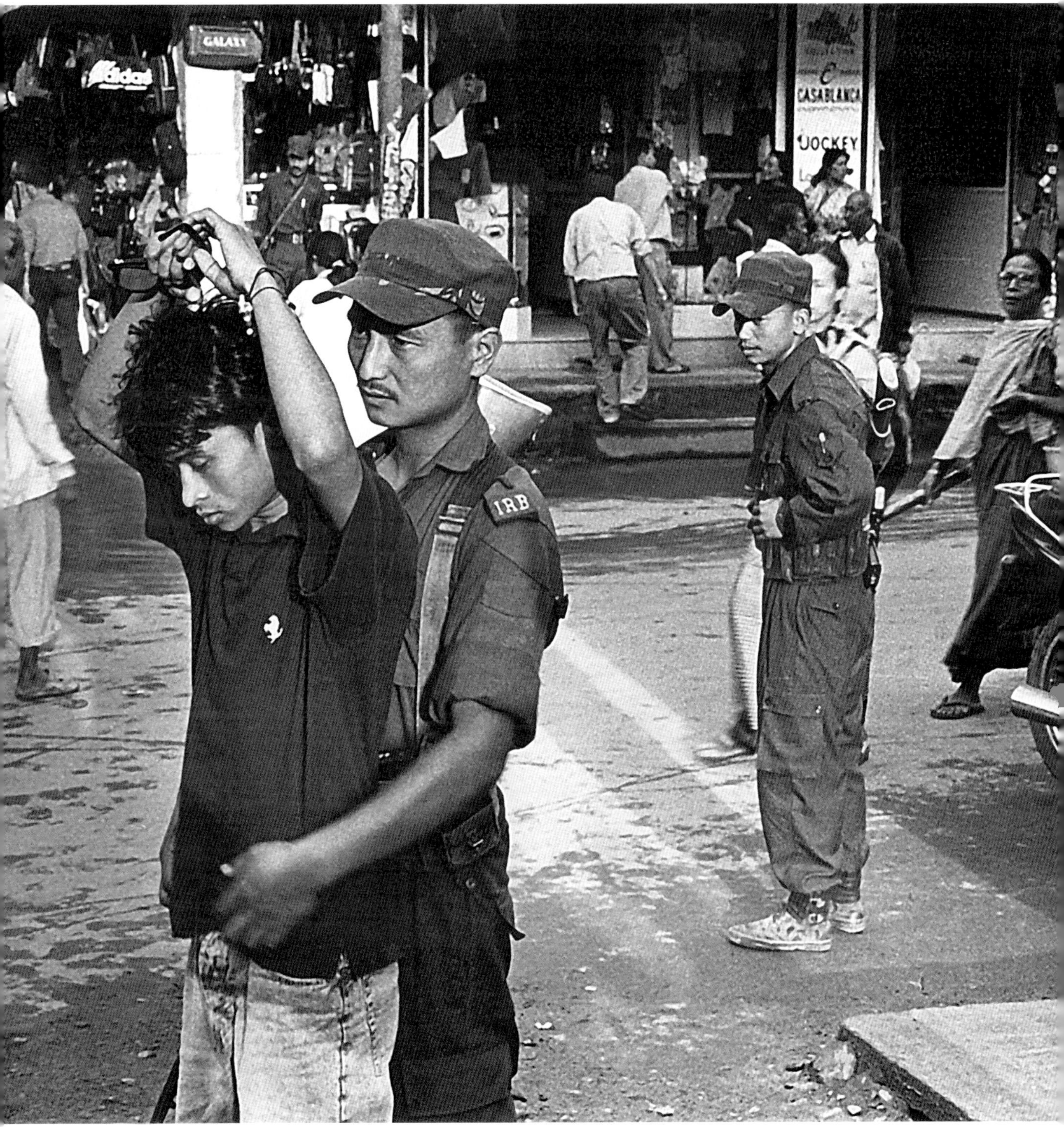
GALAXY
CASABLANCA
JOCKEY
IRB

what's happening to our children and women?'

Imdongla walked to the field thinking about the debate and was sure that her dream had something to do with this. She resolved to tell her daughter to repay only half of what they owed, so that after paying the underground they would still have enough rice for themselves to last till January – when her husband could look for work on the road-building projects or even in the army camp where they constantly needed labourers to mend fences or carry loads from the big trucks which brought supplies regularly. But when she reached home in the evening she was told that a group of soldiers had come and dragged away all the elders, including her husband, to the army camp, on charges of giving supplies to the underground. It was a cold night and to her surprise she saw that her husband's red blanket was lying in a corner. Knowing how susceptible he was to the cold, she grabbed it, and also his red-and-black jacket, and started for the army camp. While she was leaving her daughter came out of the inner room and said, 'The army man pulled it off father's shoulder saying that he did not deserve to wear it because he was supporting the jungle men.'

Imdongla walked resolutely towards the camp with the warm clothing. When she reached the gate the sentry would not allow her in, but she began to shout at him in her dialect pointing to the captain's hut and saying, 'Sahib, sahib.' The sentry, thinking that she might be an informer, let her through. When she entered the hut there seemed to be no one around, but she heard voices from a room beyond a partially open door. She peeped in and saw an enclosure of bamboo stakes where all the elders were being held captive. Only her husband was in a separate enclosure. As soon as she spotted him, she threw the blanket and jacket through the opening between the stakes. She was so quick that by the time the captain realized what was happening, Tekaba had put on the jacket and wrapped himself with the blanket. The captain turned to his soldiers and started to shout at them asking who had let this mad woman into the camp. He made as if to open Tekaba's cubicle but Imdongla, talking rapidly, jumped between him and the makeshift lock-up. The captain turned to someone in the shadows and asked him to interpret what she was saying. He told the captain that she had come to take her husband home and would not leave without him.

Imdongla sat in front of her husband's enclosure. When the captain approached her, she stood up and made as if to take off her waist-cloth, which was the ultimate insult a Naga woman could hurl at a man signifying his emasculation. He turned round and left the room. Imdongla again squatted on the earthen floor, pulled out her metal pipe with a bamboo nozzle and filled it with home-grown tobacco. She saw a box of matches on the captain's table and crossed over to snatch it. She lit her pipe and dragging on it deeply, sat down to continue her vigil, having tucked the match-box in her tobacco pouch. She had decided that as long as she was there, the soldiers would not dare beat up her husband and the other elders.

Outside, the captain was mulling over what the interpreter had told him. Imdongla had asked: 'Don't you people have fathers? Or are you all bastards? How would you feel if your fathers were punished for acting out of fear? Fear of you Indian soldiers and fear of the mongrels of the jungle.' For the first time in his career in these hills, he was made to see the impossible situation faced by the villagers. This apparently simple village woman was stating an essential truth and at the same time raising some fundamental questions. Abruptly he turned to the sentry, and told him to release Tekaba and to escort the couple beyond the perimeter of the camp. He decided to keep the others overnight as a face-saving measure for the army.

After the couple left, he felt like smoking and began to look for the match-box, which was by now nestling in Imdongla's tobacco pouch.

Bullet in the Eye

E.M. Jose

Rebecca's life was shattered on the night of 24 March 2008 when a bullet from the guns of militants from the People's Revolutionary Party of Kangleipak (PREPAK) pierced through her right eye, damaging her eyesight, while she was playing *holi* (*Thabal Chongba*) with her friends in Kairembikhok village in Manipur, braving the dictat of the militants.

Though Rebecca sees only shadows now, induced by hope that she would regain her sight, she came to Bawri Netralya, Shillong, along with her mother and relatives, on 20th May, for treatment. 'I am hopeful that I can regain my eyesight,' 16-year-old W. Rebecca Devi said during her visit.

Her anger against those who had unleashed the terror on the night of 24th March has not subsided yet. She remembers what happened. The revelry of the *holi* celebration was turned into cries of anguish after the militants fired at the merry-makers. Rebecca was among many injured in the firing.

'I feel I may not be able to study further like my friends', said Rebecca who is a class IX student of Eastern Popular English School, Heirok in Manipur. After the bullet pierced through her right eye, it had got stuck in the left eye. Soon after the incident, she was admitted to a hospital in Imphal for treatment for some time. When she was brought to the check-up room at Bawri Netralaya, she was assisted by two helpers as she could not walk alone. The Medical Director and Trustee of Bawri Netralaya, Dr S.P. Saikia, checked Rebecca. Considering the pain and the agony that she and her family members, who are from the poor strata of the society, had to undergo, he recommended that the Trust should sponsor her treatment. Bawri Netralaya took care of the patient's stay, medication and surgery.

As the bullet pierced through the right eye, it damaged the nerves and also the retina of that eye. Vision in the left eye is negligible. The doctors hope that they will be able to correct the problem in the right eye. The prayers and concern of Rebecca's parents are that her condition should improve, even if they have to stay back in Shillong until the treatment is completed.

W. Shanti, Rebecca's mother who had accompanied her to Bawri Netralaya, said that the family is praying to God every day for her early recovery. With the meagre amount that Shanti gets from weaving clothes at home, she cannot afford her daughter's treatment. Moreover, there is not much income generated by Rebecca's father W. Inaobi Singh, who is a carpenter.

The family is glad that at least Bawri Netralaya came forward to reduce their sufferings. They are also thankful to Royal Riders Manipur, an adventurers' association in Manipur, and also to the Manipur Chief Minister, for monetary help. 'We lost all hope and the family was devastated after the incident, but we still hope that she will regain sight and be normal again,' said Rebecca's uncle, W. Ibochouba Singh.

Rebecca has come to symbolize those who are deprived of basic human rights in Manipur and the rest of the North Eastern states, caught between militants and government security forces.

Panchnamas of Fear

Nandini Sundar

VILLAGE KORCHOLI

The Salwa Judum started in 2005. What does the Salwa Judum do? It beats people, burns their houses, takes away their goats, pigs and poultry, rapes women, and catches and kills men. This is the only work of Salwa Judum. They kill not only able-bodied adults but people across all age groups, from children to the old. The Salwa Judum not only kills, but slits people's tongues and hearts after killing. They take out people's eyes and cut their ears. Even those who are taken to the camps are not treated properly, and people are killed and thrown away. Going to the police does not help as the officers do not listen to the villagers. The frightened villagers of Gangaloor, Cherpal and Bijapur have fled into forests. The Salwa Judum burns their food stock, houses and clothes. They break the cooking utensils. Raping women, slitting people's throat to kill them, killing people by drowning them in water, robbing them, etc., are the main activities of the Salwa Judum leaders. Why is this happening in our country? Why is this happening in Chhattisgarh? Why has the Chhattisgarh administration been running this? Has our chief minister been elected only for this?

Damages done by the Salwa Judum in Korcholi village, Post Gangalur, Tehsil Bijapur:

Those killed: 1. Potam Toka, 2. Tati Chola, 3. Tati Moda, 4. Tati Munna (10 years).

Salwa Judum has taken away Rs 20,000, 15 goats, 100 poultry, 15 pigs, 200 eggs and 100 sacks of paddy.

Those who are running Salwa Judum in Bijapur are Mahendra Karma, Chika Maji, Kanna Nete. People who go to the market are caught and beaten up, their belongings and resources looted, and they are forced into camps. Five cycles were destroyed. My pen fails me as I write.

Signed, 100 people from Korcholi village.

VILLAGE PALNAR

It has been 2 years since the ordinary people (*aam janta*) have started facing a lot of trouble. The Salwa Judum takes away our animals – goats, pigs, hens, and their eggs too. They do this along with the CRPF, SPOs and Naga forces. All of them harass us a lot. If anyone falls into their hands, they get killed. Women, even older women, get raped and killed. Small children are thrown into houses that have been set on fire by these forces. Household items like pots, plates, glasses, etc., are ruthlessly destroyed. Salwa Judum also cuts away our limbs and organs, like the heart, lungs, tongue, etc. Even women are not spared. So far, 12 people have been killed, 500 houses have been set on fire and around 3,000 sacks of paddy have been burnt by them. Our chickens and beans (*barbatti*) seeds are also taken away. They also take away pulses like *kulti, tilli,* etc., along with bags and everything else. When they loot, they scatter things all over. The Salwa Judum, CRPF and SPOs forcibly take people away. They are in camps now – please free them and send them back to the village. Why is all this happening to innocent farmers? Send back the CRPF and the Naga forces. These criminal activities are being carried out the behest of Mahendra Karma – killing people, firing blindly at ordinary people and killing them. They take away our bicycles and machines. They snatch away the money that our women carry around their waist. Clothes, such as *lungis*, saris, blouses, are also taken away. Due to all these reasons, please end the Salwa Judum.

Thank you.

Signed, People of Palnar village

VILLAGE PAKELA

In the attack on our village, 20 out of the 30 houses were burnt down by the Salwa Judum. Everything in the houses – rice, clothes, utensils and money – got reduced to ashes. Just in this village, 75 sacks of grain and 20 houses have been burnt. Two residents, Golla Potti and Korsa Butad, were taken to jail.

The men and women living in these houses were also beaten badly. Five people were killed. All the villagers have left their homes. Some are wandering in towns and some are wandering in the dense forests. One of the residents, Bainda Lakmayya, and his father, Bainda Buchayya, died after being bitten by a snake while they were in the forests. One old woman, finding neither food nor water, died. And one resident, Korsa Bukka, died after the village was evacuated while wandering in search of food and water.

Due to fear of the Salwa Judum movement, the villagers of Pakela have been forced to become victims in the forest for at least the past three years. Some people are wandering destitute in towns and some are falling prey to the jungle. The residents of Pakela village have left all their animals – cows, goats, hens, pigs. We have not even gone back to check whether they are still there. A few who did go to check found that the Salwa Judum people had eaten them or taken the animals with them.

They also burnt eight cycles belonging to: 1. Korsa Kiran, 2. Pujari Ramulu, 3. Pujari Seenu, 4. Emla Ramesh, 5. Golla Lakshmaiyya, 6. Soyam Bhima, 7. Neelkanth Kanna, and 8. Golla Mahesh.

These cycles, which had been hidden inside for fear of the Salwa Judum, were taken out of the houses and put in the centre of the village and a bonfire was made of them.

Forgive us for our mistakes.

Thank you.

Signed (with thumb impressions)

Godgolla Kanna / Korsa Budhram / Korsa Mallaiya / Bodgollo Bhimaiyya / Neelkanth Kanna / Korsa Bandu / Korsa Dharmayya / Soyam Seenu / Korsa Marayya / Pujari Chinu

VILLAGES OF NIRAM AND ODSA

Panchnama by villagers of Niram and Odsa, Bhairamgarh block (across the Indrawati), dated 24.05.07

We the villagers of Odsa and Neeram who are living in our villages, through this panchnama state that from 2005 till 2007, we have not received any services related to health, education, agriculture, and the fisheries departments. The district administration, headed by the Collector and the heads of these departments have stopped these services to our village.

The members of Salwa Judum, along with the CRPF, SPOs and other security forces come to our villages and beat us. They do not allow us to go the bazaar. If any person tries to cross the Indrawati and go to Geedam or Tumnar bazaar, they catch that person and beat them badly. In addition to this, people from our village and neighbouring villages have been badly beaten. Our houses have been burnt.

Through this panchnama we testify that we are being blamed unnecessarily for being Naxalites and we want the government to restore these services to our villages and give us justice.

Signed (with thumb impressions and signatures)

Phagnu Veko / Shankar Veko / Manak Lekam / Srimati Sukki / Srimati Budni / Bomdaram / Gundaram / Lakshman / Somairam / Ramlal / Budhram / Srimati Kamli / Srimatai Mare / Mahesh Kumar / Venjam Budhram / Budhram Kawasi / Budhram Podiyami / Aituram / Sapperam.

VILLAGE NIRAM

To

1. The Honorable President, Republic of India, New Delhi
2. The Chief Justice, Supreme Court, New Delhi
3. Srimati Sonia Gandhi, Chairperson, Congress Party
4. The Prime Minister, Government of India
5. Chairperson, National Human Rights Commission
6. Chairperson, National Commission for Scheduled Tribes
7. Governor, Chhattisgarh
8. Chief Minister, Chhattisgarh
9. Collector, South Bastar, Dantewada
10. Collector, Bijapur
11. SP, South Bastar, Dantewada
12. SP, Bijapur.

Today 10.6.07, we the villagers of Niram village, Bhairamgarh block, district Bijapur, who are currently living in Chitalur village, Dantewada, for the past 2 years, give the panchnama below:

1. Two years ago, the *mukhia* (headman) of our village and neighbouring villages who had joined the Salwa Judum came and threatened us that if we did not leave our villages and join the Salwa Judum camps in Geedam, then the police, SPOs, Naga forces and Salwa Judum would jointly kill us. Therefore all of us left our homes out of fear and came to the Salwa Judum camp established in the *mandi* (market) of Geedam.

2. We did not find it acceptable to participate in the Salwa Judum rallies in which people are forcibly brought to Salwa Judum camps and in which all kinds of illegal, anti-human activities take place. With the intention of keeping ourselves separate from such activities, we crept out from the Geedam Salwa Judum camp and came to Chitalur village, Dantewada block. Somehow we managed to spend 2 years here. During these 2 years our families and we survived by working as daily wage labourers on development works and as labourers for other villagers.

3. Now we all wish to return to our village Niram in Bhairamgarh block, because these past 2 years survival has been very difficult. The main reason being that here we have neither our fields nor our homes.

4. We are scared that if we return to our village, the police, SPOs, CRPF and other paramilitary forces, and members of the Salwa Judum will attack and kill us, or they will forcibly capture us and take us to one of the Salwa Judum camps, or they will catch us, falsely accuse us of being Naxalites and send us to jail. The Salwa Judum has announced that if anyone from the camps or the villages near the camps tries to cross the river and go to the villages across the river, it will not be tolerated. Hence, even though we wish to, we cannot return to our village.

5. Hence, we signatories wish to claim our rights under Article 19 of the Indian Constitution – to go anywhere, and to earn our living anywhere. We demand this guarantee from the government and through our panchnama, we appeal to all constitutional authorities, the Central, State and District administration, to guarantee our constitutional rights. We are all resident adivasis of Dantewada who are suffering. This panchnama has been read to us, and we have signed it in full knowledge of its contents.

Signatories to the panchnama

Ghasiram s/o Mangalram / Sanku s/o Kosa / Kade s/o Kosa / Madko s/o Aitu / Manglu s/o Budu/ Dasaram s/o Sukda / Shrimati Bukdi w/o Kade / Shrimati Pupe w/o Mangal / Shrimati Deve w/o Aitu / Shrimati Radha w/o Sanku / Shrimati Sukko w/o Sukda / Shrimati Sundri w/o Madko/ Paike s/o Sukda / Dulsai

Missing

Swapan Nayak • Sonia Jabbar

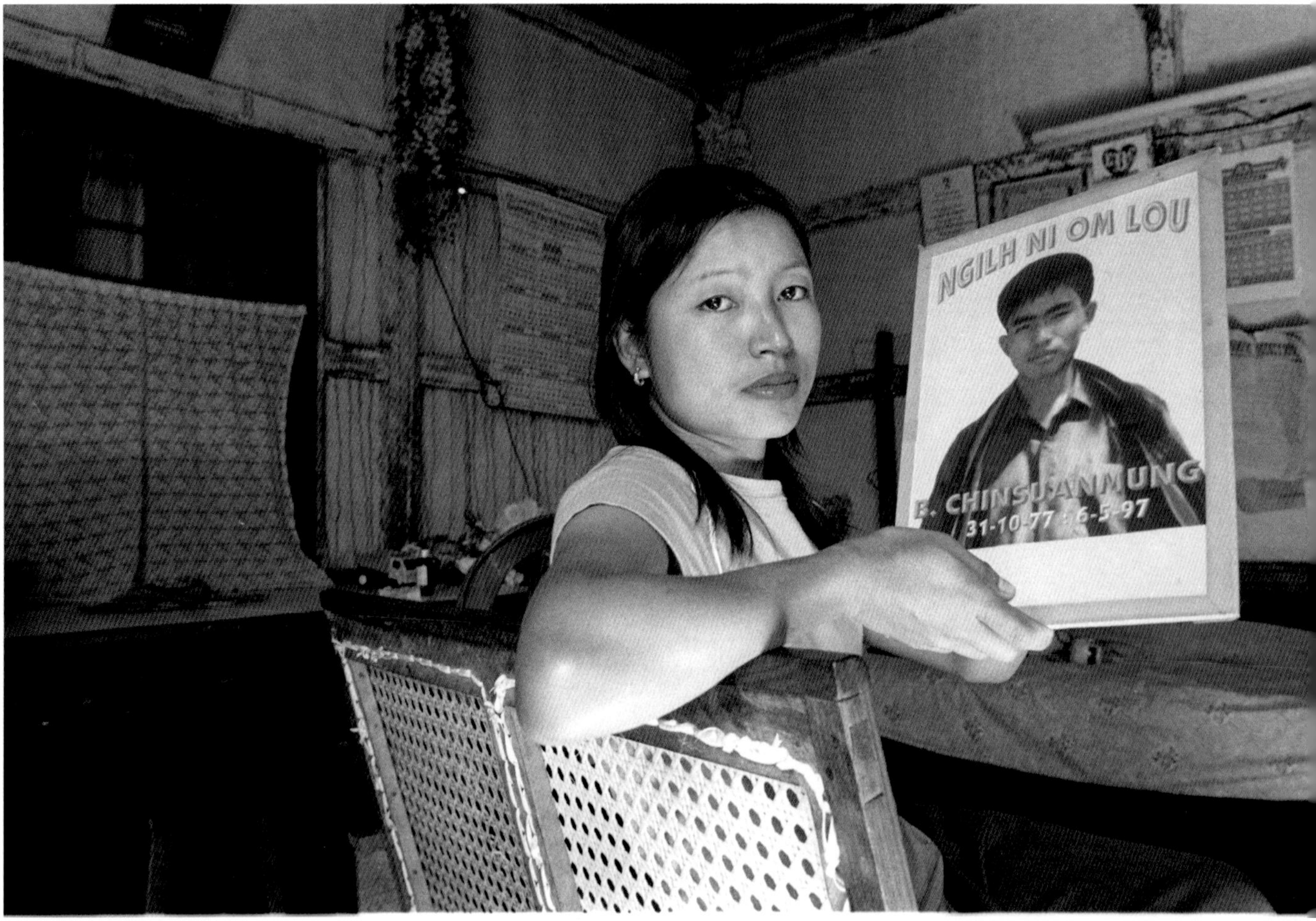

L. Muankim shows her only brother's photograph. Her brother B. Chinsuanmung was killed during a clash between the Kuki and Paite tribes in Manipur. By Swapan Nayak, India.

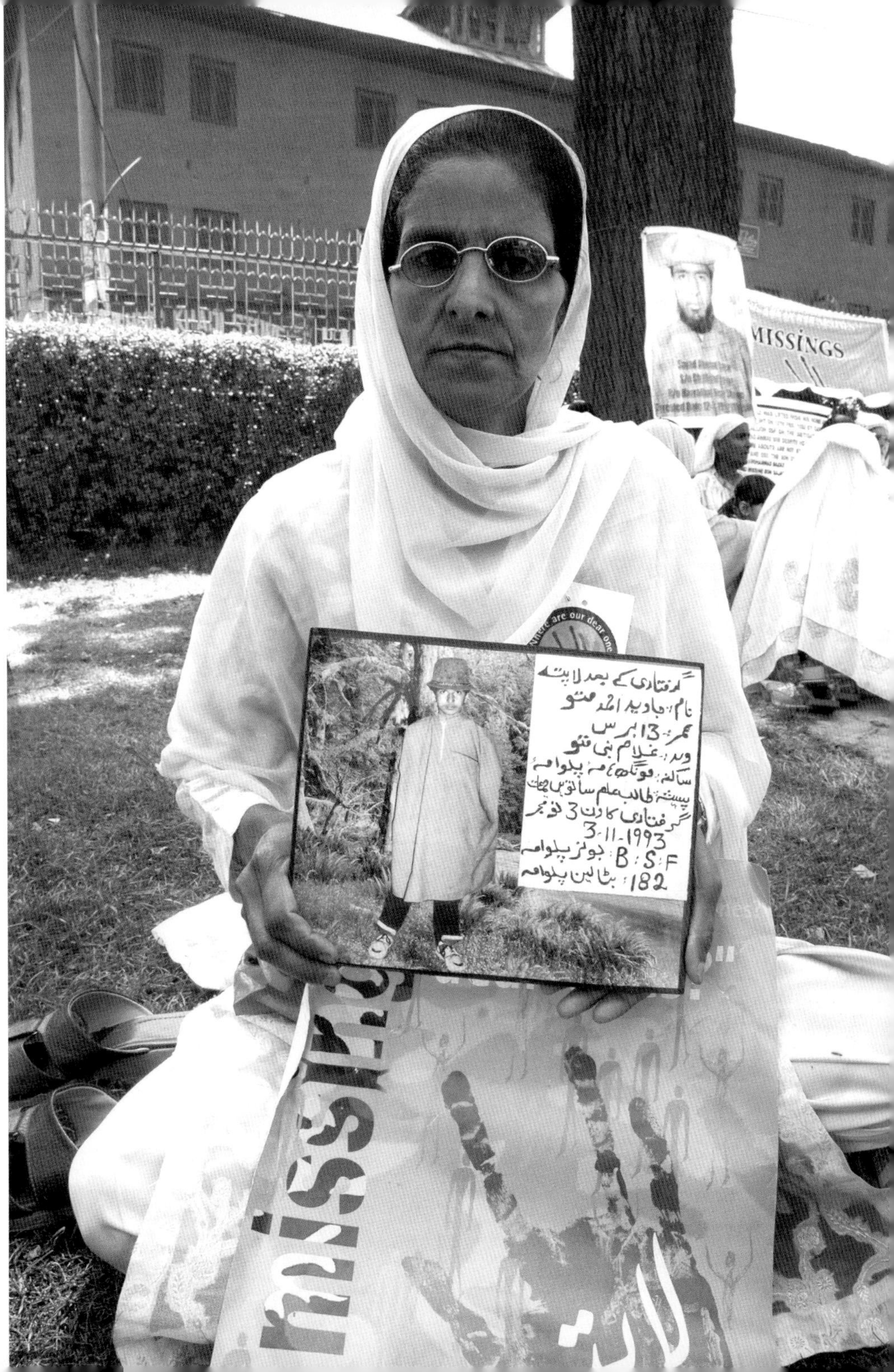

Hafeeza, resident of Bijbehara, travels to Srinagar once a month to join a protest meeting with other members of the Association of Parents of Disappeared Persons (APDP). Her son, Javed Ahmed Mattoo, was only 14 years old when he was picked up by the BSF and disappeared. By Sonia Jabbar, India.

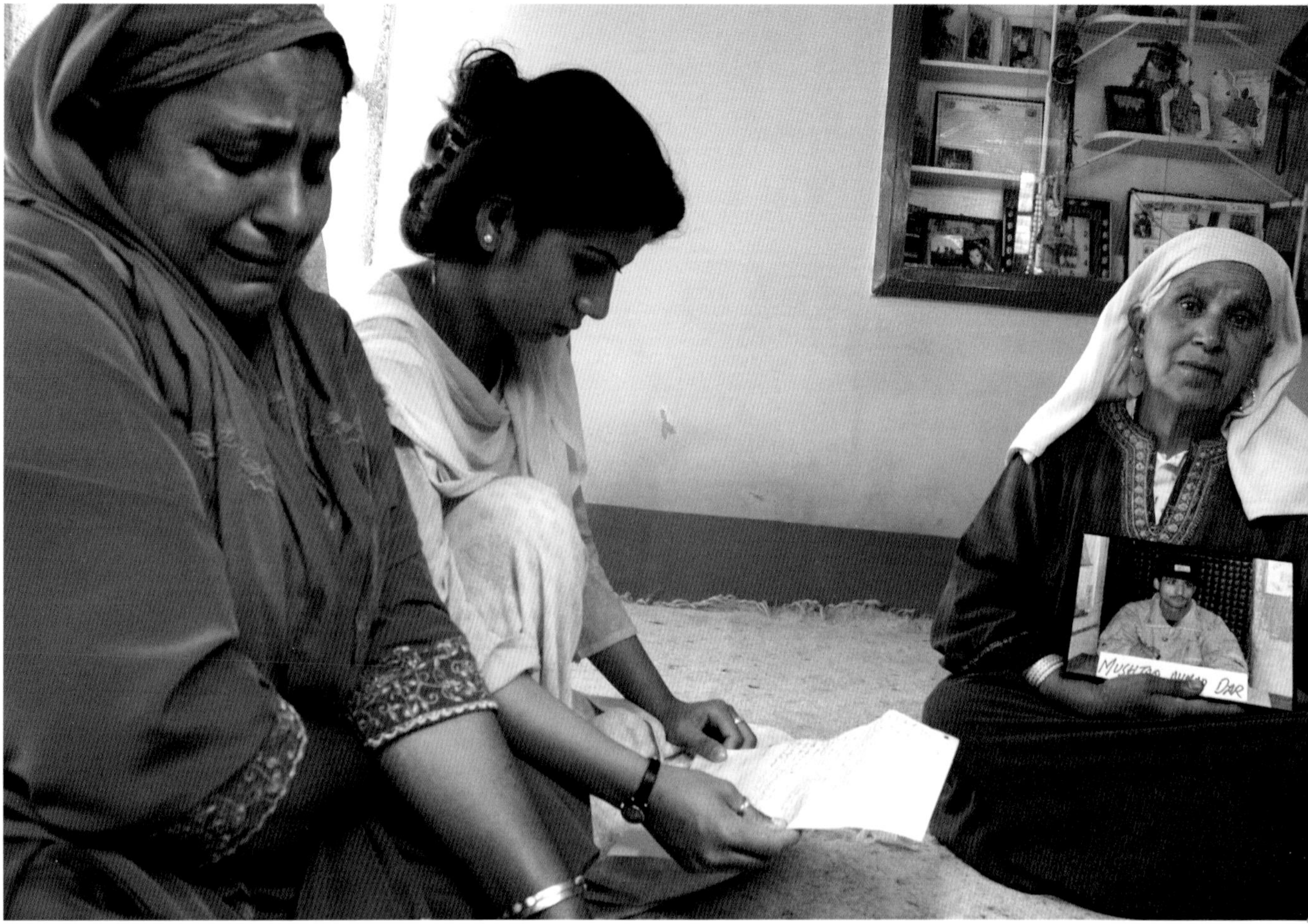

Srinagar: the sister of Mushtaq Ahmed Dar breaks down while recounting the story of his arrest, disappearance and their search for him. By Sonia Jabbar, India.

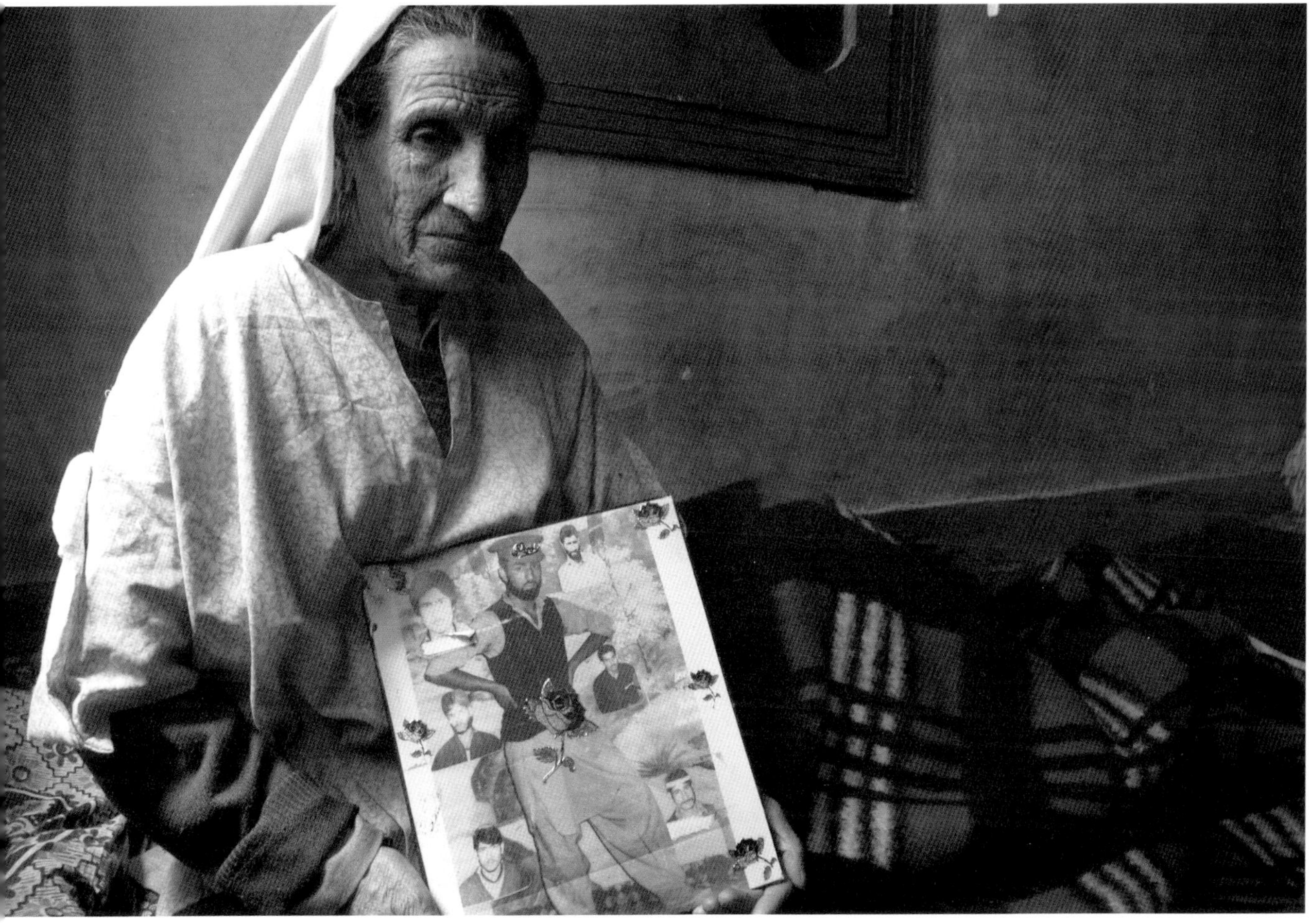

Oonagam, Bandipora district: Hajra holds a collage of photos of her four sons killed since 1990, one of whom has disappeared. By Sonia Jabbar, India.

Disappearances in Nepal

Bhai Kaji Ghimire, Managing Editor of the weekly magazine *Sama Drishti*, was arrested on 3 December 2003. For over a year his whereabouts remained unknown.

According to witnesses, at around 3 pm on 3rd December, Bhai Kaji Ghimire was travelling on a motorcycle through the Chhetrapati area of Kathmandu, Nepal, when some Royal Nepalese Army personnel, also on motorcycles, started following him. Ghimire had to stop because a white car was blocking the road. Local residents report that Bhim Giri, a 27 year-old student travelling with Bhai Kaji, called out their names and shouted that they were being arrested. He asked the onlookers to alert the press. Giri was then beaten by the security force personnel. After ten minutes, both Bhim Giri and Bhai Kaji Ghimire were bundled into a car.

Relatives of Bhim Giri contacted journalists, and informed the Nepal Bar Association and several human rights organizations. They met with the chief district officer of the area, who denied any knowledge of the arrest. The family did not receive any information about the whereabouts of Bhim Giri or Bhaikaji Ghimire for months after their arrest.

The Communist Party of Nepal (CPN) (Maoist) had launched a 'people's war' in February 1996. Reports of human rights abuses by both the security forces and the CPN (Maoist) escalated after the army was mobilized and a state of emergency imposed in 2001. Many people were arrested under the 2002 Terrorist and Disruptive Activities (Control and Punishment) Act, which gave the security forces the power to arrest without warrant and detain suspects in police custody for up to 90 days. Scores of people are reported to have been held illegally for months by the army without access to their families, lawyers or medical treatment. In 2002, Nepal recorded the highest number of 'disappearances' for any country in the world.

The situation resumed when the CPN (Maoist) announced they were withdrawing from a short ceasefire agreement. Fighting started throughout the country, and Amnesty International received reports of both sides organizing disappearances. Security forces launched a major crackdown against journalists, especially those considered to be pro-Maoist or those who were seen to have defied censorship. In most cases, no charges were filed against the journalists detained by the army.

Ghimire was freed on 25 August 2005 when Nepal's Supreme Court ruled that his detention was illegal and ordered his release. He had been secretly held for fifteen months, being moved from one barrack to another, from Bhairabnath, Shivapuri to Rajdad, all in the Kathmandu valley, and then finally to Nakkhu prison. Ghimire had been made to sleep on the bare floor, suffered frequent death threats and was even put through mock executions. Throughout, he was bound and blindfolded.

At Bhairabnath Battalion army camp in the north of Kathmandu, where he was first taken, hundreds of Maoist suspects had been held and systematically tortured. 'They placed a gun in one of my hands and five bullets in the other, and took my picture, and said that I was carrying them when I was arrested', he said. While at the camp,

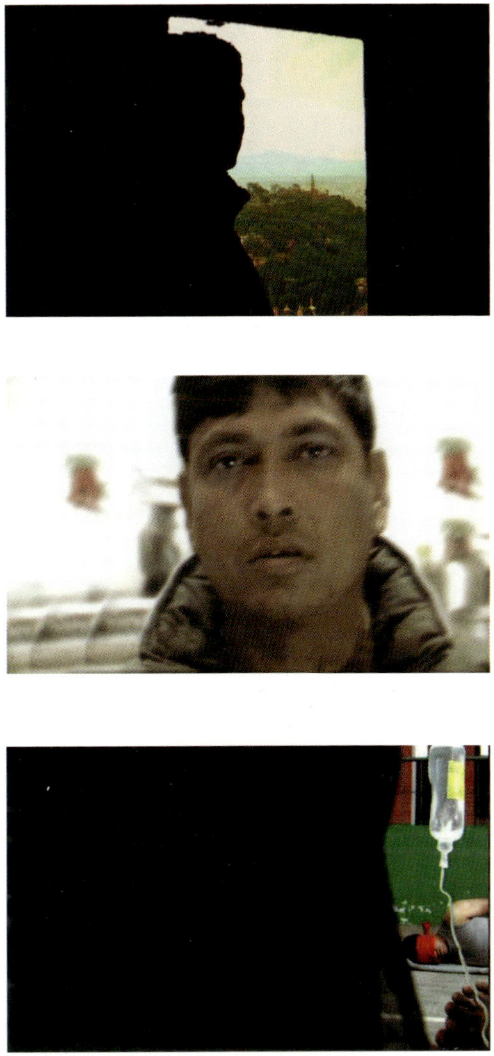

Scenes from Pranay Limbu's *Forgive! Forget Not!* Journalist Ghimire saw other detainees through the blindfold inside the Bhairabnath Battalion army camp.

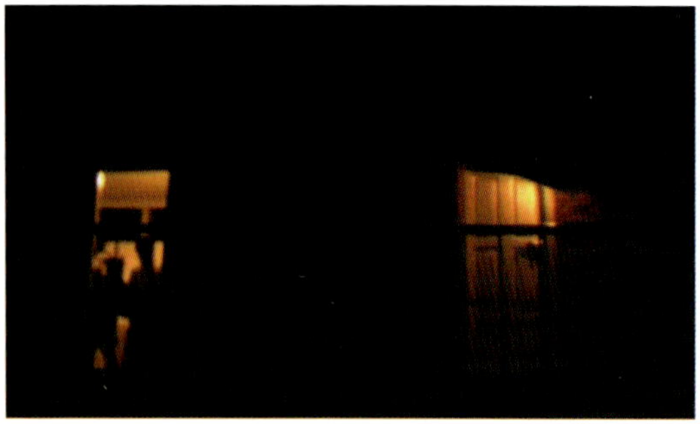

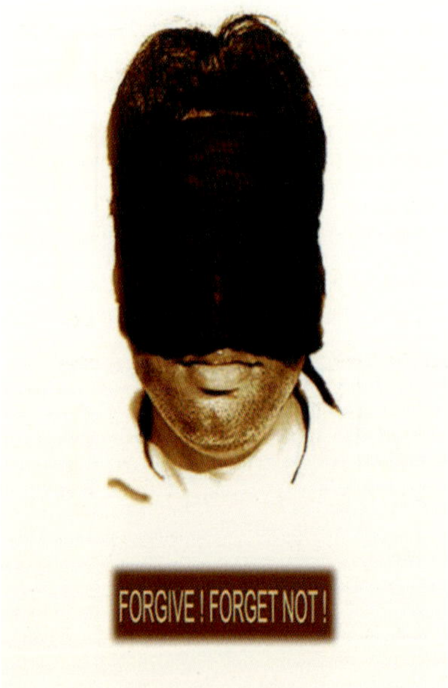

Scenes from Pranay Limbu's *Forgive! Forget Not!*

Ghimire said he was stripped naked and repeatedly ducked head first into a tub of filthy water before being given electric shocks until he fell unconscious. 'The waterboarding only happened twice, but I was severely beaten with a plastic pipe two or three times every day', said Ghimire.

Much of his experiences as an illegal detainee has been documented in a film by Pranay Limbu, *Forgive! Forget Not!*. The title of the film mirrors Ghimire's own feelings. Ghimire says it is the responsibility of the state and the Maoists to make public the names of all those who disappeared, were killed and tortured during the war, and to get the perpetrators to ask for forgiveness in public. In an interview with IPS, he said: 'No one has the right to forgive the perpetrators but the victims.' In another interview (with AFP) he was quoted as saying, 'The people in the barracks were soldiers following orders. If we start to try punishing these perpetrators, there will never be peace.'

Mirrors of Militarization

Mukul Sharma

You Kill, I Kill!

Dhaka, Bangladesh: It was the early morning of 25 February 2009, when sounds of gunshots, slogans and loudspeaker announcements began resounding for hours within the Bangladesh Rifles (BDR), Pilkhana headquarters in Dhaka. BDR Battalions had taken control of the barracks: they broke into the armoury, took all the weapons and started killing army personnel.

First, groups of armed jawans ambushed unarmed officers who were hiding and began shooting at them. Major General Shakil Ahmed was the first to be gunned down, followed by 16 other army officers. One group stormed in and killed the remaining army officers, who had not yet managed to hide. Another group went to the Major General's house, where they killed his wife, a female guest and a maidservant. They ransacked the house and looted valuables. More BDR personnel joined in. They ransacked other officers' homes, looted their valuables and took their families hostage. Another group of BDR personnel drove around in a jeep, chanting slogans supporting the killings. They used loudspeakers to brief journalists outside the Pilkhana gates, giving their reasons for the rebellion. According to media reports, they cited poor pay and conditions of service, and wanted senior BDR officers – not seconded army officers – to command them.

They massacred at least 74 people inside Pilkhana, including 57 army officers seconded to work as BDR commanders, 1 army soldier, 9 jawans (the lowest BDR rank) – who, according to BDR sources, were killed because they opposed the killings – and 3 female civilians. Three male civilians were killed outside Pilkhana. When the army moved in on 27th February, they found the bodies of army officers dumped in sewage manholes and buried in a makeshift mass grave in the Pilkhana compound. There were hostages held in horrifying conditions.

Several media reports and the government enquiry have suggested five main reasons for these killings: 'The mentality of not accepting the authority of the army had been dormant among BDR members for a long time'; 'resentment of the "luxurious" lifestyle of officials'; 'demands for increased border allowance, participation in UN peacekeeping missions, and a salary structure to match that of army officers'. And, on such flimsy grounds, they had had no hesitation in killing their 'own' people.

Bangladesh has several branches of army and armed forces that work closely with each other. The Bangladesh army is the land forces branch of the Bangladesh Armed Forces. Its primary mission is to provide the necessary forces and capabilities in support of Bangladesh's security and defence strategies, including defence against external attacks. However, the army is regularly used against 'internal' enemies. Bangladesh Rifles is a civilian force, primarily responsible for border security. It is also deployed alongside the police to uphold law and order in rural areas. The Rapid Action Battalion is a special police force, created in 2004, to tackle armed criminal activity. It is made up of police and seconded military personnel. And there are many more like these. But this does not deter them from killing each other.

This, however, is not the end of the story. We further encounter the killings of BDR people by the army in retaliation. Some time after this incident, the army moved in and took control of the headquarters. All BDR personnel were asked to come back to duty. Around 3,000 personnel were arrested, and there was no news of their whereabouts. There were allegations of torture, families were harassed, and at least 20 BDR personnel died in custody between 9 March and 6 May 2009. As of end 2009, the total count of BDR personnel who had died in custody stood at 55. Death after death in such a short span of time! Death by other means! Death continues.

You kill, I kill! This is the only language that we seem to know now, even within 'our family'.

My Killing is Better than Yours!

Kathmandu, Nepal: The Communist Party of Nepal (CPN) Maoist has been fighting a 'people's war' in Nepal since 1996, in which more than 12,000 people have died. The army and the police have been on one side, and the Maoist forces on the other. This 'people's war' has often used other terms to describe itself – class rivalry, class war, people's violence, resistance and protest – to justify killings, calling it a radical act. Language of course matters, but so does substance.

Dil Bahadur Kumal came from a poor ethnic Tharu family in Nawalparasi district. He was one of thirteen surviving children. His father, who has two wives, had twenty four children in all. Dil Bahadur Kumal grew up collecting firewood for the family from the local forest. Joining the army was a special opportunity for him, and even when his family pleaded with him to leave the military, he refused. He was unmarried and in his early twenties when, on 9 April 2009, there was a telephone message at the Thakurdhagar barracks, where Dil Bahadur Kumal was stationed, from a woman professing to be his sister, saying that his mother had died and that he should return home immediately. He was granted leave and set out straight away. That very night, a few miles from his home, Dil Bahadur Kumal was ambushed by the Maoists. His body was found shortly afterwards. He was not armed and was wearing civilian clothes. He had been blindfolded and his teeth were missing, as were one eye and an ear. He had been shot in the chest. His mother had *not*, in fact, died and no one from the family had telephoned him.

Shanker Sarki, a 29-year-old soldier, had spent six months in Congo with the UN peacekeeping operation as a military policeman. Under the UN mission, he was one among hundreds of multinational soldiers in Congo, observing compliance of the ceasefire, disengagement of forces and maintaining liaison with all members party to the ceasefire agreement. He returned to Nepal ten days before being killed on 15 May 2005. He had just been transferred to Nepalgunj and was about to leave his home, where he had been on one week's leave. He and his two friends were walking near his home when they were abducted by Maoists. Twelve armed men in civilian dress, some wearing masks and caps, intercepted the men. The victim's mother, who witnessed what happened, followed the group. She was told to go away and was asked, 'Why did you send your son to join the army?' Out of fear, neighbours did not contact the military or the police for help. Shanker Sarki's friends were released. His own body was found a few hours later on a road nearby. His gold ring and watch were missing. He was survived by a 22-year-old widow, Shanti Sarki, and two daughters aged 2 and 5.

Target the defence forces first, the police, and then the army; target political rivals, the opposition, dissenters; target the non-combatants, including military and police officers when off-duty; target the families of soldiers and the police. On 14 June 2005, six family members of soldiers, including three women and a 1-year-old child, were found dead, two days after they had been abducted by Maoists in Kailali district. Their bodies were reported to have been badly mutilated. *My (Maoist) killing is superior to the killings by the police and the army!* Such a paradigm of war distorts the relationship between change and politics.

We Will be Killed!

> 'THEY CAME FIRST for the Communists and I didn't speak up because I wasn't a Communist.
>
> THEN THEY CAME for the Jews and I didn't speak up because I wasn't a Jew.
>
> THEN THEY CAME for the trade unionists and I didn't speak up because I wasn't a trade unionist.
>
> THEN THEY CAME for me and by that time no one was left to speak up.'
>
> – Pastor Martin Niemöller (1892–1984)

Colombo, Sri Lanka: Lasantha Wickrematunge, an outspoken critic of the Sri Lankan government and editor of the newspaper *Sunday Leader*, was shot and killed on his way to work on 8 January 2009. He died a few hours later of his injuries. The *Sunday Leader* is known in Sri Lanka for its articles exposing political corruption in privatization deals, and for drawing attention to human rights abuses committed during the war between the government and the LTTE. Shortly before he was killed, Lasantha Wickrematunge wrote an obituary predicting his own death. 'People often ask me why I take such risks and tell me it is a matter of time before I am bumped off,' he wrote. 'Of course I know that: it is inevitable. But if we do not speak out now, there will be no one left to speak for those who cannot.'

Reporting and writing on war, on the military, and the suppression of truth can be fatal. Journalists have been killed, physically assaulted, abducted and harassed by both government personnel and members of armed groups. At least 15 journalists have been killed since 2006 and more than 20 have fled the country. The perpetrators of such crimes have never been brought to justice.

As recently as 24 January 2010, journalist and political analyst Prageeth Eknaligoda went missing from Homagama, near the capital Colombo. He disappeared shortly after leaving work at the *Lanka-e-News* office. Local residents told the Sri Lankan press that they saw a white van without numberplates close to his house at around this time. In the days leading up to his disappearance, he had told a close friend that he believed he was being followed. When his wife reported his disappearance to the Homagama police, she was herself detained for several hours. Prageeth Eknaligoda had been actively reporting on political events leading up to the January presidential elections, including threats to opposition activists. This was not the first time he had disappeared. On 27 August 2009, he was abducted by a group that arrived in a white van. He was bundled into the van, blindfolded, handcuffed and taken to an unknown destination before being released the following day.

There are strange cases. A high court in Sri Lanka sentenced journalist Jayaprakash Sittampalam Tissainayagam to twenty years rigorous imprisonment in September 2009, for writing and publishing articles that criticized the government's treatment of Sri Lankan Tamil civilians affected by the war. The court said the articles incited 'racial hatred' and promoted terrorism. Tissainayagam was the first Sri Lankan journalist to be formally charged and convicted under the country's draconian Prevention of Terrorism Act (PTA) for his writings. He was arrested in March 2008 and detained in police custody for five months before he was charged with an offence. He and two colleagues were eventually accused of bringing the government into disrepute, and inciting racial and ethnic animosities through material published in a short-lived magazine called the *North East Herald.*

Tissainayagam's indictment was based on passages from two articles. A July 2006 editorial headlined 'Providing Security to Tamils Now Will Define Northeastern Politics of the Future' concluded by saying: 'It is fairly obvious that the government is not going to offer them any protection. In fact it is the state security forces that are the main perpetrator of the killings.' And a second article, published in November 2006, accused the government of starving and endangering civilians in the town of Vaharai to further political and strategic military objectives. The state prosecutor also put forth, as evidence, an alleged confession made by Tissainayagam while in police custody. Tissainayagam maintains that he was tortured by the police and that the confession was forced. The court, however, ruled that the evidence was admissible. Under the PTA, the burden of proof rests with the accused to prove that the confession was made under duress or torture.

These wars and conflicts, involving the government, the army, the police and the LTTE, have a corrosive effect on democratic rights, such as the right to information, the right to expression and the right to dissent. It often leads to a situation where, as Sunada Deshapriya, a Sri Lankan journalist, says, 'Everyone is censoring themselves, some willingly because they support the system, and some unwillingly.'

Wounds

Surviving Massacre

Parthiv Shah • Sohrab Hura • Abdul Rahman Roslan

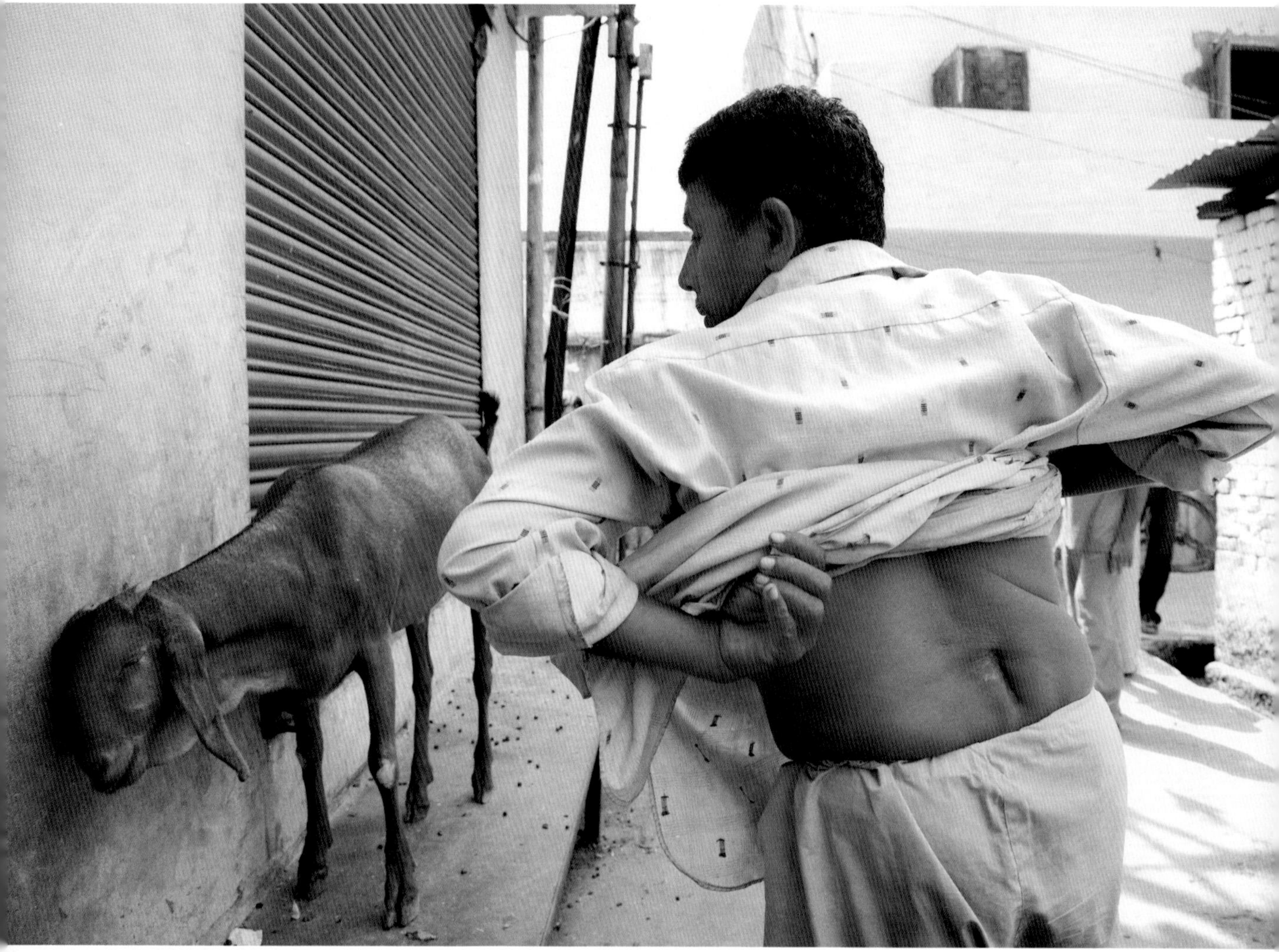

Mohd. Usman who survived the massacre turns his wound to the camera. He was the third to be shot near the canal in Hashimpura. From the *Hashimpura* series by Parthiv Shah, India, 2008.

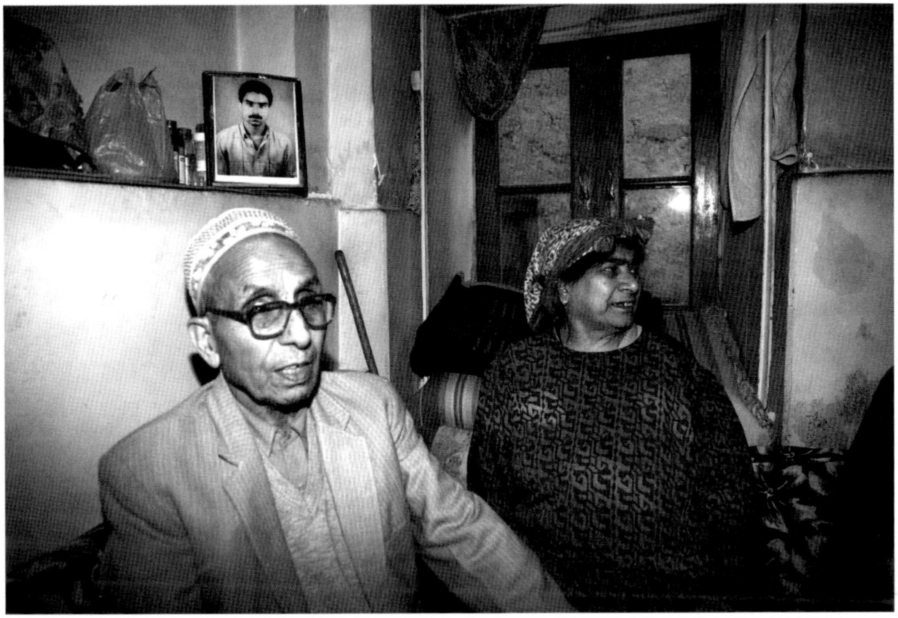

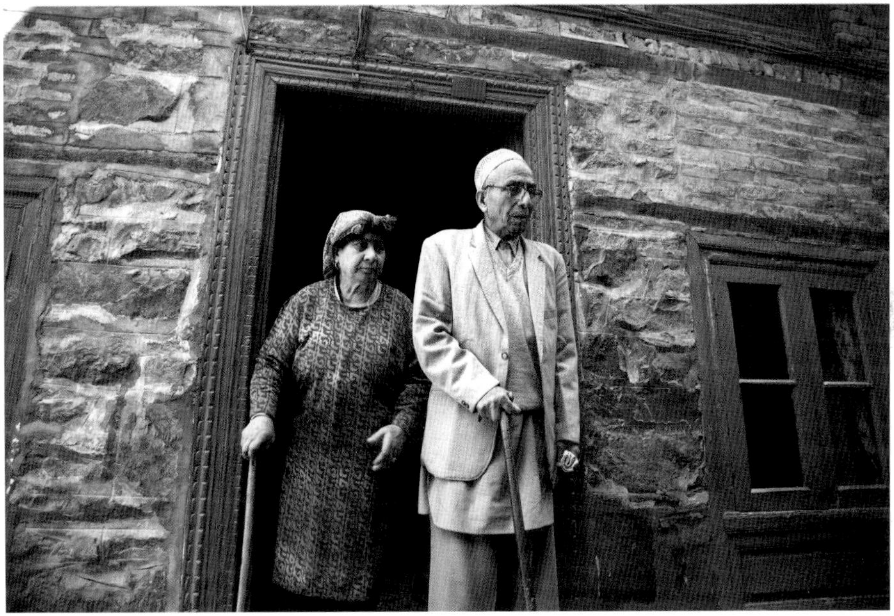

75-year-old Ghulam Mohd. Shah and his wife, from Rainawari, Kashmir. Their son, Shameem, was killed in 1990 by Rashtriya Rifles, and they have no other children. They lodged an FIR, 1260 F-90. So far they have received no respite from any quarter. By Parthiv Shah, India, 2008.

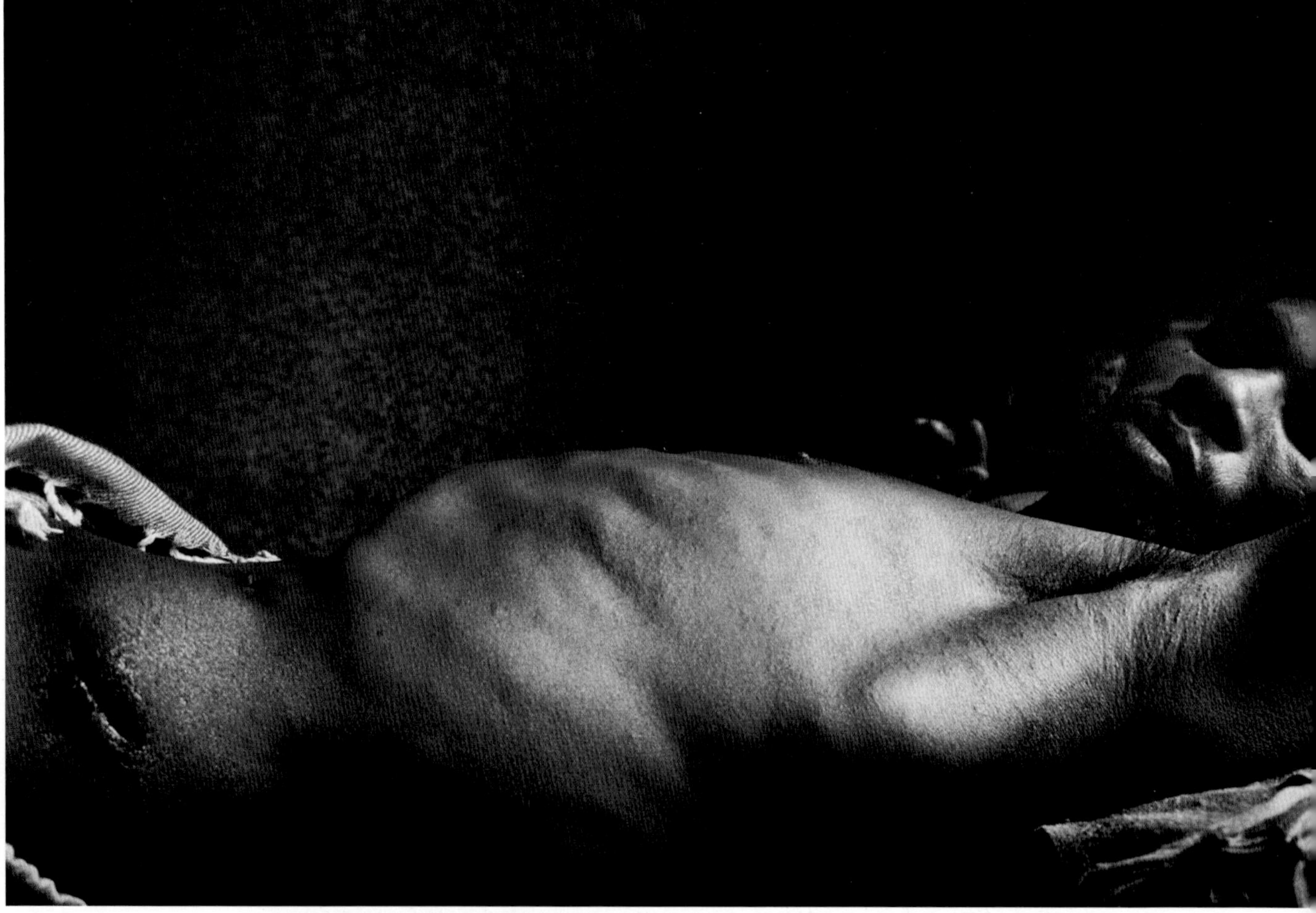

Kalinganagar, Orissa, 2 January 2006: The police opened fire on unarmed people, including women and children, who were protesting against the inauguration of a newly built boundary wall around a piece of disputed land by an Indian steel major. Thirteen were killed and several seriously injured. Ganesh Banara was one of the survivors. He was shot through his stomach. By Sohrab Hura, India, 2006.

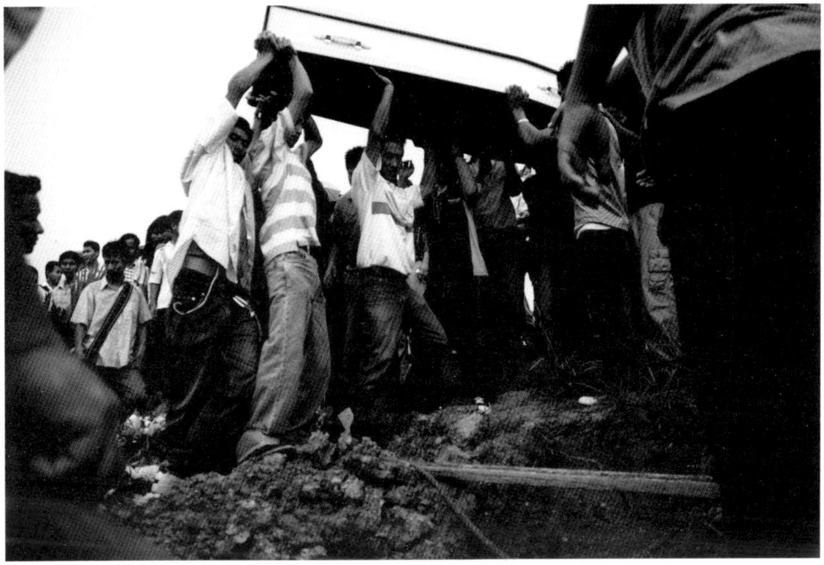

Malaysia, October 2007: The refugee community offers support to each other during a funeral procession. Chin refugees from Burma have sought shelter in Kuala Lumpur, the capital of Malaysia. By Abdul Rahman Roslan, Malaysia, 2007, DRIK.

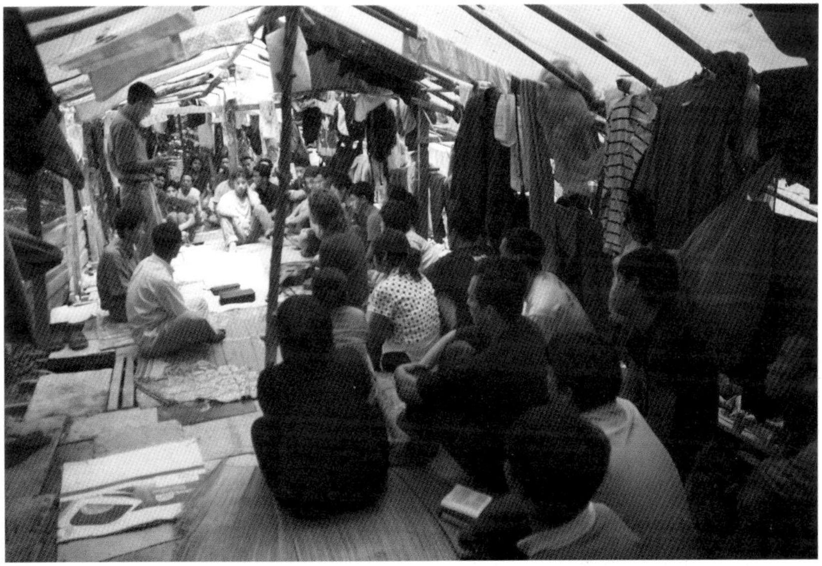

Malaysia, October 2007: Chin refugees gather in a makeshift camp on the outskirts of the city of Kuala Lumpur. By Abdul Rahman Roslan, Malaysia, 2007, DRIK.

Hidden Haemorrhage

Inder Salim

A thin gauze of words,
In Kashmir, is Kashmiri;
Anything else is more or less
A bullet proof jacket.

Death penetrates,
Wear what you want, Body
Makes it clear that it chooses
To be on the negotiation table.

Questions could have found
Right answers in those Hammams
Where we all are naked; but alas,
Dead solutions perform: the skin.

Even, during the month of Ramazan,
The thread from one's bed-room
To the woodcutter's axe on logs
Never cuts.

Although skilled to cut the Bread
And serve his dependants.
He would love to talk about his
hidden haemorrhage.

History, like camera on the crane
Stooping, while omitting out
The bullying players; blades of grass were
Never so magnified.

The Marks of Toil

Sohrab Hura

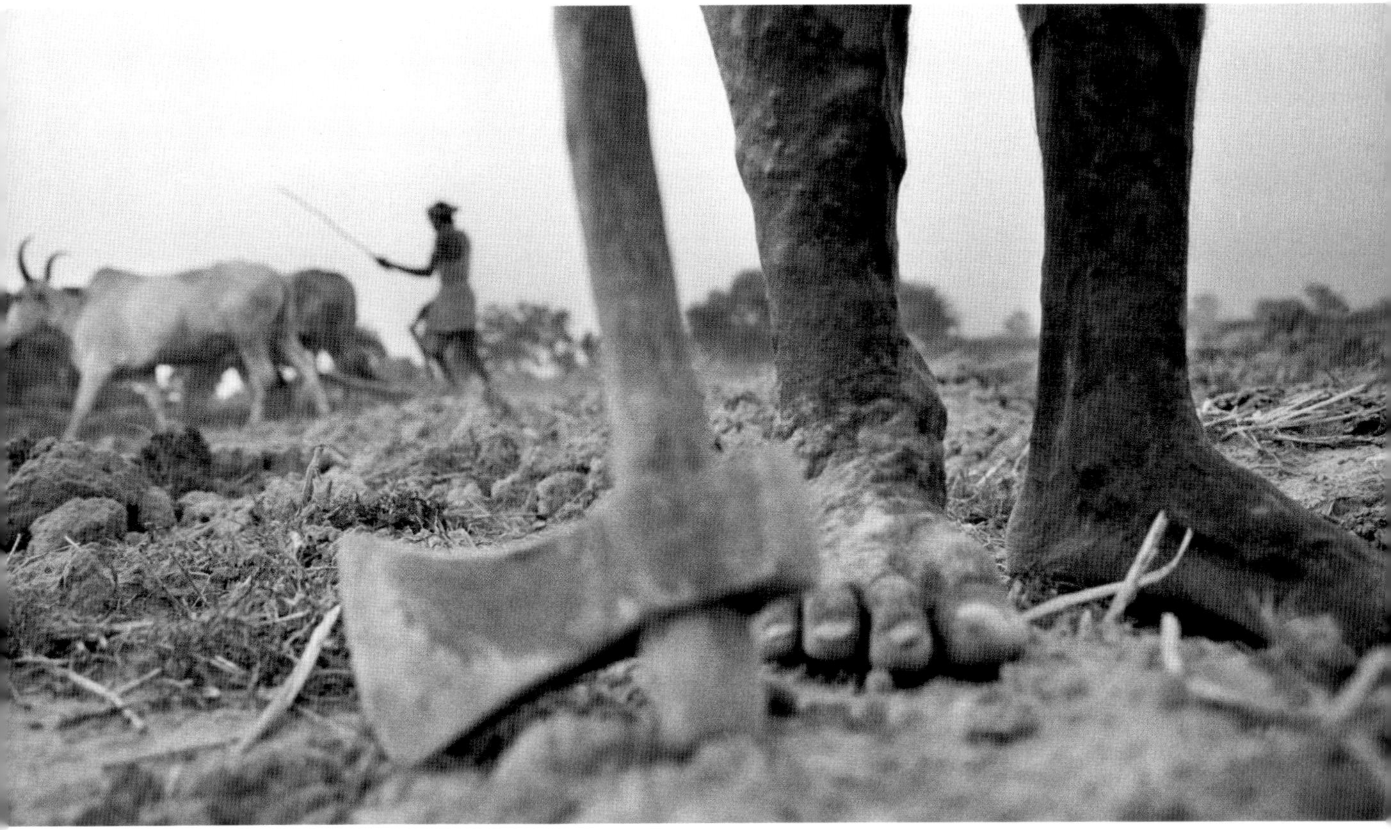

Bokaro, Jharkhand: Two brothers toil hard for subsistence on their small piece of land. The soil is infertile and with the absence of irrigation, hardly anything grows. This is the situation in an overwhelmingly large part of rural India where innumerable farmers still struggle on subsistence agriculture and the land remains the only source of livelihood. By Sohrab Hura, India.

The *Chaddar* and the Mask

Suhas Borker

Please remove the new mask
There is no need for that *chaddar* at the *Dargah*
We know you must woo us to be anointed
  again
the high priest of the temple.

Our pen is not dipped in vitriol
It drips our blood
burning in the pyres in our heart
etched on the dusty coffins of our dreams.

Gujarat was a mistake you say
But you will not touch the perpetrator
who cut up our womb with
cold calculated scalpel swipes
and disrobed by Vikramaditya's dictat
still struts unfazed and brazenly spewing
the devil's venom on our soul.

We will not let it happen again you say
But you will not rein in
your storm troopers who ravage
the psyche of our living
and the peace of our dead.

Remember what the Sardar said:
You may not have killed Gandhi
but you created the laboratory
which brought forth a Godse.

You say you are the harbinger of peace
with Pakistan and Musharraf
But please do tell us for Ram's sake
what that has to do with *quam* ?
Do you want to reopen the wounds of partition
each time you speak of peace to us?

We ring the Church bell
but there is an eerie silence
When JP died you said
He reminded you of Christ on the Cross
Please show that Cross to your storm troopers
while we await the next assault.

Please make a pilgrimage
to lay that *chaddar* on the Best Bakery graves
before time peels away the smug-mask of history
Remember your ashes will be swept away
but our bones will remain here forever.

Nanaji's Disappearance

Showkat Kathjoo

After the year 1991, my sensibilities and responses to events in life could not remain the same. I remember growing up with a deep-seated sense of not only cultural but religious confluence, and sliding between these two. The year 1991 began altering that negotiation. The turmoil left a vacuum in our minds – a wound that is still fresh and yet to be healed. That year, when the Valley witnessed mass migration to the plains, every household was a witness to pain and suffering. The urgency caught the Pandits of the Valley in its clutches. Such events were unheard of in the vicinity of my space, around the orbits of which revolved secure and secular living experiences. Ever since my involvement with this cultural space, I have played a part that I inherited from my ancestors, in which I solely believed. This space often lurks in my memory and I am amazed to realize that each time I remember it, I do so with greater clarity and precision.

The Razdan family was not merely living adjacent to my house but was a part of us, as an extended family and they considered themselves to be so. Ramannath, alias Nanaji, of the Razdan family worked in the Forecast Department. The man, not willing to leave this space, created a difference of opinion within his immediate family, consisting of his wife, son and daughter. The three of them left with the wave of Pandit migration, but Nanaji decided to continue living next to us. It was after long negotiations that his family yielded to let him stay back. This extended the responsibility into our family to take care of him. I can still recall the grief and sense of loss which his death brought not only to his family, far away in the plains, but to all of us, including others in the neighbourhood, who knew Nanaji by face or by name. Like my community folk of Rainawari, I am yet to reconcile with this loss.

I remember the ease with which Nanaji would enter into cross-cultural negotiations in his personal space, which was a sign of a larger cultural collective and integration.

This nourishing confluence would facilitate us to overcome prejudices on either side. Despite hardened resistance in religious affairs elsewhere, his was a departure of ease and liberty. I do not hesitate in referring to the liberal enthusiasm shared by many others like Nanaji in that period in our area. I have known the ease with which Nanaji would come on the occasion of Eid-ul-Zuha to participate in the feast. I grew up learning this ease and feelings that increased one's understanding of the complexities of life in cultural admixture, rather than in alienation or hostility.

It was an unfortunate day when Nanaji was dragged away by two armed men. I remember only too clearly how he was being dragged (and I still feel the pain), and then the struggle between my uncle and the armed men to let Nanaji go. This was not a mere demonstration of sorrow but of heartfelt human compassion. With rage, as they lurched at him, my uncle was trying hard to loosen the clutches fastened upon Nanaji's neck. As their faces became apoplectic with rage, one of them grabbed my uncle's shirt, which, by his violent gesture, was ripped open, tearing the fabric and throwing him off balance in a sudden, angry bout. Before my uncle could regain his posture, the armed man took a huge swing at his head and fisted him down in his by now uncontrollable rage, threatening to kill him. I immediately propped up and secured my uncle who had fallen on his back, and whose nose by now was spouting an alarming red stream of blood. The two men went away, dragging innocent Nanaji. I kept staring in that direction long after my uncle regained his posture. Nanaji was taken away without even giving him a chance to bid farewell to any of us. Had he ever forecast his own death at the hands of time? Has his not bidding farewell left us in doubt about his returning? I cannot remove the image of his departure from my mind since the questions it has put forth continue to confront me.

There is no doubt that the 1991 mass migration was an act of brutalization, causing angst to the Muslims as well as the Pandits in the Valley. No one was left unaffected by the violence. This puts me at the crossroads to forecast the future of the Valley in reconciliation with whatever is lost – a valuable cultural legacy, a secular space and common spiritual strands.

Who Will Muzzle the Cry from Vidarbha?

Suhas Borker

Eight more Kisan suicides in one day
Gajanan Sadashiv Chaudhari of Nandura Khurd
Atul Manohar Sabre of Manakwadi
Naresh Bakaram Meshram of Walgaon
Gajanan Babarao Thombre of Amti
Laxman Bapurao Chaudhari of Barzadi
Natthu Raghoji Shrirame of Dahoti
Shaligram Farfat of Khandvi
Ajabrao Ramji Sonone of Sukanda

The count this year, till now
Nine hundred and nine.
Thousands and thousands more
are on a vigil unto death.
How many more Gajanans will it take
for the altar bells to toll?

Do you want to kill yourself here?
Or migrate to the Megapolis to a slow death?
Who is next? Please line up.
A firing squad
with silencer muzzled guns
will be more painless, silent and instant.

Your cries will never pass muster
through the cordons of the Temple
usurped by pygmies
wallowing in farcical one-upmanship.

There is a cost to everything
a price to pay
someone, somewhere, someday will pay for this.
It won't be long!
It won't be long!

Burma Headed the Wrong Way

Daniel Pepper

Thousands of displaced villagers spend their lives on the run, choosing to wander relentlessly through the teeming jungle rather than live under the repression of the Burmese military regime. 'Living under their control means forced labour', said Saw Pa Pwe's sister-in-law, Naw Pi Htoo, 44, who lost three of her seven children to disease in these malaria-infested hills. Their family and about 60 others arrived in a refugee camp inside Burma near the Thai border late September 2006, after a twelve-day trek through the jungle, subsisting on handfuls of boiled rice and bamboo shoots.

Since 1996, the United States and the European Union have implemented various economic sanctions against the military regime, citing the house arrest of democracy advocate and 1991 Nobel Peace Prize winner Aung San Suu Kyi for ten of the last seventeen years. But this is a regime notoriously unresponsive to outside pressure, and public rhetoric notwithstanding, certain signs point to it becoming more reclusive, not less. 'This is a regime impervious to outside influence – whether positive or negative. They don't care what the world thinks of them.'

The 2006 military offensive in eastern Burma, against the Karen ethnic minority, was the worst that was seen in ten years, displacing about 18,000 people since the end of last year, according to the Thailand Burma Border Consortium, an advocacy group based in Bangkok. Karen rebels have been fighting for autonomy in eastern Burma for half a century in one of the longest-running insurgencies in the world.

'The military's strategy for the last ten years has been to bring the entire civilian population under direct control for forced labour and monitoring', said Kevin Heppner with the Karen Human Rights Group, another advocacy group based in Thailand. 'And everyone who lives beyond that immediate control has to be relocated or killed.'

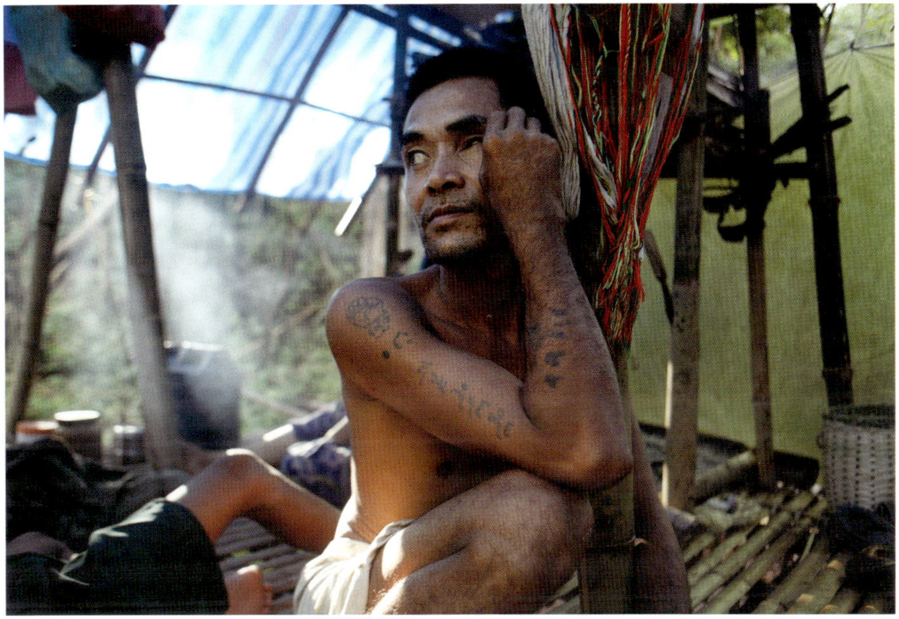

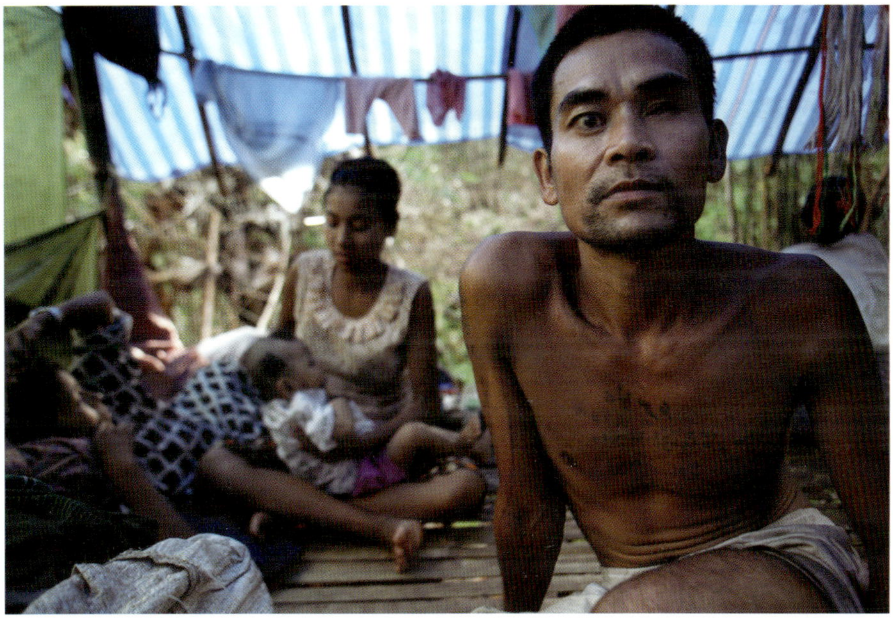

One of the many thousands of refugees living in the Burmese jungle, this man also has to live with the brutal loss of an eye. By Daniel Pepper, USA.

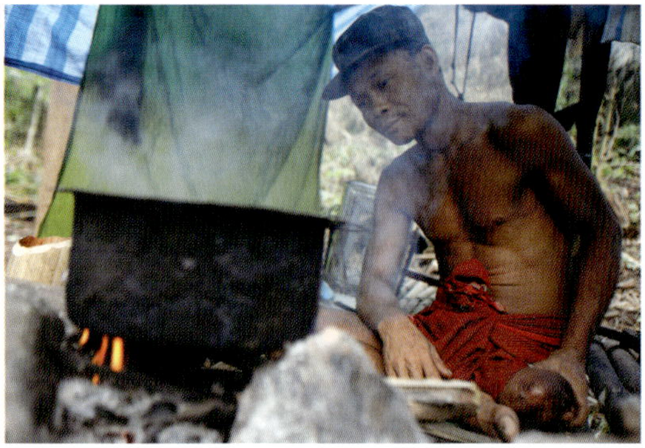

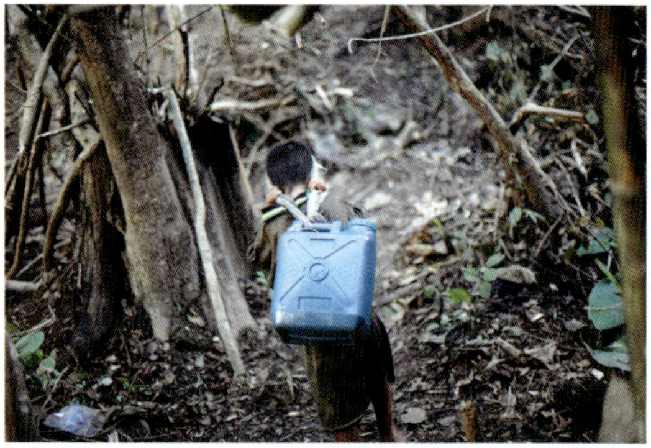

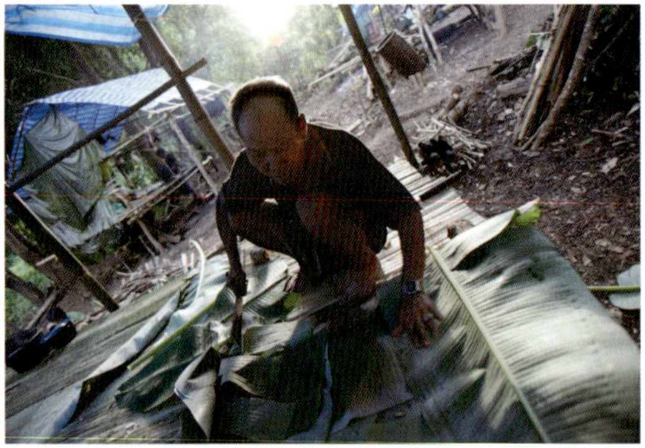

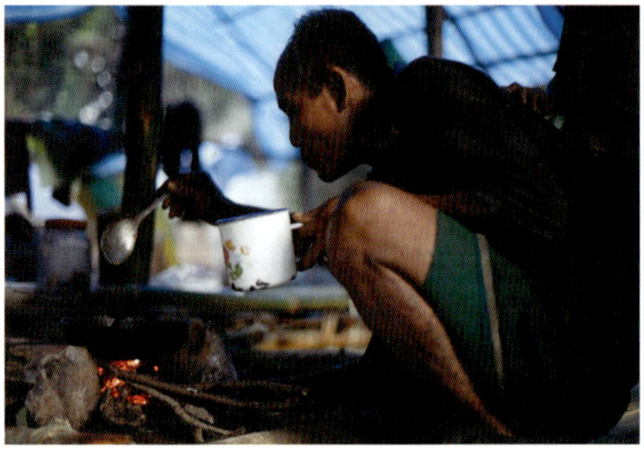

Despite living in the jungle camps, life must go on: meals must be cooked, roofs must be thatched, water must be fetched. By Daniel Pepper, USA.

Half a million Burmese are displaced within eastern Burma, of which only a fraction have access to cross-border medical care on the militarized Thai–Burma border.

Any foreign direct investment in Burma's natural gas fields by governments, such as by India and China, and companies, results in investment in further repression and displacement rather than in health and education.

(Extract from Daniel Pepper's article originally published as 'Burma Headed the Wrong Way, Watchers Say/Regime Seen as Increasingly Repressive and Isolated'. Copyright 2006 SF Chronicle, Sunday, 15 October 2006, Chronicle Foreign Service)

The Gauze and the Gallows

The Spy, the *Quran* and the Death Sentence

Gowhar Fazili

Kashmir Singh was an Indian spy. He was caught by the Pakistani authorities and sentenced to death in 1973. He spent 35 years of his life in Pakistani prisons before he was released by a presidential pardon by General Pervez Musharraf, then President of Pakistan. Gowhar Fazili from Amnesty International India interviewed him and his wife, Paramjit Kaur, in their village Nangal Choran, Punjab.

Gowhar Fazili (GF): This interview is for a book about people who have been given the death penalty and those who have gone missing in our part of the world. The book argues that we should legally abolish all forms of death penalty.
Kashmir Singh (KS): I shall answer your questions in Urdu. I have come back after thirty five years in Pakistan and forgotten much of my Punjabi!

GF: Tell us how you came to be in prison.
KS: I used to go to Pakistan to do intelligence work for the Indian Government. I used to be sent to photograph particular strategic sites. After some time the Pakistanis arrested me. I had been careless. My case was registered in the military court and I was given the death penalty. For three years I was kept in different Pakistani jails, then for seventeen years I was serving a life imprisonment sentence. I was always kept handcuffed and my legs were always shackled with 15-pound iron chains. I still have their marks on my body. I was kept in a 7x7 feet cell and was not even able to see sunlight. There was a small hole in the door of the cell through which they used to pass me water, tea and food. The food in jail was very good. We got chicken, beef and *chapattis*. I think they are soft towards Indians! For one-and-a-half months in Lahore I shared my cell but for most of the thirty four years, I was kept alone in my cell.

GF: How did you manage to survive in those conditions for thirty five years?
KS: If a person has a strong will, then

nothing is impossible. I used to read the *Quran-e-Pak* all the time. I never tried to escape but for thirty five years I hoped to get out.

GF: Did people talk to you?
KS: People did talk to me. If that wasn't there I would certainly have lost my sanity. I also thought of God a lot. One who remembers God does not feel scared. Most importantly, reciting the *Surah Yaseen* [a chapter in the *Quran*] heals every worry. I fasted regularly, and did the *tahjud* [early morning prayers]. They respected me for all this as they considered me a religious person. I used to sleep only after reciting all the *kalmias*. How many *kalmias* do you remember?

GF: Not even three I guess.
KS: [Much giggling] I remember all six.

GF: Who taught you so much from the *Quran*?
KS: There was a man accused of murder. At that time for half an hour we would have to clean the toilets in each other's cell. Within the twenty three days I went to his room I learnt it all. Then I taught the *Quran* to others for eighteen years.

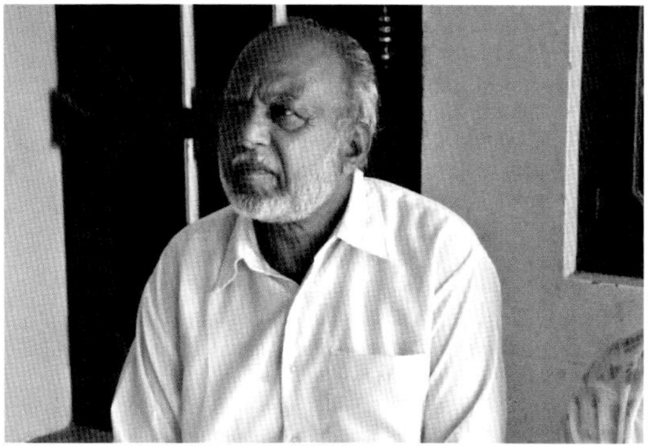

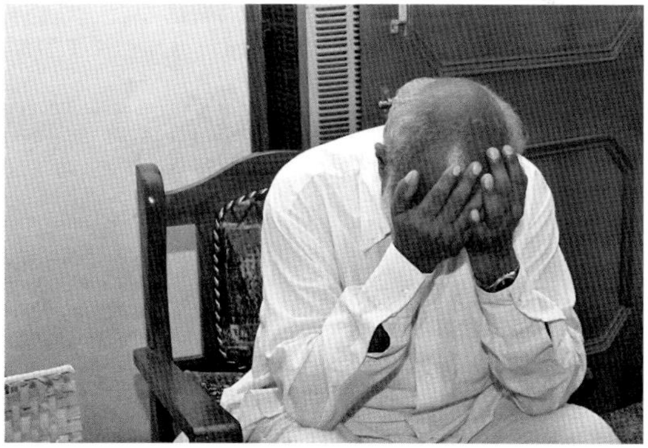

Kashmir Singh breaks down during the interview as he recollects his days in prison. By Gowhar Fazili, India.

GF: We would like you to come to Kashmir some day.
KS: Oh, if you invite me, I will surely come. Where in Kashmir are you from? The Valley! Oh I have lived in Baramulla, Chowkibal and Teetwal, I have seen Kashmir from both sides. I served as an army commando and crossed the five rivers from both sides of the border!

GF: You stayed thirty five years in prison and saw it all?
KS: I have seen all of Pakistan. Lahore was like a second home. I have even gone to Afghanistan and Iran.

GF: Do you remember specific incidents from those years you would like to share?
KS: When I was first caught they interrogated me for six months. Despite being tortured I did not speak up and I was still pretending to be Mohammed Rafeeq. One day I was in the cell sleeping when a *havaldar* came to me and told me to tell the truth that I was Kashmir Singh. His name was Saadiq Baloch and he was a Pathan from Peshawar. I continued to deny that I was Kashmir Singh.

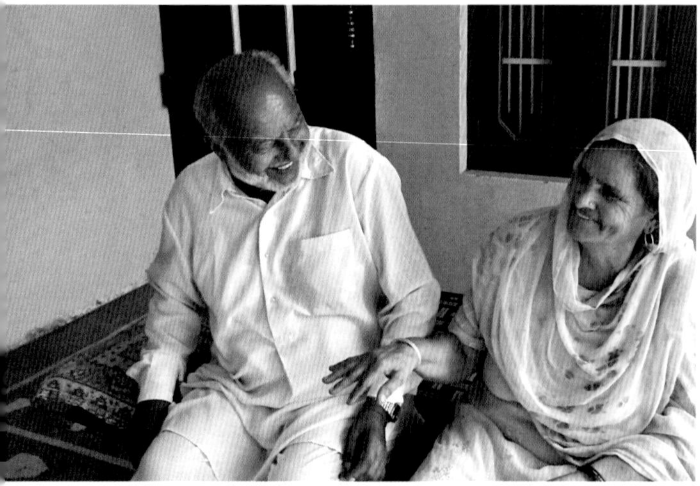

Kashmir Singh shares a lighter moment with his wife, Paramjit Kaur. By Gowhar Fazili, India.

Baloch released me from my chains for a while. The major who ran the prison came to the cell at that point and saw me like that, and demanded to know what was going on. But Baloch made some excuse and covered up. At night the Pathan came again. I asked him, 'Have you gone mad?' He said, 'I have stayed as a *jangi qaidi* [prisoner of war] in Bangladesh. My son was 11 years old when he died and I found out only years later.'

Then he said. 'By 10 o'clock tomorrow you will be shot. They have given me ten rounds to shoot you. We will take you to the round room on the hills and you will be shot. There is no way you can escape unless you do what I tell you to do.'

'When I take you there I will loosen your chains. We will be accompanied by two guards. I want you to kick me on the feet, trip me as we are climbing and run away. Or else you will not be saved.' Then he went away. The next morning, at a minute past 10 am, the Pathan came to take me. It was raining on the hill. I asked to speak to someone in charge and then confessed that yes, I am Kashmir Singh from India. My life was spared that day.

GF: What do you think about the death sentence?
KS: There are thousands sentenced to death in Pakistan and very few are non-Pakistani. Ideally a country should not have the death penalty and it certainly should not impose it on someone who is not a citizen of the country. I did my duty by my government. It was only my good fortune and Ansar *bhai*'s [the Pakistani human rights activist, Ansar Burney] kindness that he took up my case to the President and my life got spared.

Ideally, there should be no death penalty at all. But in Pakistan there is Muslim law and the *Quran* says God can forgive all crimes but not murder. Only the murder victim's family can forgive the crime. The murderer might even pay blood money and have the family withdraw charges. That might work, but otherwise for Muslims, the response to murder is murder.

Yes, there should be no death penalty. I have heard that Pakistan is also going to abolish the death penalty, is that true? As if Ali Zardari [President of Pakistan] wants to abolish the death penalty in Pakistan!

GF: Yes, they are saying that all the persons who are on death row, nearly 7,000 people, will be pardoned.
KS: For those who are on death row lots of time gets wasted. Some wait for twenty years. The families suffer in the meanwhile, begging before authorities for pardon. Though Muslims may not agree, the work you are doing is good. You should give them [Pakistanis] some advice.

Interview with Paramjeet Kaur, Kashmir Singh's wife

GF: How did you deal with your husband's absence for so long?
PK: I worked in the fields and did all kinds of work.

GF: When you came to know that your husband has been given the death penalty, how did you react?
PK: I experienced terrible feelings all the time. I had a lot of responsibilities and worried about my small children, three children all under the age of 10. I wondered how I would be able to fend for them.

GF: How did you manage to keep the house running during that period?

PK: My brother used to give me money to run the house. The government did not give us a single penny.

GF: How did you hear that he had been given the death penalty?
PK: For eight years we did not know anything about him or his whereabouts. In 1983, a prisoner who just been freed from Pakistani jail came to Firozepur. It was from him that we came to know that Kashmir Singh is still alive. After that we started our efforts to bring him back. Once we got a letter from him. Every now and then we used to get messages through prisoners who had been released. Otherwise we would have thought that he had died. The Indian government never helped us, neither at that time nor are they helping us now.

GF: His hanging was cancelled twice. Did you know anything about it?
PK: No! No! We knew nothing about what was happening with him in Pakistan.

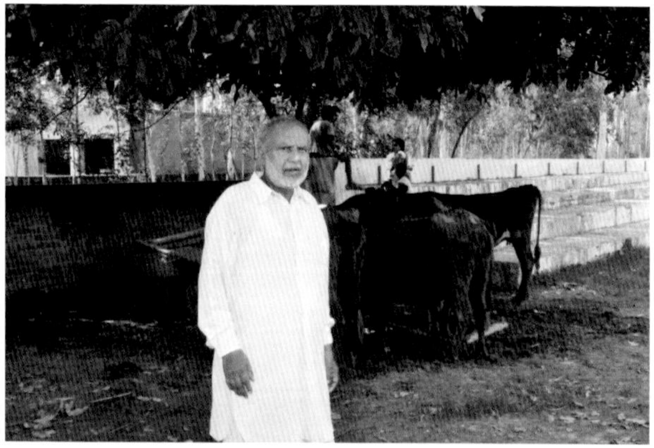

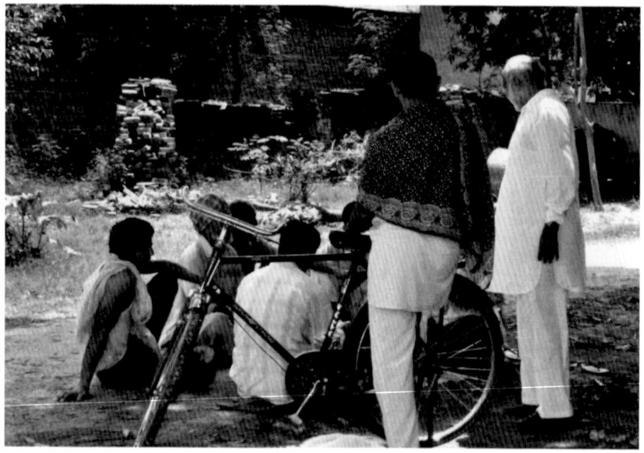

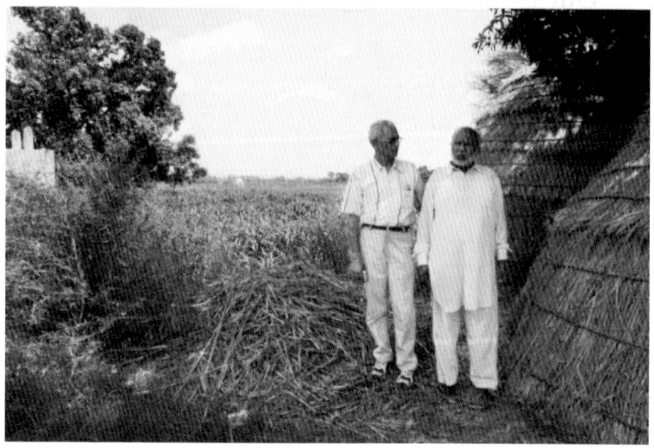

Kashmir Singh taking a stroll in his village in Nangal Choran, Punjab. By Gowhar Fazili, India.

A Crime and a Criminal

Sabrina Lall

Jessica Lall, a model in New Delhi, was working as a celebrity barmaid at a party when she was shot dead on 29 April 1999 by Manu Sharma, the son of Vinod Sharma, a wealthy Congress politician in Haryana. In this piece, written in 2008, Sabrina Lall, Jessica's sister, gives her views on the death penalty and the Indian legal system from the point of view of a 'murder victim family'. Initially acquitted by a trial court in Delhi in 2006, Manu Sharma has now been given the life sentence by the Supreme Court, on 19 April 2010 for the murder committed eleven years ago.

Our first reaction after finding out who killed Jessica Lall was shock because things like these don't happen in the normal course of life, and, of course, that the person who did it was a politician's son and was influential also scared us to a certain extent because then we knew what we were up against.

My family was never really keen on the revenge factor, it was more about punishing the boy – making sure that he was held accountable for what he did and punished accordingly. It wasn't about lynching or hanging or any such thing. It was more about acknowledging the fact that Manu Sharma had shot Jessica and punishing him for the same.

The only other form of punishment would have been life imprisonment as there is no other punishment for this – it's either life or death.

We were never for the death penalty. It could have been because of our Christian upbringing where forgiveness is a huge part of the religion or because of the take we had on it, as I always felt that killing him would be more of a punishment for his family than for him. If you want somebody to realize their mistake and do something, then you need to punish the boy and not the family.

The punishment that one wants to be given to the criminal is very personal. I don't blame anybody for wanting the death penalty or wanting someone hung if they have taken the life of a loved one. Personally I do not believe in the death penalty, because I do believe that the death penalty is more of a punishment for the people who are left behind, the loved ones rather than the person himself.

My fight for justice was very clear, that's exactly what it was – justice. I wanted the state to acknowledge that Manu Sharma shot Jessica. I didn't want a question mark hanging over his head for the rest of his life, of whether he did it or didn't, because we all knew that he had done it. The idea was for the state to acknowledge the murder, and that the state should punish him and make him pay for what he did.

The struggle involved a lot of things. Mentally, physically and emotionally, it took a toll on the entire family. I have lost my mom and dad in the bargain. They couldn't take the stress and the strain of it for so many years. But I managed to bear the brunt of it without collapsing or breaking down.

It was like a mission that had to be completed because there were too many cases in our country where these kinds of people were getting away with it, and some-one somewhere had to be held accountable for something like this. I think Jessica's case has changed the thinking of the judiciary to a certain extent because you can see that after it a lot of judgments have been passed where people have been convicted. It's a mind-set people have that the moment somebody like a politician's son is involved in a case, he is going to get away with it. These guys have all the money and power in the world, and you are just an ordinary middle-class family. That concept is wrong. I never accepted or agreed with that concept. I believed that the truth had to come out and something had to be done. That's what kept me going, and I kept my wits and will power alive.

I do not believe in the death penalty. I do not believe that the state has the right to take life. I do not believe that. I wouldn't have cared if he had received a sentence of five years or twenty years. It wasn't about the quantum of punishment as much as it was about acknowledging the fact that some-body had done something wrong and punishing him. Whether he is a politician's son or somebody on the road, it should be the same.

I don't think that having a network of people wanting punishment, but at the same time not wanting the death penalty to be given, would make much of a difference, because the courts decide the quantum of punishment and in our legal system the death penalty is given in the rarest of rare cases. It might not have any effect on the legal system.

The Slayers and the Slain

Chittaroopa Palit

My feelings about capital punishment have not changed since I was old enough to think about such things. I have always felt that to hang a person for a crime is a futile act, fraught with malice, serving no purpose and opposed to the essential sanctity of life. Nothing in my experience, including my parents' murder, has changed that.

When the telephone call came, I was in a meeting of women activists in Raipur. 'There has been a burglary in M-6, you must leave for Delhi immediately', the friend who had called up said. 'Again?' I asked, amused (the last time, there had been a theft when my parents had gone to Calcutta for a visit). 'What did they take this time?'

He repeated, 'It's serious. You have to leave for Delhi immediately.' 'Why must I go to Delhi? I'll just speak to Daddy and Ma.' 'They are not there', Rakesh said. 'Not there?' I asked. 'Then where are they?' 'They were injured during the burglary.' 'Are they in hospital?' I asked. He kept quiet.

Puzzled, I put down the phone and called my uncle's home, close to our house in Delhi. My aunt picked up the phone. 'Where are you Silvy?' she asked. 'Come right away, your parents have been murdered.'

It was difficult to comprehend what she was saying. My parents, so full of life, of love, murdered? Only four days ago, I had been in Delhi with them at a cousin's wedding. After the wedding, my mother, while driving me to the station to catch the train, was unable to resist, even at her age of 55 years, racing another car down the road. I remember my father, on the last night I spent with them at home, telling my mother, 'She's going away tomorrow, ask her to sleep here with you. I'll sleep in the outside room.' My mother beseeching me at the station, 'You'll come home next month, won't you, for your birthday?' Me replying, irritated. 'No, I'll come in April, not before that. As if I don't have any work to do.'

Now here I was, four days later, going home, crushed under an impossible weight pushing me down. And the only people I could have turned to, in order to comprehend this terrible thing that had happened, were gone. Now one would always be with strangers, in exile, for the rest of one's life. Always correct, proper, gallant, with no one to make unreasonable claims on.

There had been painters in our house, apparently, working late on the evening of 21 January 1993. My mother, returning from a walk, was killed by them first. My father, coming in later and let in by the painters, after that. My aunt, shrill with loss and anger, told me and my twin sister, my only sibling who had flown down from the US where she taught, 'It's all your mother's fault. She was never careful, never cautious. Always chatting with strangers, with workmen. Now see what happened!'

My sister and I turned to each other and laughed. We thought of our parents crying in our home in Gauhati, when we were about 4 years old, as the body of our brother was brought in. The speeding school bus had braked in time, so as not to run him over. But the fall from the cycle which he was learning to use had been enough to kill him instantly. We left him under the gaze of the mighty Brahmaputra, his body consigned to flames. We thought of how our parents had cherished us and protected us from their sorrow, mourning their first-born and trying to overcome their loss in the only way possible for anyone: by being industrious, working hard, accepting the loss and taking joy in simple things, with the deep scar of their loss uncorking them in some strange way, until they were unable any more to control or conceal their love, tenderness, vulnerability – unable to stop themselves from being moved by all things.

Memories of revelling in the red earth, fields of golden rice, the forests and streams of Chhattisgarh, the nippy cold and the mists of Lucknow, sitting out late in the evenings with our parents singing Rabindra Sangeet, seeing my mother correcting her students' test papers, then watching her set them aside to climb the guava tree in our garden to look for ripe guavas – the deep connectedness of our life seeped into us.

We laughed at our aunt's comment, my sister and I, thinking together – as we always did – through our childhood. Divining what was in each other's mind, we laughed in defence of the innocence of our parents. That afternoon, we wrote out a card to be printed, a card we sent to our friends and relatives, informing them of our parents' death. It said:

> We wish to inform you that our beloved parents, Shri Bimal Kumar Palit and Smt. Sulekha Palit, passed away in Delhi on the 21st of January 1993, under tragic circumstances. May love and trust prevail.

So this what I have to say about capital punishment: we live in this world only on the basis of trust, sheltered in the grace of the earth's bounty, cradled in other people's love and caring – both known and unknown. If some people have made up their minds to kill me and rob me, it is almost definite that I will be killed. There is no way we can defend ourselves against deliberate malice. There are not enough guns or guards in the world for that. The only way to break that malice, that intention to hurt, is by building more love and trust, by building a world that more firmly affirms the connectedness and the sacredness of all life. There is no other way.

When the painters, who were migrants from Faizabad in Uttar Pradesh, were apprehended, I went to meet them in police custody. While narrating the entire sequence of events to me, they kept referring to my parents as uncle and aunty. I could not understand how they could do that when, at the same time, they had treated them as less than human and killed them. I asked them, '*Lekin aapne unko mara kyon?*' ('But why did you kill them?') One of them said with a little derision, '*Hamne socha tha, bangla hai, mal milega, lekin kuch nahi mila. Hame kya malum ki kuch nahi milna.*' ('Looking at the house we thought it would be quite a loot, but we had no idea there would be nothing.') Another man, a 22-year-old, told me that he had been in love with a Hindu girl but had not been allowed to marry her. He showed me a tattoo of her name on his body, and said that was why he had become like that. I looked at him and wondered how a man who claimed to have known love and loss could injure and kill two people, especially people who had undeniably been kind to him and trusted him.

I wondered at this pathological condition, this act of malice and ignorance, the denial of the common humanity that they shared with my parents and all other human beings. Among other things, this pathology stems from the current economic mould and the deepening economic schisms, which have taken away all safety from everyone. This is a world in which capitalism, a skewed development process, and the markets are creating huge deprivations and denying aspirations, which people seek to redress by annihilating other people. Not to mention the fragmentation that has come from the communalization of society. Is it possible to look at the question of increasing crime, then, as an individual question, which can be resolved only by killing the wrong doer, without looking at the issues of employment, livelihood, dispossession of lands, forced migration, ghettoization of neighbourhoods and communities, the alienation of young adults, dire poverty, obscene affluence, and so on? I think not.

In 1982, Justice Bhagwati of the Supreme Court wrote thus in Bachan Singh vs. State of Punjab:

> A society which is truly cultured ... can never harbour a feeling of revenge against a wrong doer. On the contrary, it would try to reclaim the wrong doer and find the *treasure that is in his heart*. The wrong doer is as much a part of the society as anyone else and by exterminating him, would the society not injure itself? If a limb of the human body becomes diseased, should we not try to cure it instead of amputating it?

The treasure that was in my parent's hearts, is also locked in their hearts. We are bound to each other as a society, and we have to take responsibility for each other.

The cry of the hawks for capital punishment is also a facade, completely meaningless. My friend Gayatri Sharma was raped in police custody by the District Collector and the SDO (Police). Some years ago, when she came out of jail, she filed a case against her rapists. The District Court permitted the trial on sections related to outrage of modesty, but the High Court set aside the lower court's order, saying that the District Collector could not have possibly raped her since he was an educated man. Thus her perpetrators were never tried, and are holding posts in the services even today. Speaking at the plenary gathering of the World Social Forum in Mumbai, Gayatri had said:

> As feminists, we believe in honouring life, and we oppose capital punishment. But it is ridiculous to say that capital punishment will deter rape, when most victims of rape are being denied even trial. The system is corrupt and negligent and offers few possibilities of justice. This talk of capital punishment is just to distract and take away attention from what really needs to be done with the legal establishment.

After my parents' death, we personally experienced the complete failure of the criminal justice system. For months, the police did not file a case of murder, only burglary. We could not understand what was going on. Two people were dead. The police had the postmortem report. Why were they not registering the case? Finally, after months, on the intervention of a friend's father who was then the Finance Minister, my parents' case was registered as a murder case.

However, during the trial, the evidence that our stolen belongings were found in their possession was not properly placed by the public prosecutor; the prosecution lost and my parents' killers were acquitted. The painters were not even indicted for burglary despite the fact that our belongings had been found in their house. Did money change hands? Was there a caste/community factor? Or was it simply that the case was indifferently argued?

I feel ashamed today, about how ignorant we were about the law. We did not know that we could have hired a lawyer of our own to back up the prosecution. When we asked the state to appeal the case, they refused. We then asked for permission to appeal the case ourselves. But since the authorities did not write back, I assumed that permission was refused. Years later, I found out from a lawyer friend that the state could not have refused permission. And then one day, even later, rummaging through old papers, I found an unopened letter from the office of the public prosecutor, stating that we were at liberty to appeal the case ourselves. By then it was too late. Years had passed. In 2006, when I heard that Manu Sharma had been sentenced to life for murdering Jessica Lall, I experienced such terrible pangs. Jessica's sister Sabrina must have been as ignorant about the law as I had been, but she had persisted to win justice for her sister. I felt that we had let down and failed my parents by failing to protect them in their old age, and by not being able to ensure that the criminals were brought to book.

I understand that this is what happens with most survivors of murder victims. In most instances, the case is not even registered as a murder case, to protect the police against ignominy. Even where the case is registered, the obligation on the state to defend murder cases is never discharged properly. The family members are never counselled about their options and choices. The evidence is never properly presented. As a result, as in our case, the persons perpetrating the crime are not even indicted for burglary. The entire police and justice system lies in shambles. It is only in the rarest cases, when family members work dedicatedly to raise the issue, that years later some justice comes through, and even that is so easily reversed.

But even a better police and justice system cannot deter crime. Capital punishment certainly cannot. Though a system of administration, of justice, law and order that coheres the society is essential, the solution does not lie in the police system. It is only by making sane and inclusive choices about our collective needs and the manner in which they are met that we can prevent deprivation. And by affirming love and connectedness, the cost of a human being's life may be restored to what it is – priceless.

The *Kathopanishad* says:

> The slayer thinks he has killed and the slain thinks he has been killed but both are wrong. When the body is destroyed, the Self within is not destroyed.

Life is indestructible, even when the clay garment is shed. Often I feel my parents are not dead, and I feel their palpable presence when I most need them. I often feel that they have come to live within me.

The Death Machine

Sana Das

The popular nineteenth-century poet, William Wordsworth, wrote fourteen sonnets to explore the personal aspects of the death penalty and its impact on the condemned, titled *Sonnets upon the Punishment of Death.* One of the sonnets, 'The Last Walk' (1839), describes to us a place called 'Weeping Hill' that thousands of condemned persons, bound in chains, pass by on their walk to Lancaster Towers to be hanged; as they look upon the hill and see its beauty, they begin to cry and are blinded by their own tears which fall on their chains. Wordsworth describes these tears as 'tears of salvation and joy'. And this is the moment to pause. Could it be possible that the tears are because he who is condemned sees hope, or divine will, in his dying? That he is joyous, not fearful? Are they not tears of fear and of the loss looming before him? What did Wordsworth's readers and the society of his time make of such an interpretation? What should we make of it now, and how so, without bringing the condemned to the heart of the debate on capital punishment?

This piece traces the 'narrative construction' of capital punishment in books and films, which, perhaps more so than the real criminal justice system, shapes popular views on capital punishment. How did the aesthetic image of public execution, demonstrated in literary debates, 'trial films', and even photo-art, come to influence the death penalty sentence in the nineteenth–twentieth century and in recent imagination? Further to that, how did it groom the criminal justice system, and the legal psychology and industry of capital punishment? This brings the spotlight on three things. First, on the relationship between individual, society and culture. Second, on the present impasse created by law and public opinion regarding the 'value of life' of the condemned; not merely the mocking and taking of life, but the moral authority behind it. Third, on the recollection of a few strands from the Euro-American colonial legacy and the Christian roots of the death penalty, an inheritance we tend to mis-remember.

Execution: The Handmaiden of Deterrence and Social Order?

Execution seems to have served in the 'cultural narrative' as a symbolic 'return to order' from the chaos created by murders. In the heated debate on capital punishment in nineteenth–twentieth-century Europe and America, we find that some of the popular and loved poets of the time were against its total abolition precisely for reasons of 'order' and what may be called 'deterrence', the preventive value of capital punishment. Though more and more countries are now abolishing capital punishment, this earlier logic continues to have quite a grip on the popular and legal imagination, easily seen in India in the fervent demand for death to all those allegedly involved in the 2001 attack on the Parliament or in the 26/11 Mumbai attacks of 2008.

Hidden in the very act of capital punishment, in its public–secret nature, and in all literary and other works that defend it, is a belief in the theory of deterrence. Deterrence theorists believe that death is the commonality of social planning, and that all social policy decisions – including whether to have capital punishment – determine who will live and who will die. That some innocent people will die should not interfere with the fact that without the death penalty some innocent people will be killed. Believers in this theory are anti-abolitionists, and they cite the hazards of mere imprisonment or letting free a killer-convict through convincing statistics on murders/deaths of jail inmates and murders committed outside within a few years of their release. Today, though two-thirds of the world's countries have abolished the death penalty in law or in practice, 69 countries and territories still uphold the death penalty and uphold this punishment on grounds of deterrence, or divine justice and the moral–social order. Heading the list of users of the death penalty are China, Iran, Saudi Arabia and the United States, though they vary in the extent of secrecy or publicness of the acts. The theory of deterrence is a 'consequentialist' argument that influences almost everybody.

In contrast to such a 'consequentialist' argument, there is a 'normative' one made at the level of moral belief. There is, however, scepticism regarding the extent to which moral arguments actually influence adult beliefs or actions. All the same, the power of the state to execute, which had such a central role to play in the nineteenth century, is attributed to its religious authority and sanction, and such normative arguments do continue to be invoked in the death-penalty trials of murderers today in different parts of the world, with varying degrees of support and opposition by religious groups. Sanction for the death penalty in the Euro–American tradition has been seen as grounded in theology and biblical arguments in the Old Testament: that the death penalty is perhaps not against God's will. Theological surveys reveal a deep-rooted competition between the Jewish and Christian religions: that if death had not been so strikingly represented as a divinely ordained penalty for dozens of human misdeeds in the Hebrew Bible, the practice of executing wayward fellow human beings would never have gained the central position it did in Christian history.

Nineteenth- and twentieth-century literary narratives reveal some of these fissures, particularly articulated in the strain between believers and non-believers in deterrence, and the possibilities and impossibilities of knowing what divine authority may ultimately feel about the matter. We focus, though, more on the consequentialist arguments as they are a site where we may anticipate quicker changes in views.

In the nineteenth century, executions were generally conducted by hanging in public. Gregg Mayer, in *The Poet and Death: Literary Reflections on Capital Punishment through the Sonnets of William Wordsworth* (2007), points out that unlike writers like Charles Dickens, William Makepeace Thackeray, Leo Tolstoy and his contemporaries who opposed public hangings, Wordsworth staunchly resisted, through his poetry, the government's inching closer to abolition in its criminal law reform plan. Arguing that preservation of the state compels executions and that the death penalty as a punishing crime is necessary to 'fortify the moral sense of all', Wordsworth broadened the idea of 'the harmed' from the victim-individual to all of society – duty to society must come before all other instincts. Throughout time, he said, man has relied on the death penalty to keep in check those tormented by 'fiends', warning of the danger if that ceases to be. Wordsworth believed in the deterrence value of the death penalty. Fear, rather than love, guides men's actions better, and, as he says, '... all authority on earth depends on Love and Fear ...'. Authority turns on fear and capital punishment instils fear, and thereby helps preserve moral order.

Contrarily, twentieth-century writers like Albert Camus have challenged whether deterrence and moral preservation are indeed the fruits of execution. In his classic essay, 'Reflections on the Guillotine' (1957), Camus gives an interesting interpretation to this 'spectacle' as he argues against deterrence and moral order. He says that in earlier, barbaric times – Wordsworth's, for instance – public spectacle executions were believed to subdue the public, and could act as deterrence. Witnessing the shift from the spectacle to the 'closed door butchery' of his times, Camus argues against the deterrent power of 'secret' killings. 'Today, when this ignoble death is secretly administered, what meaning can such torture have? We must either kill publicly or admit we do not feel authorized to kill.' Executions, he believes, will never be public again, meaning that the shift from 'publicness' to 'privacy' of death reflects an unconfessed bite on the conscience of the state. Obviously, Camus had not accounted for a 9/11 that could sanctify the imperial vengeance unleashed with the ventriloquism of a ruthless, co-conspiring media, by making globally public the hanging of Saddam Hussein.

Notwithstanding Camus' views on the subduing power of the spectacle, when we turn to the writings of people like James Joyce, William Makepeace Thackeray, Charles Dickens and, later, Albert Borowitz, we find that capital punishment even in its most public form – hanging / the guillotine – fails to present itself as sufficient deterrence against crime. Rather than deterring audiences of the public spectacle of hanging or ingraining in them the importance of moral order, they induce deterioration in them. James Joyce describes in 'Cyclops', Episode 12, *Ulysses* (1920), how the condemned and his lover's agony, as the former faces the grim executioner and his horrible weapon, are met with 'that monster audience that rocked with delight'. Thackeray, in 'On Going to See a Man Hanged' (1840), writes that he witnessed two little girls who had come to see an execution, and while one of them cried, the other one 'wanted to see it'. He also notes the criminal activities at the public site of the hanging itself, and totally denounces the execution. The nineteenth-century English poet, Coventry Patmore, describes how the 'mob witnesses' of a hanging disperse into individuals who return to their own violent crimes, quite unchastened. Charles Dickens, though not an anti-abolitionist, was convinced that public spectacle contaminated and corrupted the public while glorifying the executioner. Dickens – who went to a handful of executions in his lifetime, and who created a most hateful executioner, Dennis, in *Barnaby Rudge* (1841), as one of his powerful characters who loved doing away with young women, mothers and children at the scaffold – was strongly of the opinion that executions 'barbarized' the community rather than morally upgrading them. It is interesting to note that both Dickens and Borowitz (*Crimes Gone By: Collected Essays of Albert Borowitz*, 1966–2005) were convinced that public executions served more to bring notoriety to the condemned rather than deterrence. Exhibitionist murders will capitalize on the 'attendant notoreity' and provide incentive rather than deterrence.

The *Haute Couture* of Execution

If there is an official mysticism about any dimension of capital punishment, apart from the secrecy of the name and number waiting on 'death row', it is the 'fashion industry' behind capital punishment. Developed to the point of a fine art is the political economy of execution. To have capital punishment means that you need to have and maintain an official torturer, an aesthetician trained in neck-breaking,

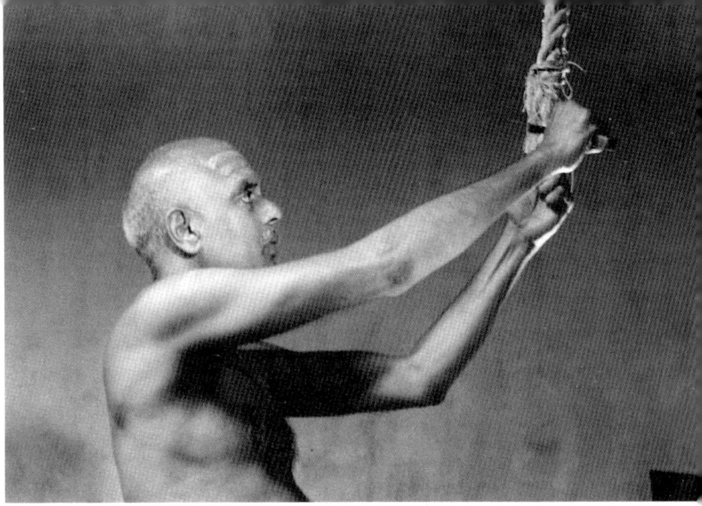

The hangman, Kaliyappan, prepares the rope for an execution. Still from Adoor Gopalakrishnan's film, *Shadow Kill.*

throttling, garroting, strangling, asphyxiation, decapitation and electrocution, not to mention the right moral clothes to justify it.

The *haute couture* of capital punishment is a bitter *mélange* of the rope-and-trapdoor form of execution of the English, as well as the more forensics-based, more efficient, medically sophisticated, 'private' and detached forms such as electrocution or the lethal injection of the US, although the former were always looked down upon for their earlier hole-and-corner hangings. Presently, Egypt, India, Iran, Iraq, Japan, Jordan, Pakistan and Singapore are some of the countries who still prefer hanging as the mode of capital punishment, while others prefer stoning, electrocution and decapitation.

Along with the fashioning of official torturers, the industry of capital punishment had to create an official grapevine that would 'lynch and tell all' through an elaborate spectacle of public hanging no doubt, but also through the 'lynching photography' and 'lynching media' evolved to great populist heights in the early twentieth century. Here, we stand before a long legacy of punishment as pornography and the pornography of the state, where media and aesthetics act as a surrogate for the mob or crowd.

Charles Duff, the author of *A Handbook on Hanging* (2001) and one of the influential, early twentieth-century anti-abolitionist writers, mentions that from any prison gallows, news of an impending hanging would reach the homes of people. Special excursion trains were run and special editions run off the presses to see the 'treat'. The press could build great excitement by reminding all that the object of the excitement could be burned alive. Bob Dylan's haunting lament, 'They're selling postcards of the hanging', in 'Desolation Row', stands as lyrical proof of such lynching photography. Dylan wrote and performed this for the first time, as part of the album *Highway 61 Revisited*, at the Forest Hills Music Festival in Queens, New York, on 28 August 1965. It is a number influenced by the Duluth lynchings of 15 June 1920 that took place at Duluth, Minnesota – Dylan's hometown – where a mob broke three circusmen out of jail and lynched them for allegedly raping a girl in town. Dylan's song shows that lynchings were moments of gaiety …

They're selling postcards of the hanging
They're painting the passports brown
The beauty parlour is filled with sailors
The circus is in town …
… Now the moon is almost hidden
The stars are beginning to hide
The fortunetelling lady
Has even taken all her things inside
All except for Cain and Abel
And the hunchback of Notre Dame
Everybody is making love
Or else expecting rain
And the Good Samaritan, he's dressing
He's getting ready for the show
He's going to the Carnival tonight
On Desolation Row

The 'spectacle' goes against all desire for justice to be swift. What is central to 'the society of the spectacle' is perhaps the pleasure and voyeurism of the mob as in witch trials, and the more protracted it is, the better. Charles Duff writes that favourable vantage points of watching were on sale, for instance, in Hyde Park whose Marble Arch used to be a popular hanging spot. Fragments of limbs, private parts and rope became souvenirs, 'collectibles', trophies and talismans. Grisly keepsakes were commonplace. Executioners were celebrities.

The penal system of hanging and its pornography, too, in America or India draw from their colonial legacy of the British. Domestication of the spectacle happened after great turbulence – hangings were moved inside the official quarters of prisons where notices on prison walls became the public evidence. The hangman became a discreet civil servant with the British government becoming more demure in its death wish and doing away with the vulgarity of public spectacle.

Notwithstanding such transformations, in India, our own backyard, the hangman continues as a celebrity with the late twentieth-century popularization of capital punishment in the country. Nata Mullick from Kolkata, the executioner of Dhananjoy Chatterjee who was hanged in August 2004 for raping and brutally murdering a 14-year-old girl in 1990, rose to the popularity of a film star. The media put the spotlight on him as the perfect hangman and a performer for the state with ancestral abilities. Joshy Joseph's film, *One Day in the Life of a Hangman* (2005), captures the Indian *haute couture* in capital punishment by transferring society's obsessive hunger for the 'devil in the details' on to the camera, intertextually weaving in the voyeur-spectator through it. Even if the hanging spot could not be accessed, the camera, deliberately emulating the voyeuristic hunger of the public, left Mullick with no choice but to share the pornographic details of the conquest at the scaffold; the grooming for the kill undertaken by both family and state; the Faustian reconciling with guilt through his meditative alliance with Kali, the goddess of death; the preparatory rituals with sandbag bodies; the professional aspirations that lurched a father and son on to a delicate balance between guilt and duty imposed by the state.

Yet another interesting theme running through the fashion politics of capital punishment concerns the differential focus on the victim and the condemned. Who is more deserving of compassion? An assessment of the literary works of the

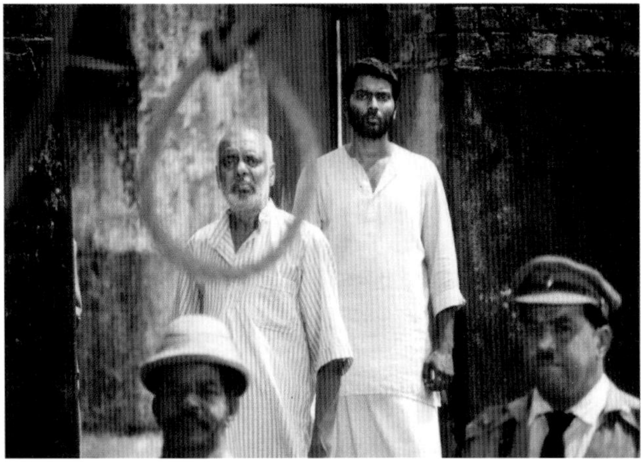

Still from Adoor Gopalakrishnan's film, *Shadow Kill.*

nineteenth–twentieth centuries seems to indicate that what prevents the development of a public conscience, a state ethic regarding the condemned, is that when we ask for someone to be killed we do not have a complete picture of the condemned or their humanity. This is precisely where Wordsworth's failure may be located. By talking about the rights of the condemned, one seeks not to belittle the suffering of the families of victims but to say that the guilty must be punished with the most important characteristic of punishment, that is, reformation. An imbalanced focus on the victim, and presenting the condemned as incapable of remorse and undeserving of sympathy, can turn a whole city into a mob – and guilt can become unimportant when the mob is coming. In Langston Hughes' 'Ballad of a Killer Boy', written between 1941 and 1950 in a pitiless style, our attention is drawn to the condemned, not on the victim, as an individual, as someone who is his own victim or the victim of his love for a woman for whom he robs and murders. In another related poem, 'The Town of Scottsboro' (1932), in four short lines, Hughes dwells on the town's legal system and its injustice which could well describe the legal system in many cities and towns.

Scottsboro's just a little place:
No shame is writ across its face –
Its court, too weak to stand against a mob
Its people's heart, too small to hold a sob.

The antithesis of the spectacle within the *haute couture* of capital punishment is the paradoxical secrecy about the breath that is waiting to be gasped. There were rituals by which the victim could be kept endlessly uncertain regarding when and how he was going to die. The situation is little different now. Human rights statistics of 2006 show that about 20,000 people are estimated to be on death row across the world, neither able to live nor die. India, which is apparently weighing the idea of a moratorium on the death penalty, passed fifty death sentences in its courts in 2009, according to Amnesty International reports. Afzal Guru, delivered the death sentence in the case of the attack on the Indian Parliament in 2001, denied a fair trial and put on death row since then, has categorically voiced his torment in his prison interviews. 'If you wanted to put me to death what was the need for such a long legal process which, to me, was totally meaningless?' Most ironically, there was an attempt to speed up his journey to execution only so that 22-year-old Ajmal Kasab, the main accused in the Mumbai Taj attacks case of 2008, could be quickly pushed towards the noose. Kasab too remains on death row after his death sentence on five counts, delivered on 6 May 2010.

Victor Hugo (*Last Days of a Condemned Man*), Vladimir Nabokov (*Invitation to a Beheading*), William Blake (*Songs of Innocence and Experience*), Franz Kafka (*In the Penal Colony*), John Steinbeck (*The Cup of Gold*) and Oscar Wilde (*The Ballad of Reading Gaol*) have all tried to bring alive the heart of the condemned before public consciousness, by highlighting their last days in prison without light and air; their last thoughts and scribbles on walls and paper; even their last vanities such as the fear of fainting as the hour drew near; their last walk in which the condemned, ironically, may try avoiding a puddle though in the next moment he is to hang; their last minutes at the scaffold when they may struggle with the noose that symbolizes the frailty of social order; or by drawing attention to their loneliness as no one offers a prayer for them or spares a thought for them as they hang.

To bring the focus on the condemned is not to talk of their innocence; they may well be evil. The death row is filled with guilty men and women, and there are, no doubt, degrees of evil. But this has nothing to do with whether it is acceptable to execute them. The question, rather, is whether the state should be in the business of killing at all. How is execution by the state any different from murders by the condemned? If it is not, how can it not be equally reprehensible? And if it is wrong for us to kill, it is surely wrong for us to have the state kill on our behalf.

Tim Robbins' film *Dead Man Walking* (1995) brings out the moral principle of this wrongness. Prejean is a nun who ministers to those on death row. She opposes the death penalty, even to Mathew Poncelot, a composite murderer who faces execution for the brutal rape and murder of two high-

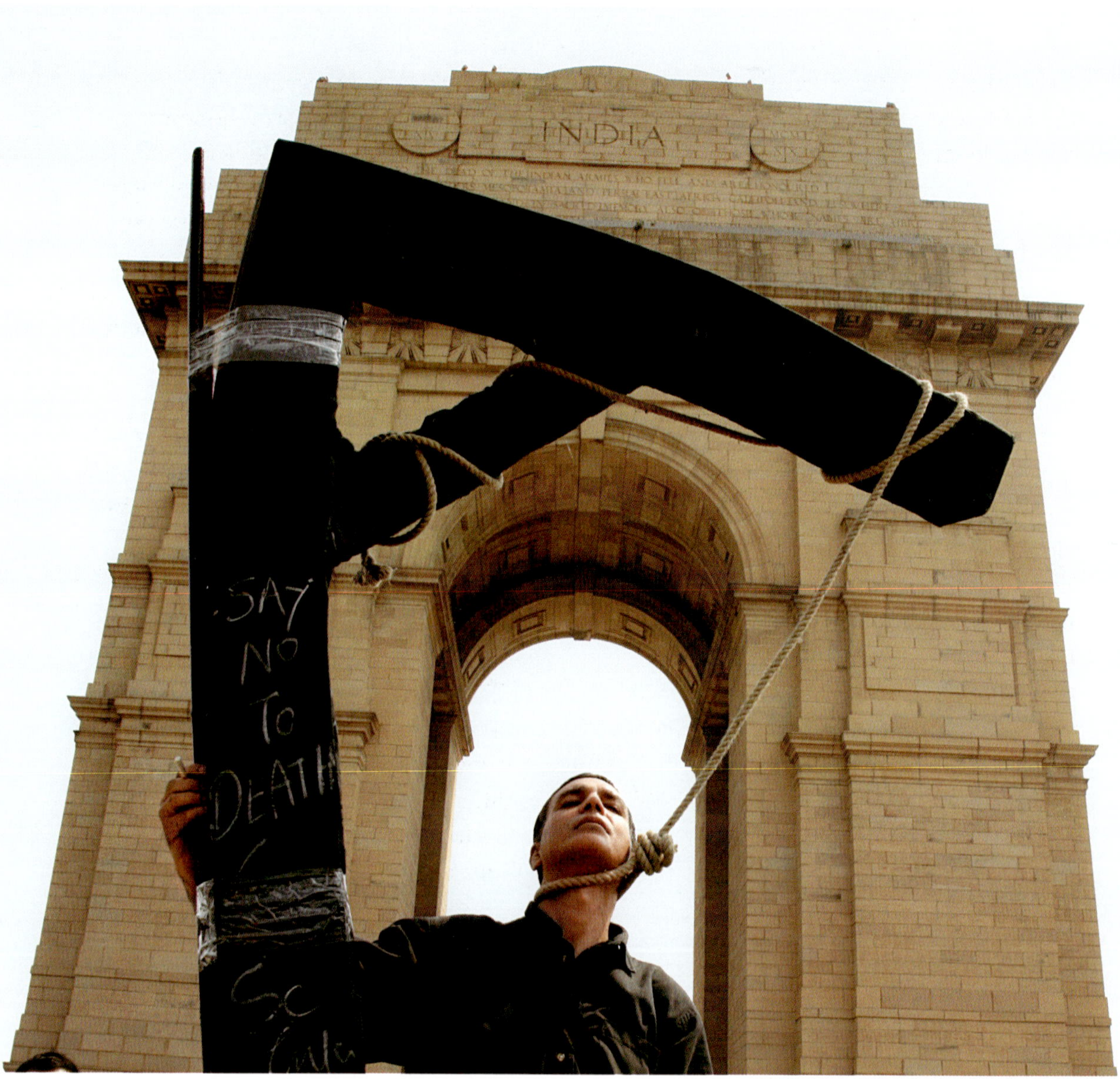

Demonstration against the death penalty at India Gate, New Delhi, on the occasion of the Sixth World Day against Death Penalty by Amnesty India. By Parthiv Shah, India, 2008.

school seniors, not because of her religion but because she believes executions 'erode the dignity of the executioner'.

The Backstage of Fear, Guilt and Bungling

Contrary to Wordsworth's poetic attempts to show the joy behind the tears of the condemned going to the gallows, Charles Duff points to the fear lurking behind the execution scene – the hangman who took a little too much to drink to steady his hand, the plastic underwear proferred to female victims; the rope that slipped and caused slow strangulation; the rope that was poorly judged and caused decapitation; the rope that broke; the second and even third attempts to finish off miscreants who didn't expire the first time; the resignations put in by clergymen or other official witnesses after some macabre piece of bungling or cruelty.

But the scaffold and the electric chair are not the only sites at which bungling occurs. There are more frontal places where it is to be seen: at the palace of clemency and the courtroom itself.

Adoor Gopalakrishnan's film, *Shadow Kill* (*Nizhalkkuthu*, 2002), brings out the fear of bungling by lampooning the king's power of clemency and its fraud. Kaliyappan, the protagonist, is a hangman who works in the service of the crown in pre-independence times. The king is someone who, to absolve himself of guilt, strategically issues a pardon or clemency order that cleverly arrives a few minutes after the hanging! Kaliyappan knows and is unhappy that the hangings he conducts are coloured by politics and the whims of the crown. There is no way he can absolve his own guilt. On similar lines, Charles Duff satirizes the powers of 'mercy' of the British Queen in the famous abolition campaign of 1953, where Members of Parliament in the campaign were helpless before the Royal Prerogative of Mercy, and Derek Bentley had to be hanged because his accomplice who killed a policeman was only 16 and couldn't be.

The right of the state or the crown to take life is a hangover from the days of divine right, of feudalism, of the ownership of human beings and the propitiation of evil spirits, and this totalitarian conception of the relationship between state and citizen has been one of the main reasons why governments like that of France sought to abolish the death penalty, as much as they used the argument of lack of deterrence. In the US it is being used in its campaign for expansion and the Global War on Terror. In Georgian and Victorian England, the death penalty was given specifically to punish crimes against property and the social order. In colonial India, it was the punishment for freedom fighters. In free India, it is a popularity weapon in the hands of politicians, wielded with justifications of civilian security, deterrence and foreign policy relations.

Yet another frontal bungling is 'judicial error', which has been a popular and dominating theme in literature and film since the mid-twentieth century. Captured by what may be called 'trial' novels and movies, they are like a mirror held up to a system of blind justice, no longer representing just one more authorized, official genre of legal tales wherein the courtroom is godly and justice is sure. Instead, they begin to present what law may mean in everyday life, and may force our confrontation with law and legal institutions we call our own but which can go on a killing overdrive.

Thackeray equates the crimes of the murderer with that of the executioner in *The Irish Sketch Book* (1848).

> I confess, for my part, to that common cant and sickly sentimentality, which, thank God!, is felt by a great number of people nowadays, and which leads them to revolt against murder, whether performed by a ruffian's knife or a hangman's rope: whether accompanied with a curse from the thief as he blows his victim's brains out, or a prayer from my lord on the bench in his wig and black cap.

Moreover, the punctuality of executions, it would seem, was deemed more important than the preservation of rights – particularly if it was the poor, the mentally ill, minorities, or members of racial, ethnic and religious communities who were literally at stake. Hughes, quite symbolically of the Harlem renaissance, put it starkly:

> *8 Black Boys in a Southern jail*
> *World, Turn Pale!*
> *8 Black Boys and one White lie*
> *Is it much to die?*

So does Goldwyn Mayer's film, *I Want to Live!* (1959), focusing as it does on a wrong execution. In Harper Lee's acclaimed trial novel, *To Kill a Mockingbird* (1960), a racial legal system is thrown open at its seams. The miscarriages of justice are satirically accounted for in Nagisa Oshima's film *Death by Hanging* (1968) in the absurd genre, where a Korean minority in Japan barely escapes the noose (not that he can re-enter an anti-minority Japanese society) after being tried for rapes he has no memory of, and in whose reminder other people end up hanging, demonstrating the convolutions and bunglings contrived by law, ideology and trial actors.

And when judges are so busy making these errors and making us believe that they were right, is it not a little too hard to believe in their theories of moral, social order and the 'rarest of the rare', criteria on which the death penalty is granted? In an article titled 'The Overproduction of Death' (*Legal Studies Forum*, Vol. 29, No. 2, 2005), Professor James S. Liebman critiques 'trials' and 'appeals'-oriented reforms that actually overproduce death sentences, condemning to death men and women who do not deserve that penalty. Such a system gives incentives to both sets of trial actors, i.e. the pro-death penalty trial actors who generate more death sentences than otherwise, and the anti-death penalty lawyers who concentrate their resources on post-trial review proceedings where, given the high rates of trial error, they prevail abnormally often.

Though it will be quite some time before the deterrence theorists stop complaining about the abolitionists' lament over the wrong cases of hanging, and the politicians stop addressing problems through the easy popularity of capital punishment; and quite some time till the courts stop overproducing death, let us halt at these lines from Bob Dylan's '11 Outlined Epitaphs' …

… it is not of me t'sit an' ponder
wonderin' an' wastin' time
thinkin' of thoughts that haven't been
thunk
thinkin' of dreams that haven't been
dreamt
an' new ideas that haven't been wrote
an' new words t'fit into rhyme […]
an' not worry about the new rules
for they ain't been made yet
an' t'shout my singin' mind
knowin' that it is me an' my kind
that will make those rules …
if the people of tomorrow
really need the rules of today
rally 'round all you prosecutin' attorneys
the world is but a courtroom
yes
but I know the defendants better 'n you
and while you're busy prosecutin'
we're busy whistlin'
cleanin' up the courtroom
sweepin' sweepin'
listenin' listenin'
winkin' t'one another
careful
careful
your spot is comin' up soon.

Artist under Attack

Parthiv Shah

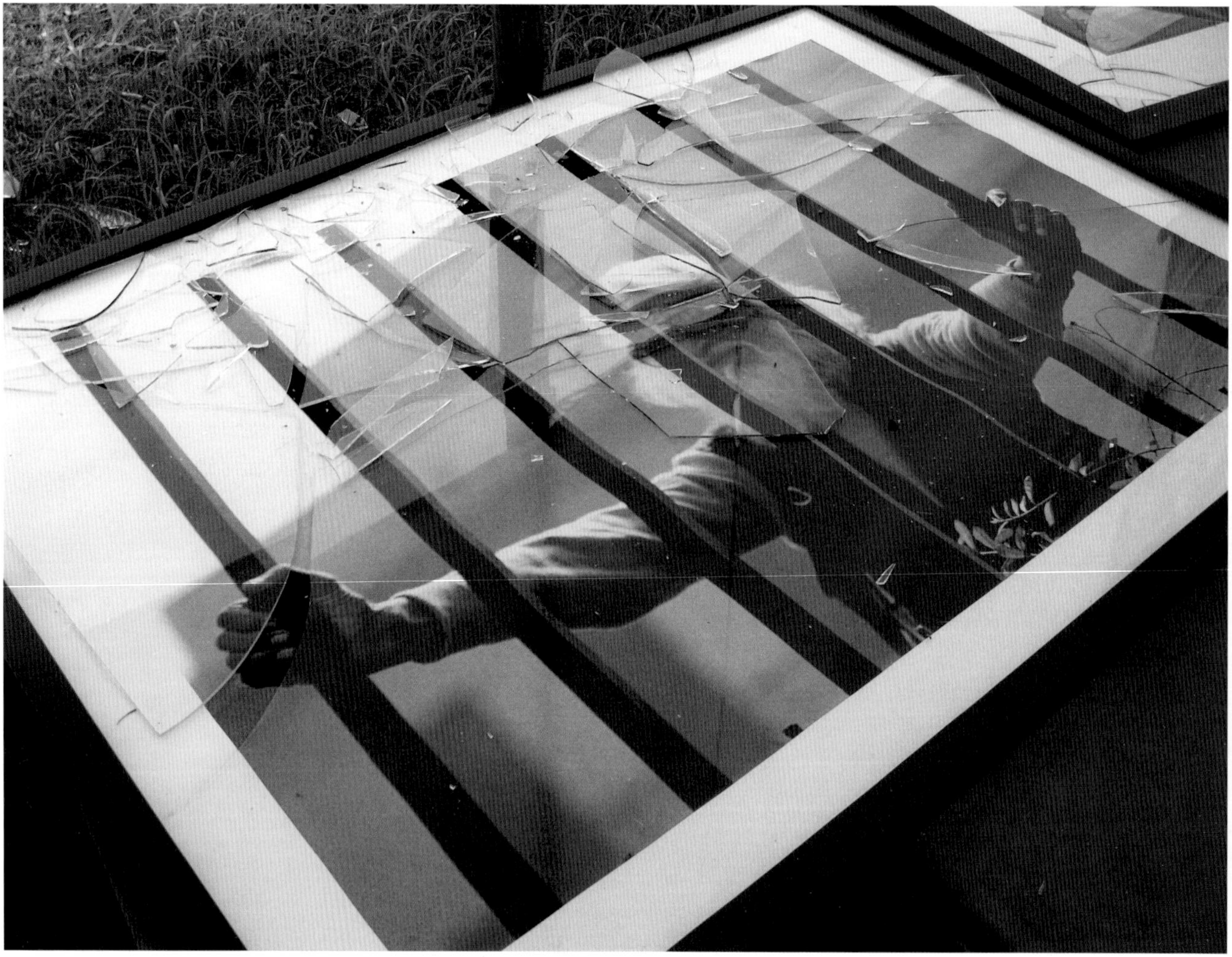

This page and the facing page: Photographs of eminent artist M.F. Husain by Parthiv Shah were attacked and vandalized by Sri Ram Sena goons during an exhibition organized by Sahmat in New Delhi, India, 2008.

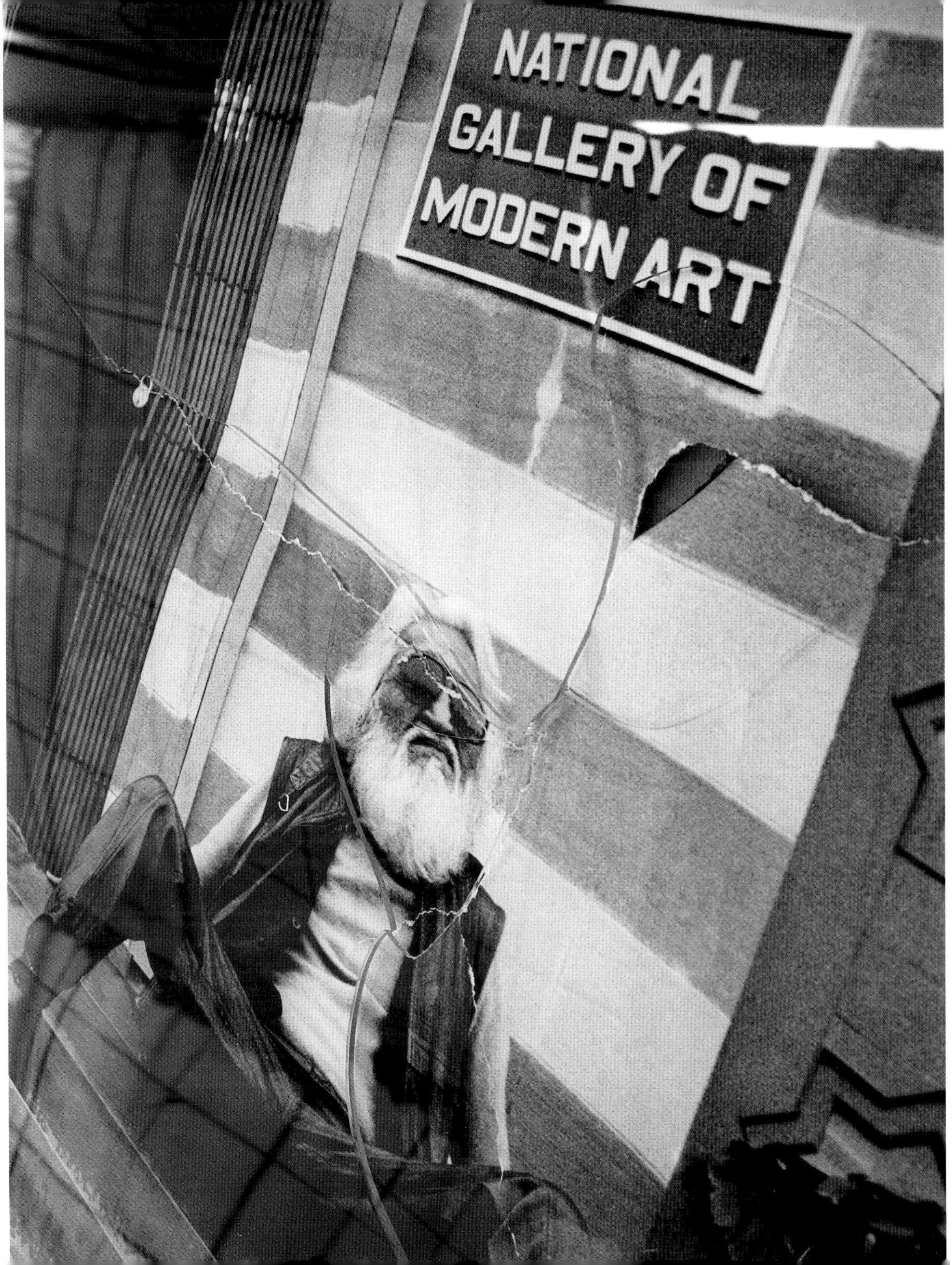
NATIONAL
GALLERY OF
MODERN ART

Contributors

Shahidul Alam is an award-winning Bangladeshi photographer and educator. He is the founder of the DRIK picture library and Pathshala, the Dhaka-based Institute of Photography, and the Director of Chobi Mela, the annual festival of photography in Asia.

Temsula Ao is a Professor in the Department of English and Dean of the School of Humanities and Education, North-Eastern Hill University, Shillong. She is also a poet and writer of fiction.

K.M. Asad is a young photographer from Dhaka, Bangladesh. In 2008, he successfully completed his degree in professional photography from Pathshala: The South Asian Media Academy.

Lipton Bhau is an activist who spent many years working with the Narmada Bachao Andolan, and is now associated with several other social justice movements.

Lachit Bordolai is a journalist and human rights activist, based in Assam.

Suhas Borker is an independent documentary filmmaker and social activist, based in New Delhi.

Suvendu Chatterjee is a photographer, media entrepreneur and human rights activist. He is the Founder and Director of DRIK India, the first overseas branch of DRIK, Bangladesh.

Sana Das is presently the Course Director of a journalism course in Bangalore called 'Archaeology of the Media' run by Educational Trust, Samvada, and is continuing a Ph.D. at the Indian Institute of Technology, New Delhi. She has been associated with Amnesty International India, Heinrich Boll Foundation and several people's movements.

Kanak Mani Dixit is the editor and publisher of *Himal Southasia*, a news and analysis magazine in Nepal.

Gowhar Fazili is a political activist and is deeply interested in ecological issues. He is the co-author of an important report on the impact of protracted violence on Kashmiri youth.

Iftikhar Gilani is a journalist and heads the New Delhi bureau of *Kashmir Times.* He is a winner of the Sahitya Akademi Award for the Urdu translation of his memoirs, *My Days in Prison.*

Vrinda Grover is a Supreme Court advocate and legal scholar.

Nandita Haksar is a Supreme Court advocate and the author of *Rogue Agent: How India's Military Intelligence Betrayed the Burmese Resistance* (2009).

Salima Hashmi is a Pakistani painter and Dean of the School of Visual Arts at the Beaconhouse National University, Lahore. She is the daughter of the renowned poet Faiz Ahmed Faiz.

Sohrab Hura is a Delhi-based photographer. He is an award winner of the Ramnath Goenka Foundation's India Press Photo and his work has been shown at the Sète Photo Festival in France.

Sonia Jabbar is an independent journalist, writer and filmmaker, based in New Delhi.

E.M. Jose is a Shillong-based journalist and author of the non-fiction book, *The Jacaranda Blooms: A True Story.*

Showkat Kathjoo is an artist based in Kashmir.

Harikrishna Katragadda is a New Delhi-based photojournalist. He currently works with the newspaper *Mint.*

Sabrina Lall, sister of the deceased model Jessica Lall, has been leading the campaign for justice against her sister's murderer Manu Sharma for nearly eleven years now.

Saroj Mohanty is an activist, poet and the editor of *Anwesha*, a progressive Oriya journal.

Swapan Nayak is an award-winning photo journalist. He works in the Outlook Group of publications.

Shahzad Noorani has worked as a freelance documentary photographer with a special focus on social issues since 1987 in Dhaka, Bangladesh. Several bodies of his work focus on the social problems of urban women and children. He received the prestigious Mother Jones International Award for Documentary Photography in 2000.

Chittaroopa Palit is a senior activist with the Narmada Bachao Andolan and lives in Madhya Pradesh.

Daniel Pepper is an American journalist and writer who has focused on human rights and social justice issues. His articles and images have appeared in major news publications around the world including *Time*, *Newsweek*, *Fortune*, *New York Times Magazine*, *The Times*, *South China Morning Post* and MSNBC.com.

Sara Rahbar is a contemporary Iranian artist, living and working between Iran and America.

Vibhuti Narain Rai is a senior Indian Police Service officer. He is the editor of a Hindi literary magazine, *Vartaman Sahitya*, and a novelist.

Abdul Rahman Roslan is a photojournalist based in Kuala Lumpur, focusing on news and documentary photography. He is presently freelancing for AFP and Reuters.

Inder Salim is a poet and performance artist based in New Delhi.

Parthiv Shah is a photographer, filmmaker and graphic designer. He is the Founder–Director of the Centre for Media and Alternative Communication (CMAC), New Delhi.

Mukul Sharma works with AIDS Society of Asia (ASAP) and the Faculty of Public Health, Mahidol University, Bangkok. Formerly the Director of Amnesty International India, he has worked as a journalist, writer, human rights activist and a development professional.

Nandini Sundar is Professor of Sociology, Delhi School of Economics, Delhi University, and co-editor of *Contributions to Indian Sociology*.

Kian Tajbakhsh is an Iranian–American social scientist and urban planner. He is the author of several books including *Social Capital: Trust, Democracy and Development*.

About 'Art for Activism'

Amnesty International's 'Art for Activism' campaign is both a tribute to freedom of expression and in defence of other freedoms. It has a long tradition of activism powered by artists. For more than 40 years, Amnesty International has devoted itself to the observance of human rights the world over. While the written and spoken word in the form of reports, letters to prisoners, governments and international organizations has proved, and still proves to be, a powerful medium for it, Amnesty International, emphatically, has never ignored the global shift towards a visual culture and its power to inform, sensitize and galvanize people. It has seen art exhibitions, film festivals and music events as a platform for human rights and human dignity – a platform for change, unity and the appeal for universality. Thus it has campaigned using images and sound to break through indifference. Amnesty Netherlands, for instance, has been the founder of the Amsterdam Film Festival, *Movies that Matter*, a well-recognized international human rights festival. One of the organization's earliest music events was *Conspiracy of Hope*, featuring Peter Gabriel, Sting, U2, Bob Dylan, Miles Davis and Madonna, among others.

Art for Activism is a platform where artists and activists can come together against persecution to deliver powerful global messages that are inspirational and invaluable to build a just and peaceful world. Under Amnesty's Art for Activism campaign, renowned Cuban artists Viredo Espinoza, Haydee and Sahara Scull, Lazaro Amaral, Eduardo Estrada, Eduardo Funes, Leandro Soto and Ali Miranda have organized exhibitions featuring their paintings and sculptures; Hollywood actor Nicolas Cage has advocated for the International Control Arms Campaign as an Amnesty International member, and worked tirelessly to raise awareness about the horrors faced by child soldiers and other human rights tragedies; Jennifer Lopez has been felicitated with Amnesty International's 'Artists for Amnesty' award in recognition of her work as producer and star of the film *Bordertown*, a film on disappearances that exposes the ongoing murders of hundreds of women in the border city of Juarez, Mexico. Edward Zwick's *Blood Diamond*, which focuses on the conditions of diamond-mine workers in Africa, is a film in whose production and distribution Amnesty International has been intimately involved. Recently, more than 50 international recording artists and over 30 record labels have united under the 'Instant Karma: The Amnesty International Campaign to Save Darfur' banner. The collection features iconic songs by legendary musician and peace activist John Lennon, recorded by an array of best-selling artists, and draws the world's attention to gross human rights atrocities in Sudan.

Amnesty International India's Art for Activism campaign is intended to strengthen the global campaigns of Amnesty International for a world without fear and torture, a world without death penalty, disappearance and custodial violence. It draws attention to the anguish of prisoners, death row victims, the displaced, homeless and landless, and the rights of human rights defenders. Its endeavours have been endorsed by Indian actor Nandita Das, Pakistani screenwriter Shahid Nadeem, filmmakers Amar Kanwar, Akansha Joshi and Pankaj Butalia, photo-artists Parthiv Shah, Sohrab Hura, Suvendu Chatterjee, Swapan Nayak, Sonia Jabbar and Harikrishna Katragadda from India, and musicians like Advaita and Sajid Akbar who have given solidarity performances at a curtain-raiser for the International Week of Justice Festival.